CAN I GET A WITNESS?

Book Clubs

If your group is reading "Can I Get a Witness? 21 Frustrations of Black Women (Including Me)" and would like a visit from Mikki C. Zimmerman, please email your contact information and group description to mikkiczimmerman@yahoo.com.

CAN I GET A WITNESS?

21 Frustrations of Black Women

(Including Me)

Mikki C. Zimmerman

To order additional copies of this book, contact:
Xlibris Corporation
1-888-795-4274
www.Xlibris.com
Orders@Xlibris.com
56703

CONTENTS

21 Fun Facts
About the Author

———————

1) I am a spoiled brat! Being the baby of four children, it was bound to happen.
2) I am a prolific procrastinator. This is really nothing to brag about, but it is true. Just ask my mom and sister. They will gladly confirm it.
3) My favorite colors are black and pink.
4) I am a *true* Scorpio . . . this may be a frightening fact.
5) From 1996-2008, I worked twelve part-time jobs. Collectively, they have given me enough material to write 10 bestselling books. And believe me, they are coming!
6) My favorite sport is football. No, it's basketball. Wait a minute; I also like swimming, tennis, and track and field. Let's just say I am a HUGE sports fan.
7) I will donate a total of ten percent of net profits from the sale of this book to two organizations designed to help at risk youth.
8) I love my New Orleans Saints and Hornets!
9) I collect bookmarks. I purchased the first piece in my collection in 1991 at Louisiana Tech University's bookstore.
10) My passion is creative non-fiction books. Don't get me wrong, I am a sucker for a great story; but I have never read a novel for pleasure. I was forced to read them in high school.
11) I am a community activist. Over the last ten years, my family and I have donated countless hours to community service activities.
12) My favorite cartoons are The Flintstones and The Smurfs. SpongeBob SquarePants cracks me up too!

13) I have ADHD (Attention Deficit Hyperactivity Disorder). I self-diagnosed myself while taking a psychology class in college. I believe the procrastination tendencies stem from it.

14) I've had the same hairstylist for more than fifteen years. Yep, fifteen years. She tried to get rid of me a few times. But thank God she did not prevail! I am still her favorite client (with the pictures).

15) I love sweet tea. My son calls me a "tea addict".

16) My mom is the sweetest woman in the world. She would do everything in her power to help someone in need. She also helped me edit this book; so if you find any mistakes, cunsult, I mean, consult her!

17) My dad is the funniest man on the planet. I believe he's responsible for my sarcastic humor. He cracks me up!

18) As a child, an elderly neighbor who my mom cared for gave me the nickname "Mikki".

19) I cried when President Barack Obama won the election on November 4, 2008. I cried again as he and First Lady Michelle walked along the inauguration parade route. And I *almost* cried as they dance their first dance as Beyonce' sung Etta James' "At Last". Okay, okay, I cried.

20) Seven adjectives describe my personality perfectly: intuitive, outspoken, passionate, aggressive, sarcastic, honest, and witty. For me, the phrase "I don't bite my tongue" is an understatement. I am very straightforward. No bluff, no beating around the bush. I cut straight through the chase and get to the point. This book is filled with truths, some are uncomfortable truths. And they were not orchestrated by me alone. I spoke with thousands of black women across the world who shared stories of happiness, heartache, regret, and pain. Some of the contents may be hard to wrap your mind around, but they are *real*. Basically, if you find it difficult to accept and embrace the truth, please proceed through the book with caution because we all know that the truth is an essential tool in the survival kit of life.

21) Regardless of your thoughts about me after reading #20, I really am a nice person!

Acknowledgments

To God be the Glory! He orchestrated the vision, title, and provided the tools to research and write the book. He gave me the strength to continue writing when I wanted to give up. And believe me, there were many times when I wanted to quit. Nevertheless, I did not. Thank you for giving me the eye to see that this book is needed in today's society. Thank You for bringing the book to life.

To my wonderful parents, Willie and Geneva Zimmerman, who shaped and molded me into the woman I am today. Thank you for providing *everything* (literally) I needed throughout my life. Thank you for providing an excellent example of a marriage meant to last forever; 50 years and counting! Thanks for listening to me go on and on about the book for the past four years. Thanks for everything. I love you!

To my son Dre', thanks for all of your support and occasional input on the book. Thank you for teaching me patience and always having my back. I love you so much. Keep God first in your life and you will cash that $60 million ticket to the NFL! Thanks Fabies!

To my traveling buddies: Rhonda (sister), Felicia (sister), LaTasha (niece), Dominique (niece), and Taylor (niece) ... thanks for all of your support, advice, criticism, and suggestions on the book. Did I say criticisms? I know you were sick and tired of me going back and forth about the book. But thanks for listening. I look forward to many more road trips (especially Saints/Hornets games and Sanctuary D'Santa spa visits) in the future. I love you all!

To my brother, Tiger and his wife Carolyn, thanks for all of your support. Carolyn, I have not forgotten about you. Thanks for everything! I love both of you guys ... Nacomas, Mack and Amber—you know I couldn't leave you out.

To the Price family (Shirley, Cleo, Granny Francis, Cornelia and Malachi), thanks for everything you've done for DeAndre' and me. We love you guys and really appreciate all of your help and support! We could not have made it without you.

To my wonderful friends, Kim, Tara (Twinkle), Tonya, and Connie of fifteen years and counting; even though you guys found out about the book a few months before it was completed, you were still very supportive and I thank you. Thanks for listening when times were hard. Thanks for your lifelong friendships. To Denita, another one of my best friends for fifteen plus year, I am glad we were able to respectfully agree to disagree. Thanks for being honest in the beginning with your opinion about the book. I am glad we were able to work out our differences. I love all of you guys!

To the men who helped raise my son from birth—Willie Zimmerman, Jr. (father), Tiger (brother), Brandon Leach (nephew), Al Leach (brother-in-law), Roosevelt Wright, Jr. (pastor), all of the men and young men of Boy Scout Troop 65—Fred Mitchell, Robert Tanzy Sr., Quincy Miliken, Marcus Beckwith, and Donnie Davis; Osaro Kyles, Jamar Enis, Lorenzo Treadway, Donald "PaPa" Winn, and Jerrick Freemont. I could not have done it without you. Yes, it takes a village to raise a child. Thanks! May God continue to bless each of you.

To my Tabernacle Baptist Church family, thanks for your support over the years. I guess all of those Easter and Christmas speeches prepared me for this moment. Who knew?

To my publishing consultant Melvin Frost and my publishing agent Christopher Co of Xlibris Corporation—thank you for everything. Thanks for encouraging me and believing in my book. Thanks to everyone with Xlibris Corporation who dedicated time and energy on this project. I could not have done it without you!

A huge thanks to LaTasha Zimmerman, Kita Wright, and my pastor—Roosevelt Wright, Jr. Kita and Tasha, thank you both for taking the time out of your busy schedules to do the photo shoot for the cover picture. You guys nailed it! And thanks Pastor Wright for lending your office as the background. It worked perfectly!

To the authors who gave me tons of advice on the writing and publishing process—LaDawn Black, Cupcake Brown, LaTonja M. Smith, Karen Q. Miller, Lamont Carey, and Shellie Tomlinson—thank you! You will never realize how much your advice helped. You guys got me on the right foot; especially in the beginning. Thanks for everything! A very special thanks to Bennett Johnson of Third World Press, Inc. for the helpful tips and advice given during the editing phase. It really came in handy!

To Dr. Henry Cole (Marketing professor—University of Louisiana—Monroe), thanks for all of your marketing advice. Good thing I made a "B" in Personal Selling!

A very special thanks to four evangelists—Bishop T. D. Jakes, Joel Osteen, Pastor Paula White and Joyce Meyers—who inspire me through Christian television. There were many nights when I felt like giving up completely on this book. But I did not thanks to an encouraging message from one of you. It was always right on time! Thank you and May God continue to bless each of you.

Last, but certainly not least, I dedicate this book to the many frustrated Black women I spoke with throughout the world. Thank you for sharing your stories with me and allowing me to share them with the world. Keep your heads up Ladies!

INTRODUCTION

"I'm not bitter. I'm mad as hell!"

Helen McCarter

"Don't judge me or think I'm bitter for the evil God's allowed me to see."

Mary J. Blige

Go ahead—talk about us. Criticize us. Ridicule us. Oh, you know who I'm talking about—angry black women. Unbelievably, black women are not biologically wired to be angry and frustrated. This seems to be a universal belief; but we are not. Anger is not encoded in our DNA at birth nor is it culturally inherited. Society caused us to become angry and bitter. Yes, society—racial injustice, black men who refuse to commit to black women; but marry non-black women in a heartbeat, absent fathers, and sexism. The list goes on and on. Everyone in the world is so quick to talk about the frowns we wear on our faces and the anger in our voices; but no one is willing to uncover the sources of our anger. Well, until now.

This conversation is about to evolve! The time has come to change the dialogue. Instead of *talking* about angry black women, why not examine the circumstances that cause anger which leads to frustrations. We are not angry and bitter just to be angry and bitter. It is not that simple. And I am not talking about a few black women. I am talking about thousands, maybe hundreds of thousands of frustrated black women. I connected with many angry and frustrated sisters throughout the world via face-to-face conversations and in cyberspace. They shared compelling stories of heartache and pain that touched every aspect of life. These testimonies of frustration led me on a grueling eighteen-month journey to find the source of anger for black women. When I began this process, my

---

13

plan was to complete only six months of research; but I was so intrigued by the testimonies of these women that I extended it for another full year.

Actually, this book was born after witnessing an incident that captivated my curiosity. It was during the summer of 2005. My sister and I were having dinner in one of my favorite seafood restaurants, in my hometown of Monroe, LA. Our table was directly across from two frustrated women who attempted to have dinner with their children. My sister and I were child-free. However, these two sisters were not.

Between the two of them, there were five, maybe six kids. They did not have dates and it seemed as though they were not expecting anyone to join them. Neither female wore wedding bands; so I concluded they were unmarried. Because we all know when a sister *finally* gets married; her wedding ring is not coming off of her finger. Not even at gunpoint.

You would think they would have enjoyed having dinner with their kids and chatting with each other; just as my sister and I were. They were not. In fact, they looked as though they were ready to hand-deliver all six kids to Child Protection Services or to whomever would welcome them. I remember thinking to myself, "Why are these women so frustrated?" You should have seen them—yelling and screaming at the kids. And the facials they were giving—oh, they were disgusted. Of course, kids will be kids. And they showed their true colors in the restaurant. They spoke loudly, got out of their seats, and clearly embarrassed their moms.

That alone is enough to drive anyone crazy; but I knew it was more than those bad kids who got on their last nerve. Understandably, dealing with kids, especially bad kids, is frustrating. But it was more to their stories. I felt it. These women wrestled bigger problems. And I was on a mission to find out.

My initial reaction was to quickly go to their table, introduce myself and start a conversation with them to *discreetly* probe deeper into their frustrations. But in fear of getting righteously cursed out, I did not bulge. Instead, I used my keen investigative skills to monitor them. I watched them the entire time. I listened to the tone of their voices when they spoke to the children, I watched their facial expressions and body language—everything. Each time one of them looked in our direction, I quickly looked at my sister as if we were in the midst of a heated conversation. Being a master at persuasion, I convinced my sister to watch them too.

The kids were restless. They continued to move around at the table and walk around the restaurant. I felt badly for both women. Finally, they finished dinner, rounded up the kids and headed for the door. After they left, my attention shifted back to the gossip session with my sister. We eventually finished our dinner and returned home as well.

Later that night, I could not forget the incident that I had witnessed earlier in the day. I called my sister and asked her opinion on the source of frustration for the two women. She felt the kids were the source. But for some strange reason, I knew it was more. Their facial expressions and body language spoke volumes. The kids were not the source of their frustration; they only *added* to it.

That is when the idea hit me! I reflected on the many frustrated sisters that I witnessed over my lifetime. Heck, I reflected on the many times that I've worn that same disgusted look on my face. Black women are frustrated and angry. Some of us have worn frowns on our faces so long that the strongest dose of Botox could not smooth the wrinkles. Again, I asked myself, "Why are we so angry?" Do we feel abandoned? Are we angry at being forced to become single mothers to our babies due to lack of support from absent fathers? Are we frustrated because black women have become the face of HIV/AIDS in America? The answer? All of the above.

I have always been a people-watcher; but I became obsessed with the task of finding the sources of frustration for black women. For eighteen months, I observed and chatted with black women around the world. I unnoticeable listened as they complained about "no-good boyfriends" and "back-stabbing friends and co-workers". I watched as they scolded their children in public. And living in the friendly South, many of them began conversations with me as well. We discussed raising kids, financial debt, or "bills" as they referred to it, and school.

Without revealing my motive, I asked the question: "What causes the most frustration in your life?" The response was overwhelming.

"Baby, you don't have enough time for me to tell you all of my frustrations" one sisters answered.

My sister, Rhonda, laughed as she answered the question. My mom had a short list of frustrations. I even listed a few of my own.

I did not stop with regional conversations. I needed a broader perspective from a variety of black women. So, I hit the internet. I received tons of feedback from black women throughout the world. I logged onto discussion forums and message boards on African-American websites and chatted with tens of thousands of frustrated black women. The "cyber-sisters" were open and candid about frustrations that disrupted their daily lives just as the regional women. These forums were filled with angry and frustrated sisters. If you don't believe it, log on for yourself. Day after day, they logged on to share their frustrations with the world. For one full year beginning October 2005 and ending October 2006, they talked and I listened. I allowed them to vent their frustrations without judgment.

I spoke with black women from all walks of life—educated, uneducated, professional, single moms, broke college students, high school drop-outs, and even housewives. True enough, they resided in different parts of the world; but their stories were similar in nature. From South Africa to South Carolina, they were frustrated with unhealthy relationships, racial injustices, financial debt . . . just plain frustrated!

Am I implying that all black women are angry and frustrated? Not at all. I am in no way implying that all black women are frustrated because we are not. Many sisters were perfectly satisfied with their lives and would not dare change one aspect of it. And that's great. I wish all of the women had expressed this notion; but they did not.

Am I implying that only black women are frustrated? Once again, no. All women regardless of race or ethnicity get frustrated every now and then. But sisters seem to be *more* frustrated than any other race. Go to a shopping mall, any shopping mall and observe white women. They are just as happy as they want to be. You know why? Most times, they have help. Help with the kids, help with finances, and help with everything! Now, check out the sisters. Look at the frowns and scowls on their faces. Do they have help? Are they alone with kids? Are they left alone to pay for everything *themselves*? Now, do you understand why we are so frustrated?

Yes, it was a grueling journey; but I accomplished my goal. After approximately 720 hours of extensive online research and years of "Girl I know he didn't" conversations with girlfriends and ordinary sisters, I have uncovered the sources of frustration for African-American women and black women throughout the world. This unique collection of personal testimonies from sisters worldwide identifies many topics that not only affect black women; they affect the black community as a collective unit.

The twenty-one topics in *"Can I Get a Witness? 21 Things Frustrations of Black Women (Including Me)"* answer the age-old question—why are black women so angry and frustrated? It also dispels the negative and stereotypical myths that are associated with black women—being loud in public, promiscuous, and overly aggressive.

Just as many of the women I spoke with, I have witnessed and overcome many of life's frustrations. I am 34-years-old and *still* single, waiting for Mr. Right. I am a single mother. I struggled through college while working several stressful and unsatisfying jobs. I represent the face of many frustrated black women. In the book, I share a few personal stories in chapters including "Meeting Too Many Mr. Wrongs" "Hard-Headed Kids" and "Past-Due Bills". Follow me as I uncover the circumstances that cause the most frustration in the lives of black women worldwide.

Not only will it keep you laughing, it gives vivid insight to the daily frustrations that black women face. It also offers "Mikki's tips" to successfully overcome them. *Can I Get a Witness?* will engage, enlighten and entertain its readers from start to finish.

There is a common belief in today's society that all black women are "negative" and have "bad attitudes". This myth is simply not true. Many sisters, young and old, are only frustrated. Frustrated about what you may ask—please allow me to explain.

CHAPTER 1

Absent Fathers

"My father left me to do it all by myself. Just me and Mama."
Ray Lewis

"Any fool can make a baby;
but, it takes a real man to raise his children."
Jason "Furious" Styles

"Never knowed a child to come out right unless there's a man around
. . . children gots to have a Pa!"
Shug Avery

"Child, where is your mother?" Most often, this is the initial question uttered when an African-American child is reprimanded at school, church, or in their respective neighborhoods. The dialogue is quite different on the other side of the tracks. And it's really not a question, more like a comment—"Just wait until your father gets home!" With the growing number of black households headed by single women, "Wait until your father gets home" does not carry much weight. It is more like an idle threat. It would not mean a thing to many black kids because they know "father" never comes home. Hell, most of them would not recognize "father" if he stepped through their front door because they have never seen him before. In our community, it is almost as if we, black women, conceive babies alone. As if "father" does not exist. But what defines a father? Is he a provider? A teacher or role model? The head of his family?

Well, on Easter Sunday 2006, my pastor, Roosevelt Wright, Jr. preached the sermon "You Can't Keep a Good Man Down". In it, he described characteristics of a good father. His message discussed the trials and tribulations of Christ, as a man, which included—disappointment, betrayal, abuse (both mental and physical), persecution, and many of the same problems that we face today. Jesus was subjected to all of these things; but still gathered the strength to overcome them. He concluded the sermon by explaining the definition of Christ's resurrection.

"The resurrection is about rising from setbacks." he stated. "It's about starting all over, when it seems though it is *hopeless.*"

If only absent fathers carried the mentality of Christ—the world would be a much happier place. Angry children who resent their fathers for leaving would not feel a need to vent in other ways like fighting and causing trouble at school. And single mothers, we would be grateful. It would lighten the load that we carry each day—emotionally and financially.

Yes, a father's presence makes all the difference in the world. But, in many cases, especially in the African-American community, fathers are not present. Why? Great question. Many of them feel they are not father-material; which should have been considered before conceiving children. Some are unemployed and feel they cannot support a family. But, once again, this should have been considered before becoming fathers. Actually, many absent fathers are financially and emotionally able to care for their children. They choose—for whatever reason—to be absent from their kid's lives. There are also fathers who insist they were "trapped" into fatherhood which, in my world, is just another excuse for their absence.

Speaking of excuses, absent fathers possess more than a recovering crack addict who's discovered in a crack house four months into his recovery. The bottom line is, there is no excuse for being an absent father—none. Absent fathers abandon their kids and leave them to maunder through life and wonder if they have what it takes to bring daddy home. Lost is the best definition to describe father-less kids. They go through life feeling like an incomplete jigsaw puzzle knowing only half of their family's history. Mama is the only caregiver they know. Yes, many fatherless kids can relate to NFL linebacker Ray Lewis when he said, "Just me and mama."

Lost children and fragmented families are prevalent throughout the black community. I have witnessed it. You have witnessed it. It is a sad reality.

Some kids don't know their father's name—first or last. And that is really sad. My son's friend, Tre, can identify with this concept.

"I don't have a daddy", he said when I asked if he lived with his father.

Without going into graphic details of how babies are conceived, I said, "Everyone has a father Tre." I added, "You may not know your father; but you do have one."

Instantly, his eyes lit up. The look on his face was as if I have given him the best news in the world. He did not say a word. He simply smiled and walked into my son's room. Apparently his mom did not tell him anything about his absent father. He did not even know the man existed.

My son knows all to well the feeling of abandonment. His father left when he was just a toddler. Of course, at two-years-old he did not understand the affects of his father's absence. But as he grew older, he felt it. In March 2006, he used writing to release his frustration. He wrote a poem entitled "Black Men". I found it one day while rummaging through his backpack after school. He wrote, "Black men are there to make the baby but not there to take care of the baby. I wonder how they move so quickly. If you look at the clock it hadn't moved a tick." He continued, "If you can stay long enough to make a baby, be there to take care of the baby." And on the far edge of the paper he wrote the words "true story". It is such a shame that at the tender age of twelve, he too recognized the growing trend of absent black fathers.

Fathers who willingly disconnect themselves from their children seem to be the norm among African-American households. Dedicated black fathers are slowly becoming an endangered species. According to the 2000 Census, single female-headed families are far more likely in black homes than in all other groups. They account for 45.4%. White households have a rate of 13.7% and Hispanics have a 22.3% rate of single female-headed families. It also stated that black families are less likely to contain a married couple than all other groups at 46% compared to 81% in white families. The rate for Hispanics families is 67%.

One does not have to travel far to validate these grim statistics. There is significant evidence across the country. Look at the growing number of black men incarcerated. Many of them are fathers—absent fathers. And many of their fathers were absent as well. Drug addiction is another obstacle that devastates the lives of black men and snatch them from their families.

As I mentioned before, I am a single parent. My son's father has been absent for most of his life. He is a teenager now, fourteen. But he was always surrounded by positive men. I made certain of it. Whether at church, school or at home, he was always surrounded by positive men.

And being his mother's son, he is very active in sports. He loves sports! Since the age of four, he was affiliated with sports and coaches who disciplined him and kept him in line. One particular program that he participates in annually is the Monroe Youth Baseball Association. It is a predominately white league with approximately 5% black players, if that many. With practice beginning three weeks before the season began, parents always participated in a "Meet and Greet" sessions. I mentioned this league because of the mass amount of parent participation it has each season. It was always great; especially among fathers. They did everything. They coached the teams. They worked the concession stands. They even performed ground keeping duties on the baseball diamond. I mean they did everything. Each father did their part to support his son's team.

Just as many of the previous seasons, last season was no different. My son was the only black player on his team; meaning I was the only black parent present. This was so interesting to me because I was the only female who was not accompanied by a man—a husband. My dad and brother were present as male supporters; but my son's *father* was not there. It hurt badly to see all of the women grinning and smiling with their husbands; but I did not dare show it. I did not want my son to feel bad; so I hid it. I acted as though it did not bother me. However, it was all a front.

Each time I saw the boys walking with their fathers, it hurt. Each time I saw a father walking with his son to the concession stand to buy snacks, it hurt. And each time I saw my son stick to his coach like glue, it hurt. But I refused to allow my frustrations with his absent father to interfere with his performance on the diamond; so I concealed them. I redirected all of the negative energy and used it to cheer his team to victory. Besides, his entire family—grandparents, aunts, uncles, and cousins—were present at all of his games.

Even though it hurt to see their father's presence, I was amazed by it. They were there for every game throughout the season—no excuses. If they were running late, they still showed up. In some cases, they had kids playing on different teams simultaneously. That did not stop them. They'd spend time at one game; then leave and watched the second half of the other game. They did everything in their power to support their boys and I was so impressed. It all came down to one word—dedication. These fathers were dedicated to their boys. And that's how it should be, regardless of color. Fathers should be there for their kids, especially for their sons.

Baseball is not the only sport my son played. Just as his father, football is his passion. He is athletically gifted . . . naturally talented. It was passed from generations before him—his grandfather to his father and from his father to him. If you ask him, he'll quickly inform you that he has the speed of the Heisman Trophy winning running back Reggie Bush of the New Orleans Saints; but at the quarterback position. He began playing football when he was eight years old—flag football. So, each year after baseball season, I registered him to play football with the local YMCA. This was our routine year after year.

About four years ago, I missed the registration deadline because it was moved up a week or two. Due to the mix-up, he was not able to play for the YMCA. Of course, he was very disappointed and so was I. His passion for the game would not allow him to miss the season. So, we researched to find another football program. I researched a few places and found a program affiliated with the city recreational department. As a child, I enjoyed playing at the local recreation centers and worked as a summer camp counselor for years. I assumed he would enjoy "the rec", as we called it back in the day, too. So, I signed him up. Bad decision.

From the very beginning, there were ominous signs that this program was a bad idea. The first day of practice was a disaster. We waited for nearly two hours for the coach, who by the way did not contact the parents prior to the meeting. We waited and waited; still, no one arrived. Disgusted, I called the center the very next day to inquire about the program and the coach. No one knew anything. Not even the center director. He didn't know if my son's application had been processed. He didn't know the coach's name. Nothing.

I insisted on getting information, at least regarding my son's application. Finally, he retrieved the coach's information and called him. He gave a tentative schedule of the games for the season and asked me to return the following day for the first day of practice.

Just as the registration process, the first day of practice was a joke. Being an African-American sponsored program, I was so disappointed to see the lack of parent participation—especially from the fathers. It was minimal; almost non-existent. The only men present were the coaches—three of them. I saw a few mothers and grand-mothers; but not many. Sadly, parent support was the total opposite of the other program.

Everything seemed to be wrong with this program. The boys were not properly equipped to play football in this league. There was not a uniformed dress code enforced; so the players wore anything to practice and even games. I even noticed one child playing in a pair of black house slippers that were flattened at the back because he walked on the back of the shoes. If I recall correctly, my son was the sole child with a pair of football cleats on the field. At the end of the initial practice, most of the kids either walked home in the dark or needed a ride; so I offered a ride to whoever lived closest to our house.

Just as with everything else, my son and I were disgusted with this new found program. After only one practice, he was not feeling it. Actually, he hated it. He hated the lack of organization, the low parent participation and the fact that they did not have equipment to play football. And I hated it too. But his love of football and new teammates were the only thing that kept him interested in the program. He felt sorry for the players who did not have cleats. He asked if he could give a pair of his old cleats to one of his teammates. I thought it was a generous gesture; so I allowed it. On the second day of practice, he gave the cleats to one of his teammates and they were a perfect fit.

I thought the parent participation would increase the second day of practice. It did not. It was the same—one or two mothers, the players, the coaches and no fathers in sight. Twelve to fifteen boys were on the team, and not one father present to support them. Game day was no different. The fathers still didn't show up. I could not believe it.

On some days, it made me angry while on other days, it made me really sad. Sad to see these black boys without the love and guidance of a father. The coaches stepped up though. They did an excellent job with the team and I applauded them for their effort. They did not have any kids who played on the team nor were they paid to coach the team. They volunteered when no one else would. They needed more help though. The task was too great for them to do it alone. I offered help whenever possible; but they needed men. They needed men to help coach, carry equipment, and drive players to and from the games. They needed help from the so-called men who fathered these boys.

It was so disheartening to witness that my son and I did not remain with the program. We dropped out after the second game. He quit the team and I supported his decision 100%. It was ridiculous—unorganized and dysfunctional. Thankfully, this experience did not discourage him from playing the sport that he loves dearly. The following year, I made certain to sign him up for the YMCA program. I was probably one of the first parents to inquire about the registration deadline. He completed two successful seasons with the program and now plays quarterback for his high school team.

Kids will be kids regardless of race or ethnicity; but parental guidance and discipline are key factors in raising children—especially from fathers. I have worked with children of all races for more than ten years in recreational, reading, and volunteer programs. But I had never encountered a group of kids like the group I met in the fall of 2005. "Tutors needed" was inscribed on a colorful flyer in the stairwell of the Administration Building on the University of Louisiana—Monroe's campus. Enthusiastically, I applied for a part-time position with a non-profit organization. After only the first interview, I knew I had the position. Why wouldn't they hire me? I had years of experience working with "at risk youth", whatever that meant, and I was my usual self-confident, charming and very persuasive. Sure enough, I was offered the position and I began training immediately.

The kids, whose grades ranged from 1st to 12th, were divided into two groups. Group one consisted of grades 1st through 6th and group two consisted of grades 7th through 12th. Fortunately, I was able to choose my grade level. I chose the older group of students because I felt they would be more mature. And yes, I was fully aware that the students in the program were at risk kids; but I had worked with problem kids most of my life. I was not concerned about my new position as tutor and mentor. But maybe I should have been.

The first week was great. I breezed through it. It consisted of team building skills and getting familiar with team members. Oh, this was the fun part of the experience—learning the programs' policies, group activities, and games. During this week, we were introduced to the students, but had very little contact with them. I was eager to meet them. And when I met them, it was a very, shall I say, eye-opening experience for me indeed.

You could not tell just by observation alone that this was an undisciplined group of kids. There were approximately fifteen students with two team members per group to supervise them. "This isn't too bad" I thought to myself as they introduced themselves to us. Besides, I had worked with larger groups of kids before. Boy was I wrong! The group size was not the problem. Their behavior was awful. They were disrespectful, vulgar, and ill-mannered. Instead of hiring two female college students, they should have recruited three Five Star Marine Corps sergeants.

All of them were not bad kids. A few of them were well behaved. A few. But the bad over-shadowed the good. I tried every possible technique to get them to participate in learning activities. They were not interested. Most of them were more interested in clowning around and calling each other names like "Nigga" or "Bitch". And basketball held their attention longer than any other activity.

Despite the ill-behavior of most of the kids, there were two or three who I enjoyed working with. They were respectful and they addressed me as "Ms. Zimmerman". On one particular day after accomplishing absolutely nothing in the learning center, we proceeded to the gym for recreation. I closely monitored each child's behavior. I was intrigued by one student whose behavior was the total opposite of his peers. Michael was his name. He was very well-mannered at the center and a star athlete on his high school football team. Michael was a very articulate young man who dressed neatly.

Michael was well liked by his peers, so he assisted me in controlling the group because they listened to him. All of them except one. And he was the worse of the bunch. He dressed with his pants hanging below his butt; which I constantly disciplined him for. He loved attention. But unlike Michael, he gained attention by acting out. This kid stayed in trouble. I noticed that he lacked the self-confidence that Michael displayed and it bothered him. He argued with Michael every chance he got. It was as if he resented Michael—envious of him for some reason which immediately raised a red flag in my mind.

Acting as a cloned Dr. Phil, I continued to monitor his behavior as well as the other kids. Each day was the same—picking fights with the other students, especially Michael, cursing, and being disrespectful to the adults. One day after returning to the learning center, I took a poll. I asked the students in my group a very interesting question.

"How many of you are being raised by your father?" I asked.

Dead silence filled the room. Then, they looked at me very strangely. Some even looked away or hung their heads to hide their faces. No one answered right away; they just looked at me. I suspected that I knew the answer; but I wanted confirmation from them.

I asked again, "Who lives with their father?"

Michael was the only student who raised his hand. That was my confirmation.

One boy asked, "Ms. Zimmerman, why did you ask that?"

I responded, "Just asking".

Their behavior instantly changed for the duration of the evening. It was as if they figured out my point in asking the question. They were still talking quietly among themselves; but they were not acting stupid as they were before.

I knew there was something different about Michael. He had a positive father figure in his life. Even if not his father, I knew the presence of a strong black man was active in his life. I sensed it. Without any knowledge of Michael's personal records, I gathered from his behavior that he was raised by a positive man. His pants were not sagging. He addressed the adults at the center with respect. And he seemed to be happier than most of the other kids. You know, like he had a good family life. The other kids seemed angry and uptight; like they had the weight of the world on their shoulders with hoarded aggression built up inside that they venomously released on each other.

I cannot confirm the family environment for any of the kids, not even Michael. But their behavior was a reflection of their home environment. Some of them may have come from good families. Some may have not. But their attitudes and behaviors spoke volumes. I am not implying that most of the students in the program were being neglected at home or that single moms can not raise children properly. I am a single mom. I know it is possible for women to raise respectable men.

Although I cannot confirm exactly what happened in their homes, I can confirm the difference in Michael's behavior and the other kids. He was no angel. There were times where I reprimanded him for his behavior too. He was talkative and aggressive—just as any teenage boy. But he displayed his aggression on the basketball court which was appropriate. He did not lash out with anger toward the other kids—downing them to build up his self-esteem. He was already confident and self-assured which was most likely taught at home.

I knew there was something different about Michael. He had the presence of a strong male figure, his father, to guide and direct his path. A father to teach him how to wear his pants properly. A father to teach him how to respectfully speak to women. A father to teach him how to be a man. These are the reasons why the young man resented Michael and always picked fights with him. He desperately wanted what Michael had at home-the guidance of a father.

Michael was one of the lucky ones. His father was home with him. But what happens to the millions of frustrated black children without fathers? Why is there such a large gap in the statistics between fatherless families in our community as opposed to other ethnicities? Some blame the large gap on the lack of male role models in the black community. Black children are not surrounded by educated, hard-working, God fearing men who plant a strong foundation for their children to learn and prosper. Instead, they are surrounded by men who father out-of-wedlock children with multiple women and men who would rather steal from others than work hard to maintain a lavish lifestyle.

Reflecting back on my research findings, I witnessed many excuses from absent fathers. Some men felt they were forced out of their kids' lives by the mother and other family members. Well, they can tell that to the judge, because I didn't buy it! If you truly love your children and want to be an active participant in their lives, nothing will stop you from pursuing a relationship with them. Not even a hell-raising baby mama.

"All men didn't up and leave on some grand ole mother ship taken away to some (a) far off land" said one fed-up online brother from Baltimore, MD. "Most were thrown out, kicked out, cussed out, beat out, cheated on, lied to, deceived, mislead, coned and broken spirited."

Sisters weighed in too. "Please, if a man decides to leave it is on him. Some men know the mother will be there for the kids regardless", suggested a Forth Worth, TX sister.

Another 21-year-old from New York stated, "Blah, Blah, Blah! You black men always cease to amaze me. There is no way in hell in America that a woman can run a man who is handling his business well away. So please stop trying to defend these immature, lazy brothers who are too incompetent to care for their offspring."

A candid Chicagoan agreed with me. She said, "A real man can't/won't be forced to do anything he doesn't want to do."

"Wow!" I thought. This was a very touchy subject indeed and everyone, male and female, got in on this heated discussion. Very strong opinions emerged online for this conversation. But this reflected how this subject affects the black community. Single mothers were angry for being just that—single mothers. And brothers were angered by the comments of the single mothers. At times, it was similar to the "Battle of the Sexes"—men against women—because genders stuck together. Men blamed women for "sleeping with the wrong brothers". And women dogged the brothers labeling them "sorry and irresponsible".

Being a single mother myself, I was angered at times by many of the comments. I responded, "Okay, instead of pointing the finger at single black mothers, let's look at how they became single black mothers. Where are the black fathers of all of these boys that we are discussing? Black men are so quick to point the finger at someone else instead of taking a long hard look at themselves. So quick to call a black woman a whore or a bitch and you wonder why our black boys are filling up jails across this country; uneducated, and any other negative statistic."

This is only a portion of my response because my parents and my pastor would have been shocked by the remainder of my comments.

My response filled an entire page and boy did I receive lots of criticism from men advising me to "Shut up". Some even cursed me out. But, it did not bother me one bit. The majority of the responses were angry; but some agreed with me.

"Yes, yes, yes, yes, yes, yes; the truth has been spoken" proclaimed an online brother. He continued, "There are so many males talking the talk and (are) the first to do the walking."

I agreed and thanked him for his positive remarks. Other guys praised me for being "candid and honest" in my opinions. This discussion lingered around the discussion board for weeks. Even months after it ended, I still received random replies on this subject.

The ill effects of absent fathers linger well into adulthood. During my research, I spoke with several women and men who explained in vivid details how it affected their lives.

"I personally don't give a shit about him", said a 33-year-old Las Vegas, NV native in reference to her absent father. "When I was 9, he and my mother got a divorce and even though he had visitation he wanted nothing to do with us."

Another frustrated sister from Washington DC stated, "I am 41 and the results of my father not being in my life hurt me dearly. I've tried to get to know him for several years; I got tired of doing all the leg work and it wasn't worth it anymore."

Even in Johannesburg, South Africa, there were problems stemming from absent fathers.

I spoke with a young woman who stated, "A lot of Black fathers are not present and this causes a lot of children to rebel and act out of character." She continued, "I do hope this bad trend of single Black families will change in the future."

And if you think only women are scared by absent fathers, you are sadly mistaken. Men maybe affected more by a father's absence. As little boys, they are left to figure out the role of a man, father and husband through the guidance of their mother and grand-mothers. But how can a woman teach a boy to be a man? Somebody, anybody, answer this question for me.

The great lyricist Tupac explained this scenario in a tribute to his single mother. He wrote, "I finally realize for a woman it aint easy trying to raise a man." Tupac knew the difficulties of single motherhood by witnessing the hardships in his life. A woman trying to raise a man alone —this statement alone sounds crazy. But this is the arduous task that we—single mothers—must perform, alone.

Women do not have penises. We do not grow beards. Our voices don't deepen as we grow older. How in the hell can we explain these physiological changes to our boys? We can explain the process to them. We can buy all of the books that our finances allow. But we cannot tell them how it feels or what they should do in many cases. The only thing we can do is make sure he receives the proper information to help him grow. That's it. We cannot relate to it. And besides, there are some lessons only a father can teach his son. So, now what?

Throughout the research process, I heard captivating testimonies from various people—men and women—regarding their invisible fathers. But no story touched me like NFL linebacker Ray Lewis's moving and heartbreaking story. The effects of his absent father were evident in a television show which profiled his life—*Beyond the Glory*. In it, he explained how he dearly missed vital life lessons that his father never taught him and how it affected him into manhood.

Early one morning in the summer of 2006, I could not fall asleep; so I decided to watch television. I flipped through channels until I rested on *FSN—Fox Sports Network* and proceeded to watch. As the show began, I set the timer because I was certain that I would fall asleep before the program concluded. But I didn't. Actually, I watched the entire show without moving an inch. I was paralyzed just looking into Ray's eyes and listening as he spoke of the pain he feels largely because his father abandoned him.

"My father left me in the hospital [at birth] and never returned" he explained with tears in his eyes. Though he did not allow them to fall, they welled up as he spoke of the pain and rejection. This 6'1" 250lb linebacker of steel who was twice named the NFL's Defensive Player of the Year was so emotional as he reflected on his father. Ray, Super Bowl MVP and eight time Pro Bowler, is one of the most feared defensive players in the league. And to see him, a *fully* grown man, tear up as he stated, "I'll do anything to have father/son relationship" convinced me of the long-term devastating effects an absent father has on his son. If Ray feels this way at the age of 33, just imagine how our children feel as babies, children, and teenagers.

When I began watching Ray Lewis' story, I was tucked tightly in my sheets. But by the end of the show, I was sitting at the edge of my bed. Glued to the television. Paralyzed by his words. His story was moving and compelling. I applauded him for sharing it with the world. He opened the door for more black men, young and old, to stand up and tell their stories as well. Their stories would definitely help millions of fatherless black boys across the world; you know, to let them know they are not alone in their struggle.

We all agreed that real fathers are rare in the black community. Not to say there are no fathers who stick around to help raise their kids. There are scores of black men who dedicate their lives to mold and shape the lives and minds of their children. I know plenty of black men—church members, neighbors, and co-workers—who are instrumental role models for their kids.

Take for example, a young man I met in June 2006. It was two days before Father's Day so you know the barber shop was packed with clients. I saw a gentleman who looked to be in his early to mid 30's holding a baby boy tightly and close to his chest. He sat quietly as he waited for his turn to get a haircut.

In my opinion, he was "Super Dad" because he did everything perfectly. He was well prepared with a diaper bag, diapers, bottles filled with baby formula, and a pacifier—you know, everything needed to care for a small infant. He was so protective of his son as if he shielded him from the world.

I watched him and I found that to be such a beautiful sight. I watched him carefully as he held his son—still close to his chest. It was such a beautiful sight. Being a unisex salon, there were plenty of female clients present. And you know how distracted men are by the presence of women. Not super dad. His focus and attention remained on his son. No one else.

I was intrigued by this father and with me being a single woman, I checked his left hand. I noticed a wedding band and thought to myself, "Yeah, just my luck".

Regardless, I struck up a conversation with him. "How old is he?" I asked. He replied, "Six months."

He was such a cute little boy. I wanted to hold him, but I decided against asking. I continued to watch him.

I was not the only person in the shop who noticed that he was the perfect candidate for "Father of the Year". My hairstylist noticed too.

She blurted out, "You should get a great Father's Day gift. Hell, I don't even know you and I want to buy you a gift."

He smiled without saying a word. I seconded that emotion. Other females in the salon smiled and nodded in agreement.

This father—super dad—is the role model desperately needed throughout our community. He could not relax while getting a haircut because he was so concerned about his son. Talk about dedication. He reminded me of the white fathers I witnessed from my son's baseball league. But he is a rare presence in our community. It is sad to admit; but many times as I witness this father in the black community, I feel the need to shake his hand and thank him for staying.

Yes, super dad is uncommon. But thug daddy is not. Who is thug daddy? He is the inverse of super dad. He lacks the parental skills needed to raise successful and productive children. He really should not be a father. But he is. And he can be found throughout the black community.

My sister encountered this father last summer and was sickened by the experience. She visited a close friend when a young man, who was introduced to her as "a friend of the family", pulled into the front yard. He drove a long Cadillac with music blaring from its speakers. He stepped out of the car, shirtless—wearing only Khaki shorts and brown flip flops. He spoke to everyone as he approached the house. He carried a 5-month-old baby boy on his right hip and a bag of Church's Chicken in his left hand. The baby wore a one piece suit and nothing else. He had nothing to care for his son. Nothing. Only a pacifier. No bottles of milk or pampers. He hurriedly handed the baby to someone, grabbed a few pieces of chicken and began to eat. The manner in which he ate the chicken disgusted my sister. With greasy hands, he reached for his tall can of beer and burped loudly after each long sip.

As he ate his meal, his son began to cry. The pacifier fell from his mouth and hit the ground. My sister attempted to wash the grit from it but she was interrupted.

He quickly informed her "You don't have to do that [rinse]". Using the can of beer, he rinsed the pacifier.

My sister and her friend yelled at him and asked again if they could wash it.

"It's nothing wrong with giving him beer" he responded. "I give him beer all of the time. That's my son!"

My sister described the manner in which the infant sucked the beer stained pacifier. She said he acted as if "he loved the taste of it." Sadly, he may have tasted it before. His little fragile body may have even craved it.

After finishing his meal, he left his son and stated that he would return "in a few minutes". A few minutes turned into an hour. As a matter of fact, he was gone so long that they finally called him on his cell phone and asked him to return for his son. The baby was fidgety and hungry. He was probably uncomfortable from his wet and soggy diaper. They could not change him or feed him because his "father" didn't bring any diapers and bottles. Thug daddy finally returned for his son and the two sped away in his booming car.

I was not present to witness his pathetic attempt at fatherhood, but I was saddened by the description. Immediately after hearing this pathetic story, a Bible verse popped into my mind. "And ye Fathers provoke not your children to wrath: but bring them up in the nurture and admonition of the Lord." Ephesians 6:4. The father that my sister described, thug daddy, did not obey this scripture at all. In fact, he did the total opposite. He placed his son's life and health in harm's way the entire evening; maybe the entire night.

Not to pass judgment, but what type of mother allows her 5-month-old son to be subjected to this type of treatment? Even if he is the baby's father. Poor thing; I suppose she was thankful that he stuck around to help her raise their son. This man clearly lacked the parental skills to serve as a positive role model for his son. This negative trend of fatherhood will be passed down to his son and his son will pass it down to his son. It is a vicious cycle that continues until someone gains the knowledge to break it.

Tearing down the family structure is a definite method of destroying a race of people. Without the guidance and leadership of strong fathers, the black community is slowly crumbling to pieces. There are not enough black men who are willing to not only step up to the plate, but hit a home run. Too many brothers are striking out on their children. Especially their boys. Leaving them to fend for themselves. Leaving their boys to figure out his role as a man.

The emotional pain and rejection a child feels knowing his father does not want him is immeasurable. Webster has yet to record a word that describes this pain. Although I have never felt this pain, I have been forced to witness it through the eyes of my son. His father is absent and it hurts him deeply. But he is very fortunate to have a large number of positive black men in his life.

Yes, it is a vicious cycle that continues from generation to generation. But, in my son's situation, the cycle ends here. He will be present to teach his daughter to ride her first bicycle. He will be present to teach his son the proper steps to tie a necktie for Sunday school. He will be there. I will make certain of it.

Sisters worldwide agreed—absent fathers cause a substantial amount of frustration for single mothers. It is, what I call, a crisis in our community.

So much, that last year on Father's Day, President Barack Obama addressed this issue while on the campaign trail in June 2008.

"They've abandoned their families", he stated in reference to absent fathers. "They're acting like boys instead of men", he added. He also mentioned the "foundation of our families (in the black community) have suffered because of it".

He was attacked in the media soon after his speech by some who were offended by his words. But he only stated the truth. Black women around the world are frustrated with raising children alone. Many times, I became frustrated by just listening to their stories which sounded so familiar to me. I became so frustrated that I decided to write a long heart-felt letter in attempt to grasp the undivided attention of absent fathers worldwide.

Hey, who knows, maybe this letter will allow me to achieve as much success as Minister Louis Farrakhan when he organized the "Million Man March" in October 2005. Maybe, just maybe, I can pull it off too! I'll call it the Million Absent Fathers March. Just my luck, I would have ten fathers show up and half of them would be late. Man, I tell you. Maybe, I should just write the letter and discuss the march at a later time. Here goes:

Dear Absent Father,

I need your help! My load is too heavy and I feel like I'm losing the battle to SMS, Single Mother Syndrome. The load I am referring to is the one I carry everyday and will continue to carry until you decide to help. I'm tired! Tired of carrying your weight in this so-called household. Tired of being an "independent woman". I need help! Besides, everything seems to flow so smoothly when you help and my back doesn't hurt from carrying all of the weight.

I'm mama and daddy all at the same time. Will you please help? Can you relieve me for just a while? I'm tired of making excuses for your absence. Your children are getting older and asking more and more questions about "daddy". And please don't get it twisted, I *am* strong enough to play both parts because I have done it for such a long time. I just need a break. That's the least you could do. Stop ducking and dodging when you come within two blocks of my house. I won't shoot at you, well, not this time anyway because I need a break. You've had your break. And it has lasted too long. You come around every now and then and expect everyone to be all giddy when we see you. You haven't done a damn thing for anyone to be giddy about.

Your kids think the world of you and for the life of me, I cannot understand why. For once in your life, stand up and be a man. It's impossible for me to fill your shoes—you wear a size 14; I only wear a 9 ½. I cannot continue to do this alone. It is a privilege to be called "Daddy" and your privilege is slowly slipping away. Do not come around years later trying to make up for lost years. You will never get those years back. And don't come around when you learn that your son will be a lottery pick in the NBA or NFL drafts. It will be too late. Once you make the choice to be an absent father, it's a done deal.

Your children did not ask to be here. We asked for them to be here. Yes, we asked. We asked when we decided to have unprotected sex. Everything was cool then. Remember? You told me how much you love me and how you would always be there for me. What happened? Did all of those feelings leave along with your sperm when you ejaculated? They must have because I haven't seen your sorry butt since that day. It is such a shame to say this but it is the naked truth. The purpose of this letter is not to make you angry enough to hunt me down and harm me but to make you angry enough to move you into action—the action of performing your fatherly duties. It should not have taken me to write this letter to get your attention but as Malcolm X put, "By any means necessary." And if it takes this letter to save the future of my child, then I am willing to write it.

If this letter is hard to digest, then it is serving its purpose. Wake up man! Your alarm clock sounded years ago but yet you are still asleep. Just because your father was not a part of your life does not mean you shouldn't be present in your kids' lives. Break the cycle. Help me provide a positive atmosphere for your children. Help me provide positive role models for your son to prevent him from looking to the neighborhood thugs or the hottest gangster rapper for guidance. Help me provide positive role models for your daughter to prevent her from looking for any man to make up for the love and affection she did not receive from you. Wake up absent fathers! Help us to help our children because they need you. We need you to survive!

Sincerely,

Single Mothers

CHAPTER 2

Meeting Too Many Mr. Wrongs

"It's so good, loving somebody and that somebody loves you back;
Said not 70-30; not 60-40; talkin' about a 50-50 love!"
Teddy Pendergrass

"I would follow his lead thinking
I would be the one he'd keep around."
Mary J. Blige

"Why do we love love, when love seems to hate us?"
Jazmine Sullivan

Ladies, has this ever happen to you? You are casually strolling through the supermarket searching for Gold Medal flour on aisle five when you spot "Him". He is tall with a smooth mocha complexion and extremely sexy. His hair is freshly cut and his goatee is shaped up just right. In a sense, he reminds you of the oh so sexy Morris Chestnut and he's headed in your direction. Immediately, your heart pounds faster. As he approaches, the aroma of Armani Black Code cologne fills the aisle. Trying to remain calm, you nonchalantly continue your search as he draws closer. Surprisingly, he starts a friendly conversation regarding the big weekend sale. You gather from his conversation that he is articulate and very smart. But you are still unsure of his marital status. Your eyes squint so tightly until they almost close; trying to get a quick glimpse of his ring finger. Still, you are unable to see it.

Regardless, this man is gorgeous and his smile lights up the entire building. As you gaze into his deep brown eyes you can't help but think "Our Father which art in Heaven". Yes Ladies, he is *that* fine! As the two of you stroll down the aisle, he suddenly reaches for a can of evaporated milk when BAMMMM! His wedding band shines brighter than Lil Wayne's grill. Your chest tightens up and you collapse in the center of the aisle. Okay, you don't actually collapse; but you certainly want to.

This scenario has happened to me so many times that it seems like a reoccurring nightmare. The setting may not have been the supermarket; but the results were the same—my leaving the situation feeling as though I will never find Mr. Right. I am not alone. I met hundreds of single black women who have the same problem as I—meeting too many Mr. Wrongs and not one Mr. Right.

So if you think "It's hard out here for a pimp", it's even harder if you are a young, single, self-respecting, sane black women waiting for her knight in shinning armor to sweep her off of her feet. The task of finding a husband is a constant struggle for black women. Statistics support this theory. The National Center for Health Statistics shows African-American women ages 14-45 are less likely than any other demographic group in the United States to get married. And at age 30, only 52% of black women are married, compared with 81% of white women and 77% of Latinos.

You see, it is hard for us to find lifetime partners. But why? Where are all of our potential husbands? Are they entangled in the prison system? Are they with non-black women? Are they on the down low? These are the responses I received from black women across the country.

"I have been here (California) many years and the brothas here have a strong obsession with white and Asian women. It's frightening", said a 28-year-old sister from San Francisco, CA.

My sister, a 40 year-old elementary school teacher, summed up her thoughts on dating and being single with two words—"It sucks".

My niece, a 22 year-old senior at Louisiana State University, was very candid with her thoughts on black men. She stated, "They are all married, gay, on drugs or in jail".

My mom, who celebrated her 50th anniversary in June 2007, commented on dating in the 21st century. "Men now are pathetic!" she said disgustedly.

The fact remains there are many single black women who seek loving, honest and committed relationships. Some sisters are fortunate enough to find true love while the rest are left behind feeling lonely and abandoned. Harvard sociologist Orlando Patterson Ph.D. attributes the effects of slavery to our broken relationships. He also suggested African-American women may be the most

—

un-partnered demographic on earth. And again I pose the question—where are our partners?

So, when are you coming home?

According to a controversial *New York Times* article—"Plight Deepens for Black Men"—young black men are incarcerated at an alarming rate. This topic sparked heated debate on black websites and within black communities throughout the country. Experts at leading universities like Harvard, Columbia, and Princeton, concluded that large numbers of black men who drop out of high school will never be able to find work in the United States. It showed 6 in 10 black men in their mid 30's who are high school dropouts have fallen victim to the prison system; and in 2004, 72% of black male high school dropouts were jobless. This group represents a class of men who father children they cannot care for, do not work, and become entangled in the prison system. If these studies are correct, this is devastating news for black women. The larger the number of black men in prison, the slimmer our chances are of finding mates.

And how will these men provide for their families when they are incarcerated? What message does this send to little black boys who look up to them as role models? Not only are they negative role models; they are a burden to their families, communities, and society as well.

A young man who I met in July 2006 fit the profile of one of the men described in the study. My son and I were at the barber shop. We are always at the barbershop. Anyway, he was in his mid to late 20's, a high school drop-out, and unemployed. I'm really not sure how the subject of prison emerged in the shop, but he definitely knew the ins and outs, so to speak, of the prison system. He made it clear that he had been incarcerated a few times.

"For a simple escape charge, you'll get an extra six months" he told everyone in the barber shop as if he gave an important seminar on the legal system or something.

My initial thought while listening to him was "If only he had applied his study habits in school, he could have graduated from law school". But he did not even graduate from high school.

I asked him, "What school did you graduate from?"

"I didn't", he responded. "School was (is) not for me. I couldn't get with the a + b = c in math, you know", he continued.

No, I did not understand. He was a very intelligent young man who, with the proper guidance, could have made a big impact in the world.

He was so dramatic too. He probably could have been an actor or comedian. But his view on hard work was pathetic. He told us that he was not willing to work a 9 to 5 job because he did not want to "start at the bottom to make it to the top".

His statement was so twisted to me; you know I had to put my two sense in.

"It takes hard work to get ahead in life. Everyone has to start somewhere, you know. Even Tyler Perry started at the bottom and look at him now."

He frowned at my suggestion as if hard work was a deadly virus that he did not want to catch.

I already knew the answer; but I just had to ask him anyway. "What type of work do you do"?

Sarcastically he answered, "You graduated from high school, figure it out".

As you can imagine, that was the end of our conversation. He got a fresh cut and exited the barbershop. I have not seen the young man since that day.

So, am I too dark for you?

Another hot topic online among black women was the growing number of professional black men who prefer non-black women. Many sisters believe we are losing the ability to catch single professional black men. There were many threads, or online message boards, dedicated to the popular phenomenon.

One sassy sister from New York stated, "I am sick and tired of seeing successful black men with white women and seeing so many single black women all alone because black men will not marry them (us)".

Another fed up sister stated, "Black men lose their pride and self-respect and the respect of their people when they love white women".

Pretty harsh words. To be honest, these messages were *kind* compared to others that were posted. Many were too graphic to mention. My research revealed most black women were disgusted at the growing trend and could not understand why professional black men seemed to look in the opposite direction.

Professional brothers—attorneys, doctors, executives, and educators are rare in the black community. Not saying they do not exist; they are rare. And available sisters line up and wait for a chance to compete for one. For most of us, the opportunity never presents itself. Why is it so difficult for us to catch his attention? Hell, convincing him to glance in our direction would be a good starting place.

True enough; the idea of "good black men" dating non-black women infuriated many sisters. But I did not understand why. If black men, professional or not, chose to date Asian, Hispanic or a white women, who cares? Ethnicity should not factor into the decision of who to date or marry. In my opinion, as long as he truly loved and cared for her, that's all that really mattered.

However, there is one brother that I do have an issue with—the black man who feels the need to date or marry outside of his race to enhance his public image or boost his self-esteem. Oh, you know this brother; he is successful with looks to die for. He's on the prowl—looking for his queen to join him in his lavish mansion. He is just like his father, the product of two loving parents who taught him to be a respectful and responsible family man. But there is one problem. This insecure brother feels that his future queen cannot and will not be a black woman. His reason? She is not "good enough" for him or so he feels. He needs a non-black woman to compliment him and help him look even better. In other words, an insecure brother who only dates white, Asian or Hispanic women to help boost his self-esteem. Now this is the black man that I have a *big* problem with.

Tiger Woods' name was mentioned quite often during these online conversations. Sisters flooded the message boards criticizing him after he married his Swedish girlfriend Elin Nordegren. I'm not going to lie; I was one of his biggest critics. But one episode of *60 Minutes* changed my opinion of Tiger Woods. It was an in-depth interview with the late Ed Bradley in March 2006. Tiger candidly spoke about many aspects of his life including his father, who later passed away in May 2006, his successful golf career, and of course, his wife. It is obvious that each one played a special role in Tiger's life. But when he talked about Elin, his eyes lit up! He smiled at the slightest mention of her name. My opinion of Tiger immediately changed. It was obvious to me that he genuinely loved her and would have married her if she was a black woman who possessed the same qualities as Elin.

He said, "She is my best friend". After looking into his eyes—as he flashed that million dollar smile and expressed his love for her—I truly believed that his love was color-blind.

There is a common belief among black women that professional black men run to white women. But I beg to differ. Yeah, there are a few who run to white women; but I think the opposite is true. I think white women run to them. Not only run to them, but chase them down like Ray Lewis chases running backs on Monday Night Football! They know these men are financially able to support a family and provide a lavish lifestyle for them as well. They are drawn to these brothers, especially the professional athletes. Oh, they love professional athletes! The more money he makes, the harder they pursue them.

I often wonder if they would pursue him if he held an average job like a mail carrier or garbage man. Don't get me wrong, black women love professional black men too. But most of us would love them the same if they were average Joes. I cannot say the same for other women. For instance, the white woman who smiles and grins in the faces of NFL, MBL and NBA players. Let's examine her for a moment. Change his job status to one less glamorous and see if she's still humming "I got jungle fever; he's got jungle fever." Change only his job status from professional athlete to mail carrier or garbage man and see how the story plays out. The same man physically, mentally and emotionally; only with a different job title.

Give that brother a mail bag, the keys to the little mail truck and the blue postman uniform. Send him into her neighborhood—the smiling and grinning white woman—to deliver the mail. While peeping out of her blinds, does she A) greet him at the door with the same ear-to-ear smile that she gave him after the NBA game and offer a drink of water because she knows it's burning up outside. Or does she B) lock her door until he drives off in his little mail truck before she retrieves her mail? Many online sisters easily selected "B" as the answer. And don't get it twisted, I understand there may be a few sisters locking the door as well; but not a *real* sister.

You see, real sisters are different. Replace the smiling white woman with a real sister in that scenario and things would go a little differently. First of all, he would return to work late because she wouldn't just offer him a simple glass of water. Oh no, not a true sister. This sister would have a deluxe breakfast prepared for him. The menu would read as follows: 3 slices of French toast, 4 slices of turkey bacon, 2 scrambled eggs, a side order of grits with butter, an 8 oz. glass of freshly squeezed orange juice and a cup of dark-roast decaffeinated coffee with cream and sugar. Now that's how a real black woman would greet this mail carrying brother.

Some professional black men act as though they know nothing about real black women once they become wealthy and famous—knowing good and well they were raised by strong black women. And they truly believe these fake women would fall for them minus the money and the bling. A small percentage may honestly be attracted to black men and that is cool. Hey chocolate is delicious—especially dark chocolate. We understand. No problem at all. As a matter of fact, one of my close friends from California, who is white, only dates black men. But she has dated black men her entire life. Not only professional athletes with lots of money. She dated black men who she thought were interesting and attractive. She even found it disgusting that we were attracted to her brother; who of course was white. She just likes black men. And that is cool.

So we are not mad or hating because black men like non-black women. There are scores of black women who date non-black men. So that is not the point. Online sisters were baffled as to why black men date non-black women whose intentions are not genuine. They did not want to see these brothers taken for a wild ride by free-loading women.

"If they like it, then I love it! Just let both of them make fools out of each other. Sounds like the perfect match to me", I said to concerned online sisters.

Some men understand how these women operate; but continuously fall for them regardless. As long as she enhances his public image, he is fine with the twisted arrangement.

But how can they not love it? These women have perfected the chase down to a science. They are very smart in their pursuit. They don't wait until NBA or NFL draft night or after he graduates from medical school. No Lord! They start in their freshmen year of college. Football season—they set their eyes on the athletes who has the most potential to make it to the professional level. She spots him on the field while doing her "routine morning run". The team is practicing for the upcoming season. He runs, pivots, and catches the ball well; obviously he is tremendously talented. And she knows this critical information because she has already performed research on him. Yeah baby, he is definitely headed to the NFL. And she starts her investment with the quickness.

She dresses him with the finest threads and nourishes him with the best cuisine. He smiles so big that his teeth hang out of his mouth. The entire time he's thinking—"I've never had a female to love me like this". "Shataqua", who was his last girlfriend, "was not able to provide for me like this". All the while, Lauren, the white girl, is thinking, "Yeah, just keep running the football well without getting hurt and we'll have it made in a few years". He's still running and smiling without a clue as to what Lauren has planned. Call me crazy; but this is how I presume the courtship plays out. I told you—they are very *clever.*

We also make ourselves available to professional black men. Of course, sisters want professional black men too. But often times, it is difficult for real black women to meet professional men. It is always the imposters—fake sisters with boobs, thighs, and butt popping out everywhere posing as real women—who make themselves available. And when the imposters show up, a hotel bed, a strip club and a pole are the tools used to catch his attention.

This may catch his attention; but it will not hold his attention. Notice the difference? Running on the track or a strip club? Who do you think he will be more willing to take home to meet Mama and Big Mama? And this is how we make our mistake. I am not judging anyone. I am just saying. If we desire the same results as non-black woman, we must present much more than our physical attributes to him.

We say men only want us for sex. But we act as though sex is all we have to offer. Sisters, we must show eligible bachelors that we too are classy, intelligent and will look damn good on his arm at his high-end charity event. We must show professional black men there is no need to switch after he becomes rich. Prove to him that he does not have to "white girl shop" because there are scores of beautiful single professional black women to choose.

So, am I too desperate?

I'll ask this question again but in a different manner because this was a hot topic online. Why is it so difficult for single black women to find lifetime partners? It may be that many of us are, in the words of the 80's R&B group The Deal, "Too lonely to be alone". We are so love starved that we are willing to share men with two or three women and be miserable rather than be alone and content. Because of loneliness, we maintain unhealthy relationships with cheating partners time and time again.

Cheating partners were mentioned several times during online conversations. Topics such as "Why (do) men cheat", "Fellas, do all of you cheat", and "Are men afraid of commitment" were common among black women throughout cyberspace. Cheating is an unnerving subject that creeps its way into numerous relationships and as a recent survey shows black women are getting the short end of the stick. According to a study by Professor Edward Laumann at the University of Chicago, nearly 68% of African-American men confessed to maintaining long-term sexual relationships with at least two or more women.

Am I implying that only men cheat? No, I am not. Women cheat in relationships as well. Cheating is unacceptable regardless of who committed the offense; but it is very rare that a woman cheats with two or three men. When women cheat, we usually do it out of lack of attention and affection or out of revenge of being cheated on. But men cheat for the hell of it—her thighs were glossy and shiny, or she had a big butt, or her teeth were pearly white—any stupid reason. And when they cheat, they don't cheat with one or two women. They cheat with an NFL roster of women with each one playing for a starting position.

Man sharing is not neoteric. Men have been cheating for years in "committed" relationships and marriages. It seems as though we have become more accepting of this behavior. Which brings me to a more appropriate question—why are we so willing to stay in unhealthy relationships that eat away our spirits? Are we that desperate to be in a relationship that we are willing to indulge in man sharing? Maybe this is the reason why some men hesitate to fully commit and ask for our hand in marriage. They sense our desperation. They know we are willing to settle for an unhealthy relationship that takes everything from us mentally, emotionally, and physically and give us absolutely nothing in return.

One brother from Chicago, IL, explained, "I don't believe young brothers see the benefit to marriage. If you (we) can hook-up with a sister, get all sex you (we) want, come and go as you (we) please, why bother"?

Another black man, whose age and location were not listed in his online profile, stated, "I love black women; but they are too easy. Black women must begin to show more self respect and maybe they will begin to receive respect".

Once again Ladies, the responsibility of maintaining respect in our relationships falls into our hands. If we do not demand it, we will not get it. Period! By allowing ourselves to be cheated on, disrespected and mistreated, we give our partners the recipe for destruction in our relationship. The lack of self-respect we display opens the door for his behavior to continue.

Listen, if the signs of cheating are present in your relationship and you are sick and tired of it, do not disregard them or blow them off as if they do not exist. You only postpone the inevitable—abandoning the relationship. Gather any evidence—and if I know sisters, there is a mountain of pictures, panties, and pieces of hair weave that don't belong to you hidden in the back of the closet—and confront him with it. Present it to him and let him know his behavior must change. And if it does not, you are gone. No if's, and's, but's, or well's, about it. Leave! I know this is easier said than done, I've been there. But it is the best resolution for you.

Think of it in this fashion. What would happen to our bodies if toxic waste is not removed properly? It eventually causes illness and if conditions are severe enough, it causes hospitalization. It can even kill us. Unhealthy relationships have the same effect as toxic waste. They make us physically and emotionally sick. They send us to emergency rooms and crazy homes across the country. As women we have the power to stop man-sharing by removing ourselves from unfaithful relationships; just as we remove toxic waste from our bodies.

Let's see, if we are not busy dodging jailbirds, trying to gain the attention of a professional brother, or being cheated on, we are busy chasing men who could give less than one damn about us. They are more interested in sparing our feelings rather than being honest about the relationship. With the exception of a few, we all have experienced this type of man. He is too afraid to tell us to get lost; so he drags us on a rollercoaster ride until we get tired and decide to get off. Did you catch the underlining message in that last statement? Until *we* decide to get off. For the entire ride he pitches subliminal messages which, many times, we catch the hints but convince ourselves that we can change his negative feelings.

"Men will walk a mile for a whore", my friend's aunt always said. She said this often when referring to an ex-boyfriend who cheated on her or dogged her out. I guess the same is true for women. The type of man we should pursue, we do not want. We say, "I want an honest, faithful, hard-working, God-fearing, family man whose number one priority is to love and support his family". Yeah, that's what we say. But, when he stares us in the face, we all of a sudden become Stevie Wonder and cannot see him. Tupac was not lying when he said, "I make you laugh but you rather have what makes you cry." Yeah, he was well aware of this concept too.

James Evans from the 70's hit sitcom "Good Times" is a prime example of the type of man we should pursue. But if we had a good man like James, we would dog him out. James was the perfect husband—loved Flo to death, afro and all, and he never cheated on her. He was a good father—provided guidance and discipline for his children. And he was an excellent provider—James worked any job to support his family. It did not matter what the job duties entailed—dishwashing, construction work, custodial work, or washing cars. What ever the job may have been, if it was legal, James did it to support his family.

James was the perfect candidate for a lifetime partner and Flo knew this. That is why she respected him and treated him right. But if many of us landed a guy like James, we would ultimately leave him for a Ned the Wino type of brother. I guess my saying "be careful of what you wish for because you're doomed to not want it once you get it" takes precedence here.

We have tendencies to chase behind men who do not care about us. The less attention they show, the more we desire to be with them. The more they dog us, the more we fall in love with them. And we are quick to make excuses for his behavior. We say "Oh, his plate is full" or 'He doesn't have lots of time to spare because he's such a busy man". Really? If he cared, he would *make* time.

I know everyone plays the fools sometimes; but must we be the fool all of the time? Judging from our behavior, I actually believe some of us enjoy playing this role—the fool. There is no other rational explanation why grown women run behind men who are clearly trying to free themselves from the relationship.

And men do not help the situation at all. Do they ladies? They only make things worse by lying and suppressing their true feelings. Instead of confessing "I want out!" they break dates at the last minute, forget to call back as promised, and purposely appear in public with other females in hope of the news getting back to us.

I don't know about you, but I am tired of witnessing devastated women who are in a complete state of shock after their man gathers the courage to end their failing relationship. It is so heartbreaking to witness. And guys are probably tired of lying too. So, I developed a short list of incontrovertible scenarios to help sisters recognize signs that he wants out.

First: If he goes everywhere with everyone else besides you, this man wants out! He goes places with his family, co-workers, friends, pastor, the pastor's aide club, his Yorkie "Sugga" and the dog groomer—everyone except you. He clearly does not wish to be bothered with you.

Secondly, if you drive an hour and thirty minutes to visit this brother to spend only twenty or thirty minutes with him because he is so busy doing other things, you are clearly wasting your time, gas and energy on this man. Find something constructive to do beside visit with him. Use this time to work out, attend church revival service or catch up on some beauty rest.

Thirdly, if his idea of a romantic dinner consists of two Sam's Club pizzas and a two litter Cola; when just last week he took another "friend" on a very expensive lobster, shrimp, and Fillet Ming yon steak dinner . . . no further explanation is needed.

Fourth, if your man returns your best friend's phone call before he returns your call, he is clearly trying to send you a message. It sounds like he's keeping you around to get with your best friend. Girl, you better watch him!

Fifth, if your husband returns home at 2:00 AM, brushes his teeth, takes a shower, and washes his hair five nights each week and swears he is not cheating;

get him tested for everything from HIV/AIDS to schizophrenia. If he is not cheating on you, one of his *other* personalities is cheating.

Lastly, if your husband takes his very lovely personal assistant on a seven day "business cruise" every three months to work on a project that he insists take three years to complete. Wait a minute, every three months? Three years? Let's see, that's four cruises a year for three years. What the hell? Twelve cruises? Unless this project is reconstructing the gulf coast that Hurricane Katrina destroyed, he has no business floating up and down the gulf with this floozy! Give this man his walking papers with the quickness!

Okay, I am being a little sarcastic. But don't laugh too hard, one or two of these scenarios actually happened. I am not poking fun at anyone. I am only trying to make a valid point—we believe the stupid lies that men feed us. The bottom line is this—if your man shows signs that he wants out of the relationship or that he has lost interest, do yourself a big favor—take the hints and find out the underlying issues in your relationship. If they cannot be resolved, as hard as it may be, leave him. This man is clearly not "the one" if he is not willing to correct the problems in your relationship. Somehow, find the strength to leave. Do not stick around until he actually tells you his true feelings. You think the hints he threw around hurt your feelings, wait until you actually hear the piercing truth.

So, do you have jungle fever?

Where do sisters go to find true love? It has been suggested that we too should date outside of our race. If brothers do it, so can we. A 2006 film featuring the beautiful Sanaa Lathan touched on this subject. In the movie she tried "something new" by falling for a white guy to the dismay of her family and friends. Her character, Kenya Denise McQueen, reminds me of one of my best friends who dates interracially. For the past ten years, she has dated white guys.

"Get love where you can find it!" she said. Although she insists the idea of dating black men is still an option, she added that "it's difficult to find one {black man} who is ready for serious relationship."

Other black women agreed. "I've tried to give an intelligent brother a chance and he was trippin with commitment phobia; so I started dating a French man", stated one sister from Indianapolis, IN who was in her late twenties.

Another sister from Miami, FL believed white men appreciate black women more than black men. She asked the question, "Is it my imagination or does it seems like white men treat black women better?" She also stated, "There was no drama {when dating a white man}, no fuss, no talk about money and they don't seem to be scared of being with just one woman".

For many sisters, the idea of dating white men is somewhat intriguing. We are willing to try something new if we could find a white guy who was not married and who had not been featured on Dateline's *To Catch a Predator* with Chris Henson. Yes, white men are quick to marry; but many carry dark fantasies into their marriages—which they act out via the internet. *To Catch a Predator* profiled men, mostly white and married with children, who were busted soliciting underage children online for sex. They actually chatted with decoys with the online watchdog group Perverted Justice who posed as underage kids.

On the show, Perverted Justice worked with local law enforcement across the United States to catch sexual predators that preyed on children online. With remnants of Keith Sweat's lyrics—"You may be young but you're READY!"—playing in their heads, these predators were very tricky in their approach. Homes in five states were used as meeting places to capture them. And they came running equipped with condoms, alcohol, and duct tape . . . all of the works. The show was filmed in New York, Ohio, Virginia, Florida and California.

As I watched the four-part special, I was shocked to learn the ages of the predators—ages 19-61. And their careers were even more shocking. Teachers, counselors, coaches, police officers, and even a Rabbi were included in the round-up. Nothing stopped them from meeting the so called children they met online. Not even distance. One sick and twisted man from Ft. Meyers, FL rode a Greyhound bus four hours and brought along beer and condoms to have sex with a 14-year-old child. Four hours! Another 27—year old 6th grade teacher and track coach from Ohio traveled almost two hours to meet a 13-year-old.

A total of 150 men were busted during this child pornography sting. Many of them are still awaiting trial. Of course, they claimed their innocence and swore they would not have had sex with the children. No, they only wanted "to talk" with them. Most, if not all, were white men. I think I spotted two, maybe three brothers in this special. And no, R. Kelly was not one of them. After viewing this program and witnessing the number of white men who were busted, I am not so sure that experiencing "something new" would be a keen idea for us. But if I have a change of heart, you can believe I will perform my own online investigation to see if he takes the bait.

So, all of this just for love?

What must sisters do in order to maintain loving relationships? Protect our men from the prison system, convince professional brothers to take a chance on us, hire private detectives to ensure monogamy and periodically conduct online investigations when dating white men? Are those the answers? All of this in the name of love? Yes. Many sisters will fight like Nikki Parker fought for "the

---

Professor" in exchange for a secure and loving relationship. We hope to find partners who make us feel secure by not only his words, but his actions as well. As women we give so much of ourselves in relationships and many times receive nothing in return except heartache, disappointment, and resentment.

"Love is an action word", said one of the senior deacons of my church. "You cannot just say it, you have to show it", he added.

And sisters don't mind showing love. Often times, we give it undeservingly.

A sister from Grand Rapids, MI stated, "When I love a man and he's got my best interest at heart, I am totally in his corner".

Sisters agreed with her. That's the nature of black women. We love unconditionally. There have been many books written on the dating patterns of black women. From humor to fiction, black love is a very popular subject. Love lessons are even taught throughout the Bible. One lesson in particular is found in the 13th Chapter of the First Corinthians. It suggests "Charity", meaning love, "beareth all things, believeth all things, hopeth all things and endureth all things." In other words, if love is present in your relationship, both partners bear everything that happens within the relationship—sickness, death, loss of employment, substance abuse, everything. Now it did not mention anything about being stupid or allowing constant neglect or abuse; because if your partner really loves you, he would not employ any mistreatment at all.

According to God's law, not Mikki's, if you are involved in a loveless marriage or relationship, it has no value. Without love, everything is worthless in His eyes. So, if you are in a loveless relationship, you are wasting precious time. Love is the most powerful force in life.

To quote Mabel "Madea" Simmons—"Love is stronger than any addiction. Hell, it is one!"

But exactly what defines love? According to Webster, love is "having a strong affection for someone". Having a strong affection for someone allows enduring, believing, and bearing all things. And no other living creature shows strong affection like black women. We go through hell and high water to show love for our kids, family and especially our man. Take Mrs. Whitney Houston-Brown for example. If Whitney was not a dedicated sister, she would have left Bobby after his second or third arrest. But she did not. She stayed with him whether right or wrong. No one loves like a sister!

Black women love hard. Just as Chante Moore put it—"Even through the tears, I'm staying right here"—that is our mentality. Listen to Angela Bofill's *I'm on Your Side*—"I'll be there when times get rough and no one else can care enough. I'm on your side!" That's a black woman's mentality. Simply put, no one loves like a sister!

I'll give you another good example, Cookie Johnson. Look at all of the ups and downs that she experienced with Magic Johnson. I have a tremendous amount of respect for this beautiful sister. She could have left him. But she did not. He cheated on her several times, left her standing at the altar, and exposed her to the deadly HIV virus. I do not think anybody would not have been mad at Cookie for leaving him. But she endured, believed, and bore it all. Thank God she is still HIV negative and healthy today. Oh, did I mention—no one loves like a sister!

Speaking of love, while listening to my favorite station—Magic 97—one night, I heard the song *When Love Calls* by Atlantic Starr. As I typed and listened to the song, I was taken away by the words—"When love calls, you better answer". I laughed and thought to myself, "Sometimes instead of answering, we should let the voicemail pick up or simply let it ring because it may be the wrong call". Many sisters, myself included, have answered the wrong calls. Here is one in particular:

My Wrong Call

I answered this call in the fall of 1998. He was a senior in college. And we met through my best friend's boyfriend. They were roommates and lived in an off-campus apartment complex. We were visiting her boyfriend when he, "D2", walked in the front door. When I initially saw him, I was not attracted to him. He was a little bit taller than I, which was a turn-off, and kind of on the chubby side. He was not really "my type" so he did not catch my attention. You know, I fall for the tall athletic type. Anyway, we were watching television when he walked through the front door. He introduced himself and joined us. I cannot remember exactly what we were watching; but I'm positive it was affiliated with sports.

"D2" was very charming and had a great sense of humor. We laughed and talked for hours. I was surprised that we had so much in common because as I mentioned before, he was not my type. But we had a really nice conversation. So I was pleased. My two best friends and I left the apartment, but not before "D2" and I exchanged phone numbers.

During the thirty-five minute ride home, my girlfriends asked questioned about "D2". They wanted to know if a love connection was made. I quickly informed them that he was not my type; but I was willing to "establish a friendship with him". They immediately jumped on my case.

"What do you mean he's not your type?" asked one of my friends.

"Oh Lord, there you go again with that 'your type' mess", said the other.

They went on and on. But these comments were not new to me. I was accustomed to them because I am very picky when it comes to men. I mean *very* picky. These two women had known me for almost fifteen years, so they were very familiar with me and my type of man.

I told them, again, that I was willing to get to know him a little better before completely dismissing him. And they were cool with my decision.

My friend used her boyfriend to investigate "D2" and find out more information about him. She told me everything he shared with her. She found out that he and his younger sister were raised by his grandparents. His relationship with his mother was strained. They talked, but it was not a typical mother/son relationship.

My friend never mentioned his father; so I concluded his father was absent from his life as well. She also told me this very important piece of information—he had recently broken up with his girlfriend who now lived in Houston, TX. Out of all of the information she gave about "D2", there were at least two red flags that should have raised my eyebrow about him—his fragmented relationship with his mother and the recent break-up with his ex-girlfriend.

Despite the red flags, I proceeded with the courtship of "D2" for approximately two months. We had lots in common. We both loved music—gospel, R&B and even hip-hop. We shared a love of sports; especially basketball. And just as me, he was also in search of "the one"; well that is what he led me to believe.

We shared life stories on love, disappointment, regret, and almost every emotion we could think to share. Persuading "D2" to talk was definitely not a problem. But trusting him to be honest was a different story. He was a more seasoned dater than I. I had been in only one serious relationship with my son's father which last nearly four years. But he on the other hand had been through several bad relationships. And just as my friend mentioned, he and his ex had broken up a few weeks prior. He admitted they still contacted each other on a regular basis—red flag—but it was nothing serious. But I am not stupid. After he mentioned her name a few times, it was perfectly clear to me that his ex was not really an ex after all. Nonetheless, he reassured me the relationship was in the past and promised I had "nothing to worry about."

Although we hoped to make a love connection, the timing was horrible. We both were busy with school and work. We rarely saw each other. And the phone calls slowly ceased. After two and a half months, I decided to end the friendship. He continued to call, but I refused his phone calls. Eventually, the calls stopped and we parted ways; well, for a few years.

Five years passed without a word from "D2". But one night, my best friend and I were at the movie theater when she spotted him. It was February 2003. He and his little sister exited the movie as we entered. I did not see him because I was too busy running my mouth. But my friend saw him staring at me as he drew closer. To be honest with you, I did not recognize him because he looked so differently. He lost a substantial amount of weight. And he looked broader in the chest; like he had been working out a lot. Bottom line, he looked great!

We embraced and he introduced us to his sister. After briefly filling him in on the five years that passed, we exchanged numbers—again. He asked me to call him after I returned home.

"It'll be too late", I explained. But I promised to call the next day. And I did. We talked for hours. He graduated from college and taught history at a middle school. He was also the head basketball coach; which was very impressive. Oh, he and his girlfriend had reunited and broken up *again*. Yes, the same ex-girlfriend he had broken up with once before. But this time it was "permanent". It was obvious that breaking up and reuniting was an unhealthy pattern with him. But, in spite of that, I was still interested. I was intrigued by him and wanted to learn more. And learn more I did.

I learned that this man had too many issues that stemmed from the strained relationship with his mother; he told too many lies, and had too many women. He lied about practically everything. Once again, he led me to believe that he wanted an exclusive relationship with me; which was more like inclusive because he included Lord knows how many women into his circle of friends. I guess with the weight loss came scores of women because he had plenty. To me, it seemed like this man had a "female friend" in almost every parish in northeastern Louisiana. He maintained that they were "just friends".

As our relationship progressed, my feelings grew stronger for him. I knew the feelings were mutual but he was not willing to develop an exclusive relationship with me. He wanted to "take things slowly" and not "rush into a serious relationship". I was willing to take things slowly; but I was not going to allow him to make a complete fool of me either. You see, he wanted to play around but did not want to lose me in the process. And I did not have the time or the patience to play his little game.

I knew the status of our relationship. I knew we were not officially a couple. And that is what I desired—to be exclusively his. My family was crazy about him; especially my mom. My son admired him too. But I did not allow him to become close with "D2". I did not want to set my son up for a major disappointment—in case the relationship failed again.

Out of all the characteristics that "D2" displayed, there was one very peculiar thing about him. I found it very strange that he catered to women who mistreated him. Women who used and disrespected him, received more attention. Just like my friend's aunt said, "Men will walk a mile for a whore!" But me, on the other hand, I treated him with respect. And his response was negative. For the life of me, I could not understand why. But one day, he finally explained his fragmented relationship between him and his mother. He resented her for not being there for him as a child. She did not show him and his sister any attention or affection when they were little.

"She catered to men before taking care of her kids", he said. "I hate women who will put a man before their kids", he continued.

He knew that she loved them; but she ignored them. She had a strange way of showing love. She broke promises, lied to them all of the time, and missed important events like football and basketball games. After listening as he described his mother, a light bulb went off in my head . . . sort of like an "Ah-ha moment" that Oprah talks about.

Afterwards, I understood why relationship drama followed him throughout his life. I also understood why he chose women who dogged him and he ignored the women who genuinely cared for him.

After careful observation, I concluded that he unconsciously fell in love with women who treated him the way his mom treated him throughout his childhood. He did not want to fall for these women. But their behavior reminded him of his mother's way of showing love. So, it was like, that's all he knew. That was familiar to him. My way of showing love—respect, honesty and commitment—was foreign. How can I explain it? Just as women who, as small girls, witnessed their mom being verbally or physically abused fall for or even marry men who are abusive to them. I have seen examples of this pattern time and time again. And "D2" was no different.

To make a long story short, I ended the relationship permanently. He had so many unresolved issues that we would not have been able to move forward; only in circles. And I could no longer deal with it.

We remained friends though. We talked over the phone occasionally. But not often. My best friend calls him "Penny Wise" (the killer clown from Stephen Kings movie "It" who shows up and terrorizes unsuspecting citizens every thirty years). I care for him as a friend. And you know me; I give him advice on relationships and dating. But I am no psychiatrist; which is really what he needs. When he becomes aware of his unconscious behavior, he will begin the journey of internal healing. I hope and pray that he seeks professional help to begin the healing process and learn how to love a woman.

"D2" was not the only wrong call that I have answered. I met several men who could easily be categorized as Mr. Wrongs. And so did the women online. I called them "red flags". There are five types that I have run across who should be avoided. I suggested to online sisters to avoid them as well. Now, it may take a while for these red flags to reveal their true character; but when it emerges, do yourself a big favor . . . RUN!

Red Flag #1—The Pretender

"D2" fell into this category. He is the lying-est, planning-est, and scheming-est species known to mankind. He is very clever and great at masking his true intentions. He will do and say anything to get exactly what he wants. And without going into graphic details, we all are aware of his ultimate goal—getting into your mind, and your panties soon after.

This man is a genius at conning women. He uses his keen skills to con women for everything—sex, money, and whatever he can get. I am convinced that if the pretender used his craft on medical research instead of playing mind games with women, he could develop cures for the world's most deadly diseases like AIDS, cancer, diabetes, or Alzheimers. Yes, this man is pretty slick and if you are not on your P's and Q's, he'll get you too! The great pretender uses his expertise just as Korean nuclear scientist uses their knowledge to plot and plan ways to blow the United States clean off the map!

Yeah, it all sounds goods when The Pretender says he will take care of you, be a responsible husband and father, and be with you for the rest of your natural life. It sounds good. But guess what Ladies, it feels even better when he actually *does* it. See this is our problem, we get so excited with all of the sweet talk that we leap into actions as if The Pretender has already made good on the promises. Never mind waiting until he actually does what he promised. We are so anxious to be in a relationship that we allow The Pretender into our lives—as long as he talks a good game. His integrity could be shot straight to hell. We don't care. We listen to The Pretender because he shows us attention and affection. Yep, we are love starved; and The Pretender is waiting with open arms.

Red Flag #2—The Unhappily Married Man

I heard sisters vent about this brother time and time again. He seems so happy in public with his wife and kids; but swears he's one signature away from getting his walking papers. His sob story reminds you of the sad looking pooch *Droopy* who says "You know what? I'm happy." He constantly complains about how much his wife gets on his nerves and how he is only in the marriage "for the kids". He is also quick to reassure that you are next in line to get with him as soon as he becomes a free man. Never mind that your secret relationship is approaching its 15th anniversary; he continuously feeds the same lies year after year. And the crazy thing about this situation is we actually hang around and listen to it.

Just as I explained to everyone online, I have never been involved with a married man. What is the point? To waste precious time? But many single women take it as a compliment when married men pursue them. Personally, I am offended. It reflects his character as well as his intentions. So why get excited about him?

It is an ugly cycle; but yet many women willingly set themselves up for disappointment. Until we take the initiative to stop the cheating patterns of unhappily married men, his behavior will continue. If we, as self-respecting single women, refuse to sleep with them, who can they cheat on their wives with? Good question huh.

Red Flag #3—The Con Artist

Now this red flag is not as hard to predict as the pretender because he is so desperate to start a relationship it's almost scary. He is dubbed the con artist. He too has a hidden agenda; but he shows his hand early in the game. And he starts relationships very quickly. You can find him on any Internet dating site searching for his next victim.

He is usually unemployed; but smart enough to charm the pants or panties off any PhD candidate. The con artist seeks females, especially women who have low self esteem, who are desperate enough to take him in. His plan is strategically choreographed and he is usually equipped with false evidence to support his claims. That's why he is so convincing!

I met a guy on the Internet who fits this profile. We met on a reputable dating site, which I will not mention its name. He was born in Ghana and he lived near Boston, Massachusetts. Of course, he initiated the conversation by sending an email in response to my online profile in 2004. I noticed that he did not have a picture in his profile—red flag. I asked several times for a picture, but he told me he did not have any pictures scanned to email—red flag. He promised to mail the pictures via US mail. Instead of giving my home address, I gave a P O Box address. He eventually mailed a picture; but it was so small that I could hardly view it. It was a head shot and a total blur. I instantly became suspicious of him. Not only because he sent such a small picture, but he looked nothing like the description he gave me.

"I am very light-skinned", he said with an African accent during one of our rare conversations. He also said that he "was 37-years old". The man in the bite-size picture was black as coal and instead of 37-years old, he looked 97!

Besides his physical description, nothing added up with him. Everything he told me was a lie; even his name. My friend was convinced he was looking to marry an American woman to obtain a green card to remain in the United States. And she was right! After only two or three weeks of talking, he asked me to move to Massachusetts with him. Was he crazy or something?

I was not thinking as my friend. My thoughts were worse. I thought he was some kind of fugitive . . . you know, an elderly prison escapee or something. But I guess she was right. I wrote a long heart-felt letter expressing my feelings about his lies and deception. I also asked him to "stop preying on young African American women online". The letter contained, shall I say, harsh words. He did not respond to it; but believe me, after he read *that* letter, I am sure he changed his game plan.

Red Flag #4—The Abusive Man.

Now this one is a fool! He is jealous and very controlling. He tries his best to separate you from your family and friends. He keeps close tabs on you . . .

your every move. And he hates to see you have fun or enjoy yourself with anyone other than him. He may even be jealous of the relationship between you and your children. Some women who are involved with abusive men mistake their behavior for "overwhelming love".

My son's barber, Rufus, once said, "If a man is willing to fall out with his mama behind you, you need to leave that fool alone because he is crazy and he will kill you".

This statement is oh so true. But we think it's cute for a man to act a fool to display his love. We think he's protecting us and it makes us feel loved. While on the other hand, many abused women are afraid to leave the relationship in fear of being hurt or even killed. Even if they are fortunate enough to leave, most of them eventually return in hopes of making the relationship work. But it does not. It only gets worse.

When this subject arose, many of the women online were quick to say what they would do if someone hit them. But one never knows how they'll react if it every happened. I thank God that I have never encountered an abusive man. Hopefully, I never will. Over the years, I have heard horror stories of abuse; but there was one story that I will never ever forget. I witnessed this story one evening while watching CNN's *Nancy Grace*. The victim's name was Yvette Cade and she was a beautiful black woman who had been severely burned by her estranged husband. Before the incident occurred, she was separated from her abusive husband and had recently filed for divorce. Of course, he wanted to work it out through counseling. But she made it clear—she wanted to end their broken marriage.

She was afraid of him and received a restraining order as she proceeded with the divorce. Well, somehow, the restraining order was lifted through a "paperwork error". Still upset because she wanted to proceed with the divorce, this monster paid her a visit at work, carried a Sprite bottle filled with gasoline, poured it on her and set her on fire at work. Yes, he performed this heinous offense on her job! I saw the video and heard the 911 tape when the crime was reported. It was awful!

While watching the show, I was speechless. They showed before and after pictures of the young lady. He disfigured over 50% of her body. He wanted her dead. Despite his horrendous act, she lived to share her story with the world. Through all of the scaring, you could still see her beautiful personality. She spoke of her strong faith in God. She forgave her ex-husband for what he did to her too. He scared over half of her body; but he did not scar her faith in God. I was brought to tears listening as she spoke.

"God is going to completely heal my body", she said. And I truly believe he will.

After witnessing her story, I could not help but put myself in her shoes. What if this happened to me? What would I have done? Well, you know me. And this is my version: As soon as I realized what happened, instantly, I would have chased him around the building and into the parking lot screaming—"Why are you running? I thought you wanted us to work this thing out"? Come on, let's work it out!"

And if it looked as though he might get away, I would have leapt as if I was Jackie Joyner-Kersey performing the high jump at the Olympics, dove on him and held on for dear life! Stop, drop, and roll would not have been a productive drill to get me off of him. Together, we would have burned pot holes in the parking lot. Sometimes, you have to show this red flag just how crazy *you* are.

Red Flag #5—The Undercover Child Predator

This one had hidden secrets that he wishes no one to discover—his strong affection for small kids. He seeks single women with children because he desires the child more than the female. This predator seeks single mothers in hopes of establishing sexual relationships with her children. He is aware of her desires of finding a partner and a positive father figure for her kids. He takes full advantage of the opportunity. So be on the look-out for this sensitive and caring red-flag because he's just like Martin—he loves the kids!

As you can imagine, my research of men did not begin when I decided to write this book. It began when I was 9 or 10 years old. And I was taught well. I hung out with my brother and all of his friends. I followed them everywhere—basketball court, fishing at the pond, and recreation centers. I even followed them to places they did not want me to go. I watched over the years as they lied to their girlfriends. They even had me lying to them. From elementary school to high school I watched as they played mind games with girls.

For instance, to make their girlfriends believe they were at home "chilling", they parked the cars at my cousin's house—down the street—and left in another car with other girls. And if their girlfriends drove by the house, sure enough the cars were there; but the boys were not. They were out fooling around and doing God knows what. They asked me to "hold down the fort" while they were gone. And hold it down I did. I was great at it! I was so believable. And their girlfriends really trusted me. I know it sounds bad; but that's what happened.

High school was no different. I watched high school jocks lie and cheat on their girlfriends. It was ridiculous! I did not date very much; but I had lots of crushes though. I was different from the other girls. I had heard and seen it all before. I knew every trick in the book. Guys did not understand me at all. But I liked it that way. Football and basketball players always tried to hook up with me. But none of them succeeded. I was friendly; but not *too* friendly. I still believe they formed a pact like the brothers of "The Wood" to see who could get me first. If so, they all lost because I did not fall for any of their games.

As I stated before, I had heard and seen it all before. And it's a good thing I did. Learning how to deal with men at a very early age saved me many frustrations and heartaches. After 20 years of male observations and relationships on a personal and professional level, I have learned a lot about men. I mean a lot!

There is a certain mentality that one must have in dealing with the male species. And thanks to my 20 year male observation, I have mastered this mentality. Now, I am not implying that I know everything about men and relationships. But I know enough. And here are 21 tips that helped me move smoothly along "Interstate Relationship".

Mikki's Dating Tips:

1) Practice abstinence! Yes, I know our parents preached this when we were young. And I also know that everybody is sleeping with everybody in the twenty-first century; but abstinence is still an essential piece of the dating puzzle. So, if he is not your husband, no sex! Don't laugh, I am serious. We should return to the morals and principles of our grandmothers, mothers, and other strong black self-respecting women who came before us. They did not sleep with every man who came across their paths or cotton fields; and neither should we. Ladies, I would not advise you to do something that I am not practicing myself. I have not been with a man for four years and counting. Yes, I get lonely at times. And horny too; but I refuse to let any man wear me down before I meet my husband. Wearing me down is reserved just for him! And please, if celibacy is not an option, ALWAYS use condoms. Your health should be your primary concern. Satisfaction—second.

2) If you are looking for a long-term relationship, pay close attention to his words during the first few conversations. If sex is mentioned, do not entertain him. He has sex on the brain and his bed sheets are pressed and ready. After you leave his place you'll never hear from this Brother again.

3) Smile! Many of us are so frustrated that we have forgotten how to smile. We rock the finest threads and the best hair styles in the world; but we leave home without wearing our most beautiful attire—our smile.

4) The saying "first impressions are lasting impressions" is so true. When a new man enters your life, be yourself. Don't pretend to be someone that you are not. You will have less explaining to do once your *true* character reveals itself.

5) History tends to repeat itself. If your man was a prolific player back in the day, he is probably a more polished and smoother one today. The same rings true with an abusive man. If he hits you once, he'll hit you as long as you stay in the relationship. And if you decide to stay, you will eventually leave—on a stretcher!

6) If you ask your man to tell you the truth about anything—other women, out-of-wedlock kids, visits to strip clubs—what ever the subject may be, be strong enough to handle it. Remember, men lie to us because

they think we cannot handle the truth. Whatever the truth is, don't ask if your heart cannot bear to hear it.

7) Learn from past relationships. Do not continuously make the same stupid mistakes. We leave bad relationships feeling used, broken spirited, confused and robbed of time. And we allow them to destroy or alter our good character and integrity. Let go of the bitterness, hatred, and anger. It doesn't hurt him; it only hurts us. And believe me; he will get what's coming to him. God don't like ugly! Remember, "What goes around comes around". Regardless, take time to heal emotionally and spiritually. Learn and grow from those mistakes. They did not work in past relationships and they will not work in the future.

8) Never pressure your man into a relationship/marriage if he does not want to be in a committed relationship. It sounds simple, but we do this all of the time.

One of my best friends, Denita, said, "Men behave better when he does something because he wants to, not when he feels obligated to do it".

And my theory: "If he wants to be in a committed relationship, he will be. If he doesn't, he'll pretend until he gets tired".

9) If you have been dating a guy for more than three months and you have not met any of his friends or family, it should be obvious that he has no long term plans with you. "D2" used this line occasionally—"I want you to meet my grandmother. She would love you!" The first time he said it, I showed all of my teeth. The second time he said it, I gave a half-smile. And the third time he said it, I almost cursed him out! If he wanted me to meet his grandmother, he would have said it once and taken me to her house and introduced us. "D2" knew that I wanted to meet his grandmother. He also knew that it was never going to happen. But it sounded good when he said it.

10) Be what you are looking for in a mate. How will you meet a handsome and professional man if you are not on top of your game? What type of woman do you think he is looking to meet? He is looking for a beautiful professional woman. Get yourself together spiritually, physically and emotionally before searching for a mate. Possess the same qualities that you hope to find in a mate.

11) Now this tip may ruffle a few feathers, but it goes back to being able to handle the truth. If you allow your man to constantly cheat on you, use you for everything and basically make a complete fool of you, do you actually think he will ever stop? No, he will not! Unless God intervenes, he will continue until you put an end to his behavior by removing yourself from the situation.

12) If your man tells you he wants out of the relationship, believe him. It is rare that men honestly admit that they want to end a relationship. You will save yourself lots of frustration later on.

13) Do not, I repeat, do not use sex as a means to persuade your man into a committed relationship. Better yet—See Tip #1. The more you sleep with him, especially if the sex is good, the more you will fall for him. And guess what; you will be the only one falling. Men are experts at separating love and sex. Ladies, we have not perfected this skill yet.

14) Shut up sometimes! Sisters, we talk entirely too much and rarely listen. Lend an ear to your man. Listen to him sometimes. Whether we realize it or not, men have just as many problems and issues as we do; but they rarely get the opportunity to talk about them because we are always talking. Listen to him. If not, he'll just have to find another woman who will listen . . . like that very attractive female who's always skinning and grinning in his face at work . You know her cubical is DIRECTLY in front of his office!

15) Ladies, hear me good now—your friends and female family members' husbands or boyfriends are off limits, Period! I don't care how fine he is, how much money he makes, I don't even care if he makes you cry like *Snoopy* when he hears droopy music playing; God is not going to send you another woman's man. Take a lesson from pop-star Britney Spears. Months later, you'll find yourself bald-headed, half-crazy, and alone!

I'm begging you . . . do not go there. Especially if the other woman is your sister or best friend; that is not God sending him, that is Satan. Show some integrity and politely turn him down. He may continuously throw himself at you, but he is only testing your character. Don't be *that* desperate for a man. And while on the subject, don't fall for the "we're separated" nonsense either. A separated man is still a married man!

16) Never disclose pertinent information about random females—whether friends or co-workers—to your man. Information like "She'll sleep with anybody" or "She is a slut" can be used to his advantage one day if you know what I mean. And vice-versa, do not disclose personal information about your man to other females. She'll smile in your face one second and smile in his face the next.

17) The "perfect man" does not exist. Yeah, I know. I am very picky too; but everyone has flaws; including us. If you genuinely love someone, you will love everything about him; including his faults.

18) This is an extension from tip #7. Pray and ask God to remove any resentment and bitterness from past relationships. If not, you will carry the hurt and pain into each relationship and they will all end in disaster.

19) Do not become upset when your man glances at another woman. Notice I said "when"? Because he will look; especially if she is attractive. Oh yeah, he's gonna look. But when you get upset it shows your insecurities. Men love confident women. But keep in mind there is a difference between a glance and a stare. If he stares too long, he'll want her. So if he is starring or *consistently* looking at other women, just slap him across the head and he will get the message. I'm sorry, that was mean. Don't slap him across the head . . . slap him across the face!

20) Never put yourself in compromising positions. For example, you recently met a guy who is extremely attractive and you know if the two of you are in the right place at the right time, something physical is bound to happen. You also know that it is too early in the game for sex. Do not go to his place "to chill". We all know how this night ends. You will find yourself butt naked in his bed and unable to explain what, when, how, or why it happened. Instead, visit a crowded movie theater or a neighborhood park . . . in the daytime!

21) It took a few pathetic relationships for me to realize this last tip. But I finally got it. God selects our partners, not us! Actually, he designs them. Stop picking your husband and wait until God sends him to you. Each time I attempted to hand pick Mr. Right, I chose Mr. Stupid, Mr. Liar, Mr. Cheater, or Mr. Dummy. I decided to leave the selection process to God because I know He will send the perfect candidate. And when He sends him, he sends confirmations along with him to make certain we recognize him. The man who God hand picks will not be concerned with sex. He will be willing to wait until *after* marriage because he knows that you will have the rest of your lives for lovemaking. So waiting will not be a problem at all.

Meeting Mr. Right is such an arduous task for black women. The topics mentioned throughout this chapter were heavily discussed online and during conversations with family, friends and even strangers. The majority of our frustrations stems from the lack of available black men to choose a lifetime partner. As previously stated, several factors contribute to this shortage.

So what are sisters to do? I have asked this question throughout the chapter. I know the first thing we should do—pray. Pray and ask God to send Mr. Right our way. Just as tip #21 suggested, regardless if he is black, white, Russian, rich, poor, good looking or not so good looking, we should pray and wait for God to send him to us.

Hopelessness was the mood of many online sisters in regards to finding true love. Many were not hopeful that they would ever find Mr. Right. Many have accepted the fact that they will be alone forever. They believed black men only want sexual relationships with us, not lifetime commitments. Some have even lowered their standards and resorted to dating married men or men who are already involved in relationships. Some sisters have decided to date outside of their race.

But not me. I have not given up on love. I am very hopeful that God has a time and place where He will direct Mr. Right in my path. I don't know what he looks like, but I know he is coming! Maybe this is what Luther Vandross meant when he said, "Wait for love that you been missing, sometimes love takes a long time. But wait for love and you're gonna get the chance to love." Yeah, I guess Luther was right. Real love takes a long time. But patience is trusting in God's timing. And God will not send Mr. Right into my live until He knows that I am ready to receive him.

Many of us are not ready for Mr. Right. Just as "D2", we have too many unresolved issues that we hold inside—anger, bitterness, and resentment. Old stuff that we should have left behind years ago. If God sent Mr. Right to some of us, we would run him off after the first three days of meeting him.

After witnessing other devastating relationships and dealing with my own relationship drama, recognizing my Mr. Right will be an easy task. How will he look? What qualities will he possess? I have learned that he will be a man who is in the business of loving me unconditionally; whether I am as big as a house or as thin as Paris Hilton. He will love me whether I am as rich as Bill Gates or as poor as a homeless man who lives under a bridge. He will love me whether I am as bald as Charles Barkley or if my weave is long, wavy, and hangs down to my toes. He will be able to stomach my sometimes bad attitude and calm me down when I get upset. He will be a man who can laugh and cry with me and one who I can trust even in the most tempting circumstances. He'll be "the right kinda lover" who keeps a "permanent smile on my face" . . . like Pattie sings about.

Yes, my Mr. Right is worth waiting for. He will love and respect his mom, grandma, or any woman who had a hand in raising him as a child; because we all know that behind every good man is a good mama or "Big Mama".

My Mr. Right will remind me of my father—Willie Zimmerman, Jr. He takes great care of his family. Always have. And he continues to take care of us today. He loves and respects the women who raised him—his grandmother, mom, and aunts. He provides *everything* for me, my mom and my sisters. He is a God-fearing man who—for over 50 years of marriage—provided the perfect example of a family man for his children. He taught us how a man should love a woman. And we are forever grateful to him for it.

Now that I think back, I don't mind waiting. I am willing to wait for love—the love my father gave. And I truly believe my husband will possess all of the qualities that my father has. Yes, I am definitely willing to wait for my share of Heaven on Earth.

CHAPTER 3

Past-Due Bills

"I'm living so far beyond my income that
we may almost be said to be living apart."
e e cummings

"Can you pay my bills?"
Destiny Child

Destiny's Child said it best in their hit song *Bills, Bills, Bills*: "Can you pay my bills?" they asked.

When this song hit the airwaves in June 1995, I thought, "For these girls to be so young, they sure are asking mature questions". "Can you pay my bills? Can you pay my telephone bill?"

You think Destiny Child asked sound financial questions, online sisters modified Destiny Child's question: "Can you at least pay *half* of one of my bills?"

Bills, and the lack of money to pay them, surfaced often with online sisters. Especially for single black women who pull all of the weight in their respective households. Surprisingly, financial debt arose in conversations with married women too. This really shocked me. I assumed that married women had it much easier because they have someone to help them. Boy was I wrong! Just as single women, many married women carried the financial load in their households. Yes, they had help; but their finances were still overwhelming.

Whether single, married, divorced or separated, the bottom line is bills, especially past-due bills, destroy us both mentally and physically. They cause stress in our daily lives, break up marriages and relationships, and cause tension between family members and friends.

I vividly remember a conversation with a middle aged lady while standing in line at the bank. She expressed her resentment for payday. "I hate getting paid. It all goes to bills! So what's the point?"

I nodded in agreement. Her frustration described how many black women live financially—paycheck to paycheck.

Just as the human species, bills come in all sizes—from the forty-five hundred dollar mortgage payment to the twenty dollar credit card payment. Regardless of the amount, we struggle to pay them. Many of us sacrifice one bill to pay another; while others make payment arrangements each month to pay their utility bills, car notes, and other critical expenses.

Let's face it, until we pay them out completely and become debt-free, bills will always be a part of our lives. With a new home comes a new mortgage note for the next 15-30 years. Move into the house and more bills follow—Mr. Utility bill, Mr. Water bill, Mr. Telephone bill, and the list goes on and on. With a new car comes a car note. And if it is financed, you'll have a car payment for three to six years.

After you are dead and buried, bills will continue to flow through the US postal system and harass your loved ones who are left behind; causing their blood pressure to elevate to unimaginable levels.

We all know this is not a healthy way of life. We'll only continue to be miserable, frustrated, and raise hell every chance we get. I know it is easier said than done; but controlling your financial life is a key element to living life free of frustration. Taking control of our financial life should be a top priority for us—black women who are terribly frustrated with debt. And there are many of us who are frustrated. Noticed I said *us*?

My past due bills

I never worried about money. My entire life, I was given everything I wanted. I am the baby of a family of four children. And as you can imagine, I was a spoiled brat—in every sense of the word. It was not until one year after I purchased my first car that I began to experience financial hardship. I was not worried though—my son and I lived with my parents. So, I did not have many other bills. The car note was the only major expense at the time.

I purchased the car because I began a new job as a library assistant for an elementary school district in my hometown. And I needed transportation—badly. During this time, my credit rating was excellent. Getting a car financed was not a problem. And I was not asked to make a down payment. So I went for it!

It was the summer of 1998. The night before my first car shopping experience, I saw a dealership advertisement—"Sign and drive with no money down"—flashed across my television screen. This was wonderful news for me. I was ecstatic! I hopped out of bed; grabbed a scratch pad and pen to write the name and location of the dealership.

Early the next morning, my sister-in-law drove my mom and me thirty-five miles west to the dealership. Being a rookie at car buying, I did not know what to expect from the salesman. But my sister-in-law was a pro. She had already purchased and completely paid out two cars prior; so she knew the "ends and outs" of car buying.

She acted as my consultant and my mom was there for "moral support". Now, that's what she said. But I think she came along to make sure I stayed within my budget. My father gave me a pep talk before we left. So, I was ready to go car hunting.

Upon arriving at the dealership, I spotted a white Chevy Cavalier on the far left side of the lot. I instantly fell in love with it. My best friend and I, for some reason, were obsessed with Cavaliers during this time. So I just had to get one. It had approximately 23,000 miles. We examined it, like my father told us—checked for loose wires under the hood, checked the air condition vents, and checked all of the mirrors. We checked everything. It was in great condition.

"Would you like to take a test drive?" the salesman asked.

I looked at my consultant, she nodded yes.

"Yes I would like a test drive", I replied.

He filled the gas tank and handed over the keys. I drove home so my dad could check it too. You know, for any faults that we may have missed. He checked the tires, engine, interior and exterior. He drove it one or two blocks and gave the final okay. We headed back to the dealership for final negotiations. This car was definitely within my budget. So it was now time to "wheel and deal". Well that's what my dad called it anyway.

We pulled into the lot, walked into the office and began. The very first monthly payment amount and interest rate the salesman quoted was a bit pricey. He gave a corny explanation for the high rate.

"You don't have an established credit history or a down payment, so your payments may be a little higher than normal", he stated.

A *little* higher? The list price of the car was approximately $10,200. The monthly payment he quoted was about $425.00. If I paid $425.00 a month for five years, the total cost would more than double the list price. I would have paid a total of $25,500 for the car. Now, I loved Chevy Cavaliers. But not that much. This car was not worth $25,000.

My sister-in-law quickly informed the salesman that his payment amount was too high. "This payment will not work for us. It's too expensive", she said. "If we go to another dealership, they would gladly give us a better deal", she continued.

Of course, they did not want to lose a potential sale. So they recalculated the rate to lower my monthly payments. By the time we closed the deal, there were two salesmen and the general manager in the office. They recalculated the payment four times. We finally accepted on the fourth offer. We negotiated a monthly payment around $320.00 a month. I saved a total of $6,300! I was so excited to have purchased my very first car. I purchased it on my own. No one co-signed for me or let me borrow any money. I got it with good credit and, of course, my sister-in-laws' great negotiating skills.

For the first few months, I mailed the car payments early; even before a coupon was mailed to me. I was on point with my payments. I paid twenty-five dollars extra toward the principle balance. It lasted a while. A short while. The principle payment eventually stopped. I paid the car note though. A few months later, the payments arrived a week or two late. In order to protect my credit rating, I made certain the payments were not 30 days or more late. This was the first red flag—my finances were getting out of hand.

Keep in mind the concept of paying bills and having financial responsibilities were new to me. Really new. Remember, I was a spoiled brat. And I wanted what I wanted when I wanted it. Yes, I was an adult. But so what? That worked for me my entire life—well into adulthood—so I was just following routine.

It took a long time for me to accept the title of spoiled brat. But everyone else knew that I wore it well. Even in college, my parents mailed checks almost every week while my friends worked on-campus jobs. They knew I was a spoiled brat and called me out on several occasions.

"Mikki's way, Mikki's way everything always has to go Mikki's way!" my friend Katina often said when there was a conflict of interest within the group.

Each time she said it; I stormed out of the room and slammed the door. I guess deep down inside, I knew she was right.

My best friend Kim, who was my roommate, recalled a time when she accompanied my mom and I to the local shopping mall. I wanted a pair of earrings. And to be honest with you, I can not remember how they looked. The only thing I remember is my mom said she was not buying them. When she said it, I did not say anything at all. I quickly stormed out of the store. Storming out was my best tantrum. Crying was my second.

My mom called me back into the store. "How much are they?" she asked. And I knew those earrings were mine.

My pathetic behavior carried over into my financial life. Instead of paying my bills, I spent money on high priced designer clothes and shoes, spa visits, NFL and NBA tickets, and weekend out-of-town trips. I'd think, "I'll just ask mom and she'll pay it for me". And guess what? She did.

By giving me everything and paying my bills when I could not, she thought that she was helping me. But in reality, she hindered me from becoming a mature and responsible adult. I know my mom loved me and tried to show it by spoiling me. But as she continued to fall for all my tantrums, she also contributed to the long and hard financial fall I would soon face.

Looking back over the financial decisions of my past, I realize most of it was directly related to being a spoiled brat. I was so accustomed to my parents bailing me out of every financial jam that I got myself into.

For the next four years, my finances were out of control. I was forced to file Chapter 13 Bankruptcy in 2002 just to get back on my feet. This was so embarrassing for me. I do not think my parents knew how bad it was until it was too late. They were shocked when I announced that I filed for bankruptcy. You would think that I would have learned my lesson after filing bankruptcy. Wrong! I fell behind on my bankruptcy payments. Soon after, my case was dismissed. Luckily for me, most of the nagging collectors were paid through the bankruptcy process.

That was my story. You think that was bad. You should have heard the stories from sisters online. We are financially frustrated! And it must end.

As of now, I am not completely debt-free; but I am slowly making progress towards financial stability.

Through my financial struggles, I learned there are two key components in maintaining financial stability—discipline and consistency. I am no financial advisor nor do I claim to know everything regarding money management, stock options or 401K plans. I have a bachelor in business administration with concentrations in accounting and marketing and I am working on an MBA with a concentration in international marketing; but still, I am no financial wizard. I am merely offering tips on lessons that I have learned from past financial mistakes. The quote, "If you don't learn from the past you are doomed to repeat it" rings true in financial stability. Looking into the rear-view mirror of my life, I learned a lot about myself which helped me to understand my financial mishaps. And this is my first piece of advice.

Tip #1: Take a long and hard look at your past. Evaluate it. Learn from it; just as I did. Discover the reasons why you make financial mistakes time and time again. Don't be ashamed. Look at the circumstances that led you into this financial funk. It may shed light on thing you were not aware of. It may even bring up painful memories from your childhood; but it is the first step in taking control of your financial life. Learn from those mistakes and allow them to remain in your past and not impact your future.

Tip#2: Keep a record of your spending. Go ahead and try this for a day, a week or maybe even a month. Write down all of your purchases regardless of the amount. This gives a clear picture of where the bulk of your income is being exhausted. Believe me you will be surprised by your research. I was surprised as well. After this exercise, you will feel guilty when spending money foolishly.

When I began this exercise, it really did not have an affect on me, especially the first day. By day three, I evaluated almost every purchase. I begin to shop for bargains instead of convenience. For example, I love tea. And no one makes sweet tea like Captain D's Seafood restaurant. You remember the local restaurant I mentioned in the introduction? They make the world's best tea. I make a daily stop for a "medium sweet tea with light ice and lemons". I am not exactly sure when this habit started, but I have been doing it for years. When I enter the restaurant, the workers know what I want before I order it. A few of them reach for the medium cup as I approached to place my order. Another worker automatically adds the price of tea to my total.

Back to the exercise, I began in January of 2006. I did not buy tea for the entire month and saved $47.00. Forty-seven dollars may not seem like much; but it is too much for *sweet tea*. And multiply $47.00 by twelve months; that is a total of $569.00 a year. I could not believe I spent $569.00 a year on sweet tea. That was a wake-up call for me. Instead of daily tea runs, I now pick up my usual once or twice a week. I make freshly brewed tea at home. It is not as convenient as the tea already prepared, but I am saving money in the process.

This is why I advised you to take part in this exercise. It will be an eye opening experience for you as well. And it will lead you into the next step of moving toward financial stability.

Tip #3: Change your negative spending habits. This tip was a "lesson in discipline" as one online sister referred to it. Discipline was definitely missing in my life. I was totally out of control with spending money. I learned this negative behavior as a child because I always got my way. I was unable to accept "no" as an answer. I was in my mid twenties when I realized that I could not get my way in the real world. I had to face the financial disasters that I continuously got myself into. The lack of discipline was a major factor in my negative spending habits. I was not able to change my behavior until I finally realized it and categorized it as negative.

Tip #4: Be aware of your monthly spending amount. I despise the word "budget" because it makes me feel like I'm restricting myself. I prefer the term "spending amount". Use the knowledge gained in the first three tips to develop a monthly spending plan. Evaluate your research and divide your spending into three categories.

The first category is called real expenses. The mortgage/rent payment, car note and insurance, church tithes, water and sewage, utilities and telephone bill and groceries fall into this category. These expenses are crucial in everyday living. No one can live without food and shelter. And the majority of your income should be used on these real expenses.

The second group is called the personal and entertainment expenses. The name of this category is self-explanatory. *Designer* clothes and shoes, perfume and make-up, grooming techniques (weekly hair appointments, manicures and pedicures) are all included in this category. Now, this category caused financial hardship for many black women, including myself. I depleted the majority of my total income on this group of expenses. I neglected my real expenses by overspending on personal items and entertainment. Being a true diva of sports, I constantly attend sporting events from high school football games to professional basketball games. I am not advising to stop spending on entertainment. I am simply advising to limit the amount being spent in this category.

The last group is called convenient expenses. I labeled this group convenient because these are expenses we can live without; but they make life so much easier, or shall I say, more convenient. Cell phones, cable/satellites, Internet, I-pods, newspaper and magazine subscriptions fall into this category. I know what you're thinking, "I have to get rid of my magazine subscriptions?" I understand because I could not live without my *Essence* magazines! Once again, limit the amount that you spend in this group of expenses.

Now that your expenses are broken down, it should be clear which group of expenses is more important. Calculate your monthly income including all sources; whether wages from a part-time gig or child support payments. Subtract the total of real expenses from the total income and if the remaining amount is a positive number take a deep breath and thank God. There are many women who work full-time and are still unable to cover their real expenses. So yes, having a positive residual amount is truly a blessing. This amount can be divided accordingly between the remaining groups or even deposited into a savings account. Simple, but practical financial advice.

If you find yourself "in the red"—meaning the remaining amount is a negative number—re-calculate your real expenses. Some of your real expenses may not be *real* after all and should be categorized as either convenient or as personal expenses. Or maybe find a part-time job to cover the remaining portion each month.

Tip #5: Utilize extra refunds to pay existing bills completely out. It does not matter if you are a college student who receives financial aid refunds. Use the refunds to pay accounts that are past due. And if I know college students, you have lots of credit card debt that can be paid out. Use these extra funds to help your financial situation; not destroy it.

When possible, pay your smallest accounts first. As you clear out smaller debt, ease into the larger debt. If you cannot pay off the debt completely, pay a small amount towards the balance of the debt. Pay ten dollars every two weeks or even a month if that is all you can afford. But pay something towards it!

One thing that I have learned through experience, creditors are willing to help you if they feel that you are sincere about paying the debt. Some companies will even make payment arrangements to fit your financial situation.

This next tip is very important for sisters who religiously visit *Ace Cash Express* or any other payday loan company once a month to renew a loan instead of paying it out completely. You should pay close attention.

Tip #6: Avoid cash advance loans also known as "payday loans". These high-risk loans caused financial hardship for black women online in cities all across the country. The payday loan phenomenon emerged in the late 1990's and continues to rip us off today. And judging from the growing number of lenders that spring up in low income neighborhoods, it is only getting worse. These loans are disguised "no interest loan"; but charge a high fee and when converted into Annual Percentage Rate range from 391 to 443 percent. For instance, if you request a $100 loan for a two-week period, at the end of the two weeks you will pay a total of $115. This may seem like a small amount; but in terms of APR the $115 calculates to 360 percent interest. 360 percent! If you are unable to pay the loan out completely after the two week period, the interest continues to build up.

I know from experience the damage—mentally and financially—payday loans cause. During my financial crisis, I had three payday loans at once for almost a year. Keep a count—three! My parents had not idea until it was too late. I dreaded payday. Every two weeks, I drove to the lenders to basically pay the fee because I could not afford to pay the loans off completely. I felt so ashamed when I entered the building. Instead of parking in the front, I'd park at the back so no one would recognize me.

I recall one sister entering the building with her head down as if she was going to a funeral or something. The look on her face said it all. On another occasion, I almost bumped into another lady while she exited.

She smiled and said, "Excuse me".

"Oh, no problem", I said. I knew that she was just as embarrassed as I.

I left this payday loan company and headed to another one. And guess who I saw? Yep, the same lady that I almost bumped into at the other lender. I shook my head in disgust.

"I'm doing what I gotta do", she explained.

I concurred. I was doing the exact same thing. It took a while; but fortunately I was able to make payment arrangements to pay all of the loans completely out. Believe me, I will never allow myself to fall victim to payday loans ever again.

Online, the subject of payday loans was kind of hush-hush. Everyone was so embarrassed to even admit to having payday loans. I basically forced the issues just to get feedback. If you find yourself in debt with payday loans, do not avoid the issue like the people online. You will only fall deeper and deeper into debt with these predators. Face it just as I did. Make payment arrangements. Do anything to quickly pay them off.

And please, by all means, if you find yourself in a financial bind after you've paid them off, stay away! Please avoid cash advance, payday, and money now loans if possible. If this is impossible, borrow the money for one month. Do not stick around and allow this debt to linger. The purpose of payday loans is to borrow once and pay it out on your next payday. I know this is not an easy task. Many sisters carried the burden of payday loans far beyond payday. But everyone online agreed, if possible, borrow money from family members and friends. Get credit card advances. Do anything except a pay day loan! Trust me; borrowing money from someone other than a payday loan lender will be less costly in the long run.

Tip #7: Seek professional help. If the thought of acquiring and maintaining financial peace of mind frightens you, it may be time to seek professional help. There is help available, lots of it. The following sources are great and will help with referrals for financial assistance: The Institute of Certified Financial Planners, 800-282-7526; The American Institute of Certified Public Accountants, 888-777-7077; and The National Association of Personal Financial Advisors, 888-333-6659.

The internet is an excellent source for financial advice. Log on to any search engines and perform a search for "financial management". You will find tons of valuable and creditable information. One website I found to be very helpful is *http://www.free-financial-advice.net*. They give excellent financial management advice. Another website is *http://www.myfinancialadvice.com*. They offer great financial planning advice as well.

Sisters online agreed, regaining control of your finances is no easy task. It may take several months, sometimes years. But develop a logical plan and stick to it. You will succeed. Learn from your financial mistakes of the past, exercise discipline with impulsive spending and pay your bills in a timely manner. These steps lead to a healthy financial future. Regardless of how bad your finances are now, it is never too late to regain control. Do not allow financial debt to continuously cause stress and anxiety in your life. Take your life back. Regain the financial freedom that you deserve. Yes, you deserve to be happy and debt free!

CHAPTER 4

Hardhead Kids

*"Train up a child in the way he should go,
and when he is old he will not depart from it."*
Proverbs 22:6 (KJV)

"It is easier to build strong children than repair broken men."
Frederick Douglas

Every child is a blessing from God. Judging the behavior of some, one would think they were hand delivered by Satan himself! We call them "the Z Generation"; but I refer to them as the jittery generation. Today, kids are so restless they cannot sit still or hold a single thought for thirty seconds. Their little bodies and brains are constantly in motion. Attention Deficit Disorder and Attention Deficit Hyperactivity Disorder are common diagnosis for today's children.

According to the National Institute for Health, ADHD is the most common diagnosed behavioral disorder of childhood. Diagnosing ADHD can be difficult and requires information from a number of sources including the child's parents, doctors, and teachers. Proper diagnosis depends on the report of characteristics, behavior and observations, input from the child, and a doctor's examination. Long ago, it was believed that children out grow ADHD symptoms as they become teenagers. But 70% of children have problems with impulsivity, problem solving, and decision-making throughout their teenage years.

ADHD is a behavioral disorder, meaning it does not have clear physical symptoms. One or more common characteristics of ADHD include inattention,

---

hyperactivity, and impulsivity. Some kids with ADHD may have one of these symptoms; while others display a combination of all symptoms.

I spoke with dozens of teachers, mothers, and grandmothers who have witnessed the behavior of a hyperactive child.

"He just can't be still!" said one frustrated grandmother who was the primary caretaker of her daughter's son.

And my mom constantly instructs my son, who is also ADHD, to "rest your {his} body sometimes!"

There are many ways to treat ADHD. Medication is the most widely used. Stimulants concentrate on certain areas of the brain that control behavior, motivation, and attention. Stimulants may have positive short-term effects in dealing with the symptoms of ADHD; but some of them may cause harmful side effects.

For years, I worked with children who suffered with this disorder. Several of them were properly diagnosed with ADHD while many who displayed characteristics of the disorder went undiagnosed. I began working with children soon after high school in the summer of 1991. My very first job was a counselor/tutor with the city recreation department's Summer Youth Program.

Most of the kids in the program were raised in single parent homes and lived in drug and crime ridden neighborhoods. So, if they did not have ADHD, they carried emotional problems that stemmed from their home environment into the program. I worked the summer program each summer for six years. I enjoyed working with the summer campers and tried my hardest to motivate them. Typically, they were good kids though.

I also worked with children for three years in an elementary school—Robinson Elementary. I was the library assistant and I had contact with the entire student body because they visited the library weekly. Just as the kids in the summer program, many of them were raised in one-parent homes without fathers. Some were physically and emotionally abused at home while other were the primary care takers for themselves and their siblings because their mother was either on drugs, in jail, or simply did not care if they made it to school or not.

While at Robinson, I met a little girl who instantly caught my attention. She was a shy second grader symbolically named Star. When her class came into the library, she was always quiet. And when she spoke, she held her head down; looking toward the floor. She was a bright kid who, with the proper support system, could have been an honor roll student. A few months into the school year, I found out that Star had seven other siblings and they all lived with their grandmother because her mother was incarcerated and her father was absent from her life as well.

Star was starving for attention. She disrupted her classroom in order to gain attention from teacher and classmates. I knew her disruptive behavior was a cry for help. Therefore, I reached out to her. I met with her teacher once a week to monitor her behavior and grades. It made a significant difference. Her grades and behavior greatly improved.

One day after checking in on Star, I received a bad report from her teacher. After the recess bell ranged, I called her to the library. As punishment, I made her read to me. She read a book that I selected instead of playing with her friends. She was clearly upset. Nevertheless, I made her read anyway. I thought that I was punishing Star for being disruptive in class, but I quickly found out, it was not punishment in her eyes. I gave her what she craved the most—quality time.

After the bell rang, I walked her back to the classroom and explained, "Each time you get into trouble you're going to lose your recess". I continued, "You're going to report to the library and read to me".

She did not say anything. She just smiled and walked into her classroom.

I checked with her teacher the next day and received a good report. I was pleased to learn that my strategy worked for Star.

But one day as I prepared for lunch, the Librarian said, "Ms. Zimmerman, you have a little visitor."

I opened the door and looked into the hallway. Star stood there with her library book that she checked out earlier in the day.

"You didn't get into trouble today. You don't have to miss recess", I said.

She looked down toward the floor and said, "I want to."

Without hesitating, I opened the door. She read to me, again, the entire recess period while I ate my lunch.

We met three times a week for the remainder of the school year. Star was overjoyed! Her reading grade improved along with her communication skills. She no longer looked toward the floor when she spoke. She looked into the eyes of the person as she spoke to them. I realized that my presence made a big difference in her life. And I was so proud of her. The smile she wore every day proved that she appreciated my efforts.

She expressed her appreciation in other ways too. One year during "Teacher Appreciation Week", she gave me a gift that I will always remember. During this week, students are encouraged to bring a specific gift which represents each day. For example, Monday's gift may have been a notebook, red pens, etc. This particular year, on the last day of Teacher Appreciation Week the students were asked to bring a special gift for their teachers. And Star desperately wanted to give me a gift; but her grandmother could not afford it.

Friday was the last day of appreciation week. I was in the library making coffee with several of my co-workers when the librarian said, "Ms. Zimmerman you have a little visitor."

Star poked her head in the library, reached in her backpack and pulled out a *Glade* air freshener. It was obvious that she had gotten it from her grandmother's bathroom because it had fingerprints all over it and had a string of hair around it. But, that did not matter to me.

"Thanks Star. You didn't have to bring me anything", I said while hugging her fighting back tears.

She smiled and replied, "You're welcome."

Again, I gave her a big hug. She exited the library and I returned to my co-workers. I showed them my gift and they were touched as well.

Mrs. Brown, the Librarian, said, "That's so sweet. She wanted to get you something but couldn't afford to buy it. She probably took it from her grandmother's bathroom".

While wiping tears from our eyes, we all agreed.

During my three years at Robinson, I was so proud to have made a difference in her life and was determined to continue inspiring her each day. Keeping my promise to remain a part of her life, I maintained a relationship with Star after I resigned from the Ouachita Parish School System.

Having worked with children for a number of years, I could not help but compare today's generation to my generation. When I was in grade school, even middle and high school, there were only a handful of disruptive kids in the entire school; but today there seems to be six or seven in *every* classroom—in some instances, more than seven. They are so hyperactive that it is difficult for teachers to keep them in their seats and keep their attention. Several of them even sit in class and daydream like space babies.

At Robinson Elementary, the teachers constantly complained about the discipline problems in the classrooms. They said it was "hard to teach the few students who actually wanted to learn because the disruptive students constantly distract them". Just as Star, many of the kids misbehaved for attention. They felt that negative attention was better than no attention at all.

It was obvious that they lacked attention at home. But finding quality time for kids is especially difficult for single parents. We are so busy dealing with everything that comes along with being a single parent—work, cooking, cleaning, grocery shopping and helping with homework that we rarely find time for ourselves; so imagine squeezing quality time with our kids into the picture. But this is not an option, it is necessary. If only 15-30 minutes a day, spending time with our kids is essential. Children appreciate time with parents even if they seem agitated by it. They carry these moments with them as they grow into adults and as they reflect back on life—the fun times with mom and dad.

I hear older and wiser folks talk about the "old fashioned" way of raising children. They talk about the good ole days when everyone in the neighborhood had permission to whip your butt if you got into trouble. Back then parents knew where their kids were at all times and who they were with. I'm not sure if the mid '70's and '80's qualify as old fashion, but it worked pretty well for my siblings and me.

Speaking of quality time, some of my favorite childhood memories are summer vacations, holidays and learning to cook with my mom. My parents provided all of our needs and many of our wants; but they spent lots of quality time with us. We took summer vacations to Six Flags, Florida beaches, Disney World and every other place my older sister could think to visit.

As a child, Christmas and Easter were my favorite holidays. I helped my mom cook. And my sister, brother and I decorated the Christmas tree every year. One Christmas, I must have been around eight or nine years old, I found the hiding spot for our Christmas gifts that "Santa Claus" supposedly bought. Well, I showed my brother. The gifts were in a closet in the front bedroom. I will never forget his reaction when I showed him his first *Atari Video* game.

He was so excited! "Oh, I can't wait to press those whittle buttons", he said in an Elmer Fudge voice.

I was certain that I would get a beat down for snooping around in the closet; but thank God my mom never found out. Well, not until now.

Those are the memories a child should carry into adulthood. But for thousands of kids, quality time with family is nonexistent. Moms are too busy working, hanging out with their friends, or chasing men around to deal with their first priority—children. And please do not get me started on "daddy" and all of his issues.

There were so many children that I have worked with who shared horrifying stories about their lives with me. They were awful! One fourth grader told me that her mom sometimes leaves her and five other siblings at home while she "went out to the club with her friends". This child was no older than ten years old. And her youngest sibling was 8-months-old. If you think that was bad, it got worse. Another child told me she stayed home with seven cousins while her mother and aunts "partied". The youngest child in this scenario was 2-years-old.

I have a better example. Approximately two years ago, a young unwed mother of six moved into a home down the street from my parents. Her oldest daughter was 13-years old. One morning while preparing to take my son to school, I saw two of the kids walking down the street. The girl walked ahead of her brother. He lagged behind with his arms inside of his shirt because he was not wearing a coat. And he was crying too. It was a cold winter morning; so of course, my son and I were dressed warmly. I warmed up the car as they walked by.

"Where is his coat or jacket?" I asked his sister.

She replied, "It's at home. My mama is in the bed sleep and she won't open the door."

Are you kidding me? This little boy cried because he was so cold and his mom would not open the door to allow him to get his coat. Keep in mind, this was the heart of winter. She was unemployed; so she had ample time to cook a hot breakfast and dress them properly for school. However, she was in the bed asleep. Both children attended the same school as my son; so I gave them a ride.

Sisters online had harsh comments about unfit mothers. They talked about them badly.

And my sister blames the problem on young mothers. She said, "There should be something embedded into a woman's body to prevent her from getting pregnant until she is at least 25-years-old."

She believed by the age of twenty-five, most women are emotionally and financially able to care for a child. This would in turn allow them to be responsible mothers.

I understood her point. But I believed the maturity level and value system played a vital role in becoming good parents and raising productive children. I told her, "A mature19-year-old mother who carries strong family values will be a stronger parent than an irresponsible and immature 19-year-old mother who does not have *any* family values". A mother whose parents instilled great character building skills—respect, honesty, integrity, compassion, empathy, responsibility, self-discipline and perseverance—passed these values to her children. My sister agreed with me; but she still believed age was the biggest problem.

Mothers online raised another topic—spoiled rotten kids. I know all about spoiled rotten kids because I was one of them. Spoiled kids have false perceptions of reality. And even worse, spoiled kids become spoiled adults. They carry the "I can get anything I want when I want it" mentality with them to college, on the job and into their relationships and marriages. Even as adults, when things do not go their way, they behave just as they did when they were children—throw temper tantrums, cry, and do everything that worked just to get what they want.

It took years before I realized and accepted my spoiled brat status—thirty years to be exact. And because of it, I had a difficult time dealing with adversity. It caused a lot of frustration and aggravation for me as a young adult. However, tough times with finances, school and unsatisfying jobs brought reality to my front door. This was good for me because it helped strengthened my faith in God and helped me realize that things are not always going to go my way. Now I realize that things happen in God's time; not mine. I am perfectly content with this concept. I can say it now. I am no longer a spoiled brat; more like a rehabilitated one.

Young parents and spoiled kids are not the only problems with children today. The lack of education and our inability to focus on education is another major concern in the black community. Our number one goal as parents is to provide quality education for our kids. But for African-Americans, our focus is solely sports and entertainment; football and rapping. We do not stress education enough.

"We don't care about education! All we care about is name-brand clothing for our kids", said one mother online.

And she was not alone. Several people agreed with her. She was right too. We adorn their little bodies in designer clothing; but fail to dress their brains up with a quality education. Our kids are the best-dressed students in school; but are last in ACT and SAT scores. And many of us can barely pay mortgage and car payments monthly; but we continuously throw money away on designer clothing for our kids. Yes, we are willing to pay hundreds of dollars for Nike, Reebok, and Addias sneakers when NBA stars like Shaquille O'Neal and Stephen Marbury offer quality sneakers at reasonable prices that we fail to purchase.

Yes, we should spend more on educating our children. As parents, we should spend more on educational tools like computerized ACT and SAT programs to help improve scores on standardized test. Education is constantly stressed in white households. They believe in educating their kids. They spend thousands of dollars annually on their children's education. But unfortunately for many black children, quality education is not an option. For some, even graduating from high school seems farfetched.

Yes, there are a number of difficulties in raising children in the 21st century. As I mentioned earlier in the chapter, I have worked with variety of children and I am a single mother. So, I understand the frustrations that parents, grandparents, and teachers feel. Believe me, I *do* understand. Here's my story:

My nerves! My nerves!

I guess I should have known what to expect after my son's Kindergarten teacher pulled me to the side after the first day of school.

"Ms. Zimmerman, I need to speak with you for a minute", she said.

Even before this day, there were warning signs that my son was a very hyper child. During pregnancy, he moved constantly. I thought it was normal for a fetus to be very active. I also should have known that he was stubborn because the last three weeks of pregnancy, he got comfortable in one position and remained until birth. He did not move a lick. My obstetrician advised me to walk daily to "help him turn and move into position". Walking did not help. He did not budge. With my due date quickly approaching, Dr. Williams decided to schedule a cesarean delivery.

He weighed 7lbs 6 ounces and was 19 ¼ inches long. A healthy bouncing baby boy with skin so light his father thought he looked "like a white baby." He did not have much hair; just a light patch of straight hair on the top of his head. I thought he was perfect. So did his father. Both families were present to witness the birth and everyone was overjoyed at the little one's arrival.

—

My pediatrician warned that he was "a gassy baby". He prescribed special drops to administer before each feeding. Of course, I wanted to breast-feed because I knew it was better for him. But I decided against it. Overall, he was a healthy baby.

We added baby cereal to his formula when he was four months olds. Soon after, we began feeding him jar food—peaches, pears, and carrots. I guess another hint should have come when he started eating jar food. Each time he ate something sweet, he wiggled his little fingers together quickly as if he was trying to get something off the tips. Back then, I thought it was cute; but thinking back, I figured out it was the sugar that caused those reactions.

A few years passed. At the age of 3, he began a program called "Head Start" which is similar to Pre-K. He hated it. He did not like being away from home at all. He cried every day during the first week. The director of the center was a close friend of my father. She called home each time he cried and my father immediately picked him up.

My son was very clever so he picked up on the pattern. But Friday, the director was out of town for a business meeting. So when he cried, the teachers let him cry—all day. I picked him up after school and he never cried another day at the center.

There was another very interesting characteristic about my son. He was super smart. He learned concepts quickly and had a great memory. He was enrolled in the program for two years and gave the valedictorian speech to his class on graduation night. He was so cute in his little white cap and gown. Everyone was so impressed with him because the speech was one full page in length. After he delivered it, the crowd gave him a standing ovation. I was right there at the end of the stage waiting for him to give him a big hug!

Now, back to the first day of Kindergarten. I returned to his classroom after school to pick him up.

His teacher pulled me aside, "Ms. Zimmerman, I need to speak with you for a minute."

She told me he would not "sit still, stay in his seat, and would not stop talking". So much for a smooth transition from Pre-K to Kindergarten. Lord knows I will never forget his kindergarten teacher's name—Mrs. Russo. I will never forget it because she called me *every day*. She could not control her classroom. And I actually believed she contributed to the problem. Her "timeout" tactics and softly spoken "okay boys and girls" were not effective in the classroom. She had a room filled with active children and she'd say "okay boys and girls?" Please, try "Sit your butts down" and see if that tactic works.

I made a surprise visit to his classroom one day. DeAndre', my son, was in the corner. She told me he had been acting up all day. I don't know what happened to me at that moment. I was frustrated with his behavior the entire school year.

I talked to him everyday about his behavior and I was fed up! I spanked him in the center of the classroom with the belt that he wore to school. And I wanted to snatch her and give her a few licks for her inability to control the class. I guess I don't have to tell you, Kindergarten was a terrible year.

Thankfully, first grade was much better. He had a stronger teacher who knew how to handle her classroom. And her skin-tone was a little *darker* than Mrs. Russo. In other words, he had a strong black teacher from the old school and no one was happier than I. Thank the Lord!

She was a strong disciplinarian who rejoined the teaching profession after retirement because she loved it so much. She was great at it too. Under the guidance of Mrs. Smith, I did not receive one bad report nor did I receive a phone call during the year. First grade was a wonderful year!

Second and Third grades were okay. I received a few bad reports every now and then; but he consistently made the honor roll. He still talked in class; but I had become accustomed to it. I recognized he displayed many symptoms of ADHD. But I was in denial. My sister, who is also a teacher, expressed her concerns about his behavior. She believed he was ADHD. She insisted that I have him tested. So I did. And sure enough, he was diagnosed with ADHD.

We were faced with the decision to prescribe medicine or use alternative methods such as change his diet and make a detailed schedule to keep him on task with daily activities. We decided on both. His pediatrician prescribed a very low dosage of Concerta and we limited his intake of sugary foods. The medication helped to keep him focused in the classroom. We only gave it to him during the week; not on weekends and during the summer months.

During his fourth grade year, I felt that a change of scenery would be good for him. I decided to send him to another school. It was a great magnet school. And it was truly an adventure. We thought kindergarten was his worst year; but we were dead wrong. Fourth grade was a disaster. He called it his "worst year ever." I cannot really explain what caused his behavior to worsen and neither can he. I realized he had ongoing issues with his absent father; but I did not realize how deeply it affected him. But I quickly found out.

It seemed that my son was getting into trouble every week—suspension after suspension. Each time he returned to school from one suspension, he got in trouble again. He did everything—fight, talk back to his teachers, spray the hedgehog in the science lab with *Formula 49* cleaner—everything. It had gotten so bad that we were forced, literally, to go back to his old school for the remainder of the year. I remember thinking, "I didn't have sex with Satan so why did I have his son?" Yes, it was that bad.

I did not know which way to turn; so I turned to God. I had to draw strength from God because if I did not, I would have lost my mind. I prayed and prayed and God answered my prayers. He advised me to take my son to a psychologist.

Yes, a psychologist. I took him without questioning it. I was referred to a great psychologist and he began his sessions immediately.

After the first session, I noticed a change in his demeanor as he returned to the waiting area. When he came out of her office I noticed a few tear stains on the front of his shirt. He looked as though the world had been lifted off of his shoulders.

"Did she ask you about your daddy?" I asked.

"Yes Ma'am", he answered.

"So, would you like to see her again?" I asked.

He quickly responded, "Yes! When do I come back?"

I knew that I had found the answer—therapy. He was always a happy child; but he seemed much happier. He met with his therapist for the remainder of the semester. I had a few sessions with her too. But the biggest difference was his behavior at school. There were no more fights. No more suspensions. And no more talking back to his teacher. He did not have to do these things because he had a new method to release his frustrations—through therapy. And thank the Lord for therapy!

He is now an 8th grader. To be honest, he has not gotten into trouble or suspended since his fourth grade year. His grades are much better and his behavior improved greatly. He is a member of the football, baseball, and track teams. He is also in the marching band. I am so proud of him and grateful that with God's wisdom, we were able to identify and solve his ongoing issues.

Before I became a mother, I was not a very patient person. As a matter of fact, I was not patient at all. I believe God sent him to teach a much needed lesson in patience. And believe me, the lesson continues today. Now, I'm not perfect at this patience thing, no one is. But I am a lot better than before.

With over ten years of experience working with children of all ages and races and having gone through the trials of raising my son, I believe it is appropriate for me to give a few tips on the lessons I've learned with raising kids. No, I am not a licensed child psychologist; but I was counseled by one of the best; so that *should* account for something.

Mikki's Parenting Tips:

1) Set positive examples for children; whether you raise them in a two parent home or if you are a single parent. Sometime, we fail to realize our kids watch and emulate our behavior. Many of us set the tone in our households "Do as I say, not as I do." This confuses children. We must practice what we preach.

2) Remember, learning begins at home; not in Pre-K. We, as responsible parents, should begin teaching our kids before they enter any structured

learning institution. Really, we should start before they learn to speak. Simply teach them to recognize their facial features—eyes, nose, chin and mouth. And when they begin to speak, teach them the alphabets, numbers—maybe one through ten—and the basic colors. If they can learn the lyrics to the hottest rap song or the dance steps to the latest dance, they should be able to learn "A B C D".

3) This reminds me of a young mother that I witnessed approximately fifteen years ago while sitting in the DMV waiting to take my first driver's test. I saw a young white lady and her son in the waiting area. He looked like he was three or four years old. She practiced the alphabet with him using flash cards. I thought it was a wonderful idea. This gives him a head start before he entered kindergarten. This is what we should do. Before our kids enter a classroom, they should already know their name, address and phone number. And when I say name, I am referring to their full legal name; not a nickname like "Snackpack" or "Koolaid". I have witnessed so many children who were in Kindergarten or first grade and did not know their full name because they only knew a nickname. We, parents, are our children's first and most important teacher.

4) Provide a stable living environment for children to grow. Kids need structure and discipline in order to prosper and be successful.

5) To reiterate the opening quote of this chapter "Train up a child in the way he should go; and when he is old, he will not depart from it." The values that we instill in our children remain throughout their lives. If we teach the values of hard work, respect and responsibility, they will remain throughout our kid's lives. This tip reminds me of a homeless man that I met through the "Feed the Homeless" committee at my church. Each Saturday, we prepared lunch for the homeless people who resided in the community. When I saw the young man, I knew he was a first-timer because I did not recognize his face. I talked to him for a few minutes before we served lunch. He told me that he was originally from Florida; but he was heading to the west coast. On this particular Saturday, we served 25 to 30 people. And he was the only white person in the group. After eating, they all thanked us and exited the church. All accept one—the newcomer. He was the only person who asked if he could help clean up. He asked to take the trash out. And we allowed him to do it. He stayed around, gathered the trash, and took it out to the trash barrel outside the church. He explained that he hated the fact of not having money to pay for his meal. He wanted to pay us by doing "something to help out." He paid by taking the trash out. It was obvious to all of us that the value of hard work was instilled in him as a child. His actions displayed it; even as a homeless man.

6) Spend quality time with kids. Kids value the time we spend with them. Every minute with them is precious. Listening to them is important too. I know sometimes it seems as though their stories never end; but listen and ask questions. They love to explain things.

7) Know where kids are, who they are with, what they are doing, and the length of time it will take to do whatever it is they are doing. Seriously! Keep up with them. Especially older kids. When I was a child, my mom always knew where we were and who we were with. Before she allowed us to go anywhere with anybody, she spoke with their parents to make sure we would be supervised by an adult.

8) Keep kids occupied. Again, especially with teenagers. If they are busy doing positive things, they will not have time or energy to experiment with any negative activities such as drugs, alcohol and sex.

9) Expand children's horizon. Introduce them to new and exciting things. Take family vacations to exotic locations, visit museums and art galleries. And if finances are limited, that's no problem. Take them to the local public library. It is absolutely free! Check out books on exotic places or log onto the internet and research information together.

10) Single parents—Do not expose your children to ever person you date. I suggest introducing your kids to your new boyfriend/girlfriend only if you are serious about this person and feel he or she is "the one". Otherwise, you are setting your kids up for another disappointment after you call it quits.

11) Children look to parents for security. It is our job to provide it for them. It is our responsibility to provide a safe place for them to fall.

12) Have a sit-down dinner with children at least three nights a week. Television has become a babysitter for our kids. Having family dinner serves as quality time with them.

13) Choices and consequences are two major topics we should discuss early and often with our kids. Have frequent conversation about the importance of making good decisions. Explain the consequences of bad decisions—breaking laws, hanging with negative friends, etc. Remember, if you do the crime, you must do the time!

14) Parents must not only teach children how to deal with conflict, we must show them as well. Most African-American children know only one way to deal with conflict—fighting. Fighting does not solve anything. It leads to more anger and aggression which progresses to an even bigger conflict. Conflict resolution skills are critical and must be taught at a very young age. We must teach our black children how to disagree with one another without picking up a gun or knife. Mentoring and leadership programs are great at teaching these skills.

There are many great leadership programs across the country that focus on African-American youth. I am very fortunate to have my pastor serve as Scout Master of one of the best leadership training programs in my hometown—Top Gun Leadership Academy. My son has been an active member for four years.

15) For African-Americans, black history is relevant all year. Not only the month of February. Teach Black history throughout our kids lives. We have a cultural responsibility to teach our kids the *real* history of African Americans; not only the sad stories of how our ancestors were captured, held prisoner on slave ships and beaten by "Massa". Let them know that we hail from a strong race of people—kings and queens from the motherland. Slave ships, slave owners and plantations are all vital components in our history; but these are not the only parts of black history. Schools across the United States focus on these aspects of black history. They do not focus on the great doctors like Dr. Daniel Hale Williams. They do not focus on the great educators—W.E.B. Dubois. They do not focus on great scientist like George Washington Carver. Most times, they leave this relevant piece of African-American history out of the educational process.

16) You know the saying "Everything that glistens is not gold". This is oh so true in regards to Hollywood. It is only an illusion. Our children are blinded by the bling-bling and glamour of Hollywood. They see the cars, the money and the big mansions in movies and music videos. They do not see the ugly side of Hollywood. It is our job as parents to expose the real truth to them. It is our responsibility to let them know the difference in what is real and what is not. Hollywood is fake!

17) Let kids be just that—kids. Stop putting grown up responsibilities on kids. Yes, they will make mistakes. Teach them to learn from their mistakes. They are not perfect and neither are we. Some of us grown folks make the same mistakes over and over again. So what should we expect from children?

18) Teach children the art of good communication. Teach them to look into the eyes of a person as they talk to them. I have witnessed so many children who speak while holding their heads down toward the floor as if they have no confidence in what they are saying. Teach them to hold their heads high and speak clearly and confidently.

19) This tip is very important. Teach black boys the proper way to show love. There are many black men who view marriage as negative because as young boys they were not exposed to a loving marriage that lasted forever. As young boys, they were not taught the proper way to love women. It all begins in childhood. I explained in the introduction that

I am very observant. Over the years, I have noticed that men whose parents were married for a long period of time seek marriage themselves when they are older. They follow in the footsteps of their fathers and grandfathers. This is why it is so important that we teach them how to love properly.

20) This tip is equally important. Teach black girls the proper way to receive and give love. When she is older, she will be able to recognize *real* love. Wild girls become wild women. We must teach our daughters at an early age to respect themselves. If they respect themselves, they will never allow anyone to disrespect them.

21) Teach children the dangers of peer pressure. Peer pressure is more prevalent than ever; especially for middle and high school kids. We must teach them how to deal with it so they will know how to handle it. Believe me; they will eventually face peer pressure. Provide examples for them too. And get animated with it! Kids love exaggeration.

22) Last but not least, teach kids the power of God. God created everyone for a specific purpose. Drill this tip into their heads until they realize: "He who kneels before God can stand before *any* man".

Mothers around the world—I heard you loud and clearly! Children cause a great deal of frustration. Yes, they do. But we will go through hell and high water for them. Recently, I spoke with one of my best friends who live in Texas. She returned home for the Thanksgiving holidays. We discussed kids and she shared a story with me about her oldest son. She explained how a simple phone call from her son's principal sent both her and her husband over the edge.

"Girl, I almost lost my job that day", she said. She had a "meltdown" at her desk. The phone call ended with her screaming at the principal and threatening to pay a visit to the school. Keep in mind, my friend is a very professional woman; but she had received one too many phone calls from her son's principal. And she was fed up!

But this is the power of our children. They force your alter ego to emerge. And that's exactly what happened to my friend. Her crazy, out-of-control, sedative needing, alter ego came shining through on that particular day

Yep, our kids sometimes test our patience and our sanity; but we love them to death and will do anything for them. As I said earlier, kids will be kids and they are not perfect. So, the next time your kids test your patience and you feel like screaming DMX's lyrics—"Y'all gone make me lose my mind up in here, up in here"—and there will be a next time—take a deep breath. Think before you respond. Remember, they learn how to deal with their frustrations by observing how we deal with our frustrations.

CHAPTER 5

Feeling Unappreciated, Misunderstood, and Misrepresented

"Lately, I've been feeling unappreciated."
Cherish

"Before you can read me, you got to learn how to see me."
En Vogue

Unappreciated

Speaking of hard-headed kids, do any of these phrases sound familiar: *Mama, do you have $10? Mama, I have practice at 4:30. Can you drop me off? Mama, I'm hungry. What's for dinner?* It is always Mama, Mama, Mama. You would think mama is the only name they know. So why is "da-da" the first word our babies say when they learn to speak? I know all moms—young and old, black and white—would love to know the answer. The only logical reason that I thought of was this: they say da-da as infants because they yell for Mama, Mommie, or "Maaaaaaa!" their entire lives.

Where would our children be without us—strong mothers? Often times they take us for granted without even realizing it. They are so accustomed to having us around and doing everything for them that it sometimes slips their little minds to say "Thank you" or "I love you mom". The idea of mom missing in action is farfetched.

Being a single mother doubles the load. I don't know about you, but there is a long list of services that I perform daily without being paid a thin dime.

—

81

They include: maid, tutor, spiritual advisor, gourmet chef, counselor, bank teller, doctor, chauffeur, and head referee (between my son and niece when she is home from college).

You know sisters online agreed. "Black women work, take care of the family, cook, clean, read bedtime stories, make love to their {our} husbands, take care of their {our} parents, and get up the next morning to do it all over again", said a sister from Ft. Worth, TX.

God knew exactly what he was doing when he created mothers. He knew this world would be lost and confused without our guidance. And black mothers, we do it all, don't we? Great at multi-tasking! Ten things could go on at once and we are still in total control; and we still look great while doing all ten things.

This gift was handed to black mothers from our African ancestors—strong, bold, fierce, and resilient. These great characteristics are found throughout the female species in the black community. These distinct traits stem from great tribes throughout the motherland of Africa. Take the Yoruba tribe for instance. This tribe is known for its strong, independent women who oversee day-to-day operations in many of the cities of Southwest Nigeria and Benin.

No, our feathers are not easily ruffled. This is a known fact throughout the black community. Black women are the backbone of our families, communities and churches; yet we are often taken for granted by the very ones who should appreciate us the most—husbands and boyfriends. We manage the finances in the household. We cook and clean. Do the laundry and still find time to keep our man completely satisfied in the bedroom. And we do it all without getting one strand of hair out of place.

During my research, the subject "Black men who do not cherish black women" arose constantly online. Topics like "Why do so many black men not cherish black women?" infuriated brothers. They hated when this topic arose. They contributed to the conversation though. But most of them were "tired of hearing the same thing over and over". Many of them thought it was a "stupid topic." And you know how men are—always trying to keep the peace. On the message boards, they tried to diffuse the tension by reassuring us there are "still some good brothers out here for black women".

"I love my sisters! I have been happily married to one {black woman} for years", said one brother who was in his early fifties and from Atlanta, GA.

Another gentleman from New York agreed. He stated, "I've been screaming those same sentiments! I'm in love with all of my sistas. No question. No doubt!"

Regardless of how they reassured, some sisters still believed black men only see us for sex.

"I noticed that the average relationship in the Black community all consist of bootie calls and FWB (friends with benefits) while Black men look for trophy mates", one frustrated sister said.

The sister who started the conversation said she received "lots of hate mail for this one." And she did. But there were countless women who agreed with her.

Black beauty was another subject that found its way into this conversation. I have heard numerous people say, "Black women are the most beautiful women in the world." And we are. So beautiful, women of other races spend millions of dollars annually for physical features that we are born with—full luscious lips, beautiful brown skin, big boobs, and nice round butts. They quickly ridicule us by calling us big-lipped; but they sprint faster than Olympic gold medalist Usain Bolt to the nearest cosmetic surgeon for collagen shots. And they are quick to call us darkie; but once again, they tan and use bronzer risking deadly diseases like skin cancer in order to look darker like us. Breast implants, butt implants, any implant that you can think of are all patterned after the black woman's body.

I remember a few years ago a statement that a white guy said while dancing with me at a fraternity party on Louisiana Tech's campus. "I must admit, black women are beautiful," he said.

At the same party, a white female told my friend repeatedly, "You are so pretty!" My friend smiled and said "Thank you" each time.

We did not know what was going on. We thought maybe they were all drunk or not used to partying with black people. But that was not the case. They recognized it too—black women are beautiful!

While cleaning out some old magazines a few weeks ago, I came across the May 2000 edition of *Essence Magazine*. I keep all of my *Essence* magazines. On this cover, I saw an array of gorgeous black women—all shades of black. There was Halle Berry, in the center of course, Vivica A. Fox, Jada Pinkett Smith, Queen Latifah, Regina King, Michael Michele, Elise Neal and Loretta Divine. These women, all flavors of chocolate, were different shapes and sizes; but all beautiful black women. I looked over the cover of this magazine for a few minutes. Looking at these strong and beautiful black women, I felt like a proud parent receiving a report card with straight A's on it! I was so proud to be a black woman. And this is how we all should feel—proud to be beautiful black women. Appreciating the unique physical attributes God has blessed us with. That's right, appreciate them. Besides, there are many women who wish they had what we've got.

Misunderstood

Not only are black women frustrated with feeling unappreciated, we are grossly misunderstood. According to online sisters, we are the most misunderstood group of women on the planet. Think about it. When you picture someone cursing another out, who do you envision giving the lashing? Yep, you guessed it—a black woman. Not just any black woman; an eye and neck rolling, finger-waving sister.

That is the perception most people have about black women. We are loud, we curse everybody out and we make a big scene every place we visit. People think we fuss and complain about everything; especially in the work environment. It is virtually impossible for sisters to disagree with another colleague's idea or complain about unfair treatment. When it happens, we are said to have "bad attitudes". And sisters, please do not make the mistake of having a bad day and letting someone know about it. You are labeled as a bitch with a capital "B".

The truth is, all women regardless of race, socioeconomic status, or background experience mood-swings. Whether a direct result from PMS or Menopause, all women experience mood-swings. And some more than others. Stress alters our behavior. But when a black woman experience stress or is overwhelmed she is labeled a bitch, combative or confrontational. Why is this so? If a non-black woman has a bad day at home or at work, she's said to be "emotional" or "stressed". Why can't black women get "emotional"? Why can't we get stressed?

I guess people are less threatened when a non-black woman shows her emotions; but we instantly become the problem when we are stressed out and show the slightest bit of aggravation. I do not get it. And neither did the black women online.

Men feel this way about black women too. "Black women are too controlling and bossy", said a man online.

Another said, "Black women talk too much! And they don't know when to shut up."

Translation: black women, most of us, say exactly what is on our minds. We are not fake and we do not pretend. In most instances, we are brutally honest and it tends to hurt people's feelings. Sometimes the truth is a hard pill to digest. Nevertheless, when dealing with black women, you may need to keep an extra bottle of *Pepto Bismol* handy; because we will give it to you straight!

No, we do not talk too much. We are good at expressing our opinions. Real black women know when to speak and when to shut up. We know when to take a step back and allow our man to take control of a situation. Nonetheless, we also know when they need a little *assistance* to handle a situation. We are loving, caring, and respectable; but we also know when to be strong, tough and forceful.

Misrepresented

Here is another huge misconception about black women—we are thought of as sexual objects. Many people believe we are very promiscuous; especially in the entertainment industry. And many sisters believe black men are at the core of the problem.

One sister from New York stated, "Honestly, I see black men being equally disrespectful (if not more) to black women—especially in clubs and things like that."

Another sister believed "It's as if we are only good enough for sex. Not marriage, not a lifetime partner, but sex."

This belief was found on college campuses across the country. For example, brothers were more willing to develop long-term relationships with non-black women. But they slept with several black women without any commitment.

Years ago when I lived on a college campus, my roommate and I were friends with a young man who revealed that he only "sleeps with black women; but date white women". We were totally shocked by his comment.

When he made this statement, I did not respond because I was thinking , "No he did not just say this to two black women." No, I did not respond; but my roommate did. She cursed him out! She was so upset. She had tears in her eyes as she spoke. I was upset too. And he acted as though he could not understand why we were so upset with him. He felt that he did not disrespect us because, as he said, "I'm not sleeping with y'all". It did not matter if we were not sleeping with him. His comments disrespected black women as a whole. And it did not sit well with either of us.

Of course all black men are not guilty of this behavior. There are millions of black men who love, respect, and cherish black women. I know many brothers who do. But according to the women I spoke with, many brothers need a crash course in "Respecting Black Women 101".

White men view us as sex object too. Maybe they feel this way because of all of the misinformation from television and every other media outlet. There are scores of white men on the internet who pretend to "love black women"; but are only out to play games and mistreat us. Their online profiles read "Looking for my African princess" or "White man seeking black love". Yeah, they love us; but refuse to introduce us to their family members, colleagues, or friends. They hook up with sisters on the internet for sex and that is it. Once their mission is accomplished, they disappear and move to the next sister online.

My niece shared a very interesting story with me that dealt with this topic. She and her roommates, who are black and students who lived on campus, attended a party given by white students. They enjoyed the party and were having a great time until a guy boldly asked them if they knew how to make their "a** clap?" My niece could not believe he asked this question. It was obvious that he believed booty clapping is common knowledge among black women. He may have thought that we learn the technique as young girls. My niece recalled that she wanted "to curse him out"; but thankfully she did not. They simply walked away from this fool to enjoy the party.

This story was only one of many that I have heard regarding the stereotypes and misconceptions about black women. There were some online who believed black women are the only group of women who have kids outside of marriage. It may sound crazy, but it is true.

One discussion lasted for almost a week online regarding out of wedlock births. A white guy asked me, out of all people, to explain the high number of unwed births in black women. His exact words were, "Help me understand why there are so many unwed births, not just once but several time with several men?"

I responded, "If you are referring to black women having babies out of wedlock as opposed to white women, here's my theory: black women are not the only women who become pregnant outside of wedlock. What I've learned is that white women get pregnant before they are married; but many of them choose abortions or put their kid up for adoption; while most black women choose to keep their babies instead of killing them. I remember going to an abortion clinic a few years back with a friend. The place was packed with young UNWED white women. And there are lots of white babies who are in the foster care system looking for homes. Where are these babies coming from? Not from black women, they are born to unwed white women. They'll (white women) stand at the altar on their wedding day with a pure white dress on as if they have never been pregnant before and had three or four abortions (by different men). So don't get on this message board acting like white women only get pregnant after marriage. Because you and I both know that is far from the truth. And if you didn't know; now you do. So help me understand that."

He responded and acknowledged the fact that his question was inappropriate. He also agreed with me on both issues. He said, "Hi, my question was poorly written and offensive. I see that now. I know you are right about abortion. You are also right about giving kids away for adoption. *Both* [are] big white problems."

He agreed with me, and he was white. Black women are not the only group who make the mistake of getting pregnant before marriage. However, this is the misconception. We are exploited as sexual objects and believed to be very promiscuous. But again, these misconceptions are wrong. Now, there may be some black women who fit the profile. But guess what, there are white, Hispanic and Asian women who fall into this category as well. But for some strange reason, black women are labeled in this manner.

I mentioned earlier how the media feeds into this misconception too. Well, while watching an episode of *The Tyra Show*, I saw this misconception displayed. Not by Tyra; but through her audience. The subject of this episode, which aired on September 25, 2006, described how others see you and what they conceive about you based on your looks alone. She had four women on stage that the audience analyzed. Tyra did not give any background information on any of the women. They judged on looks only. She asked the audience, who was mostly non-black, who they felt would most likely commit a crime. At least 70% of the audience thought Crystal, the only black women on stage, would most likely commit a crime.

She also asked their thoughts on the occupation of the four women. Almost the entire audience perceived Crystal to be a "stripper." It turned out, Crystal was a medical assistant, an entrepreneur (operates a basket making business), and a sexy mother of two kids.

Now you know I have to ask—why did the majority of the audience feel that Crystal would most likely commit a crime and that she was a stripper? She did not have a frown on her face. She was not rolling her eyes and neck; nor was she moving seductively. She simply stood on the stage just as the other women. They did not perceive the other women in this manner, so why Crystal? I concluded that because she was black she had to be a stripper and have committed a crime at least once in her lifetime. That was so pathetic!

Now do you understand why this is so frustrating for black women? This is a universal misconception that people of all races share about black women. They view us as combative sexual objects with five or six baby daddies. The sister on Tyra's show was a mother of two kids, worked full-time and owned a business. An entrepreneur and full-time mother perceived as a crime-committing stripper. Now tell me, with a straight face, why black women should not be frustrated about this misconception.

Truth is, we are frustrated. Very frustrated! We are tired of being unappreciated, misunderstood and misrepresented. So once again, I have brilliantly listed 21 tips to dispel the misconceptions about black women. These 21 tips are for men, black and white, employers and everyone who negatively categorizes black women.

1) Regardless of gender, race or age, do not call us the "B" word; especially to our face. You *may* be able to get away with it behind our backs. But if at all possible, please do not let us hear it. I don't care how many firework displays you have seen in your lifetime, you aint seen sparks and flames like you will witness if you disrespect any sister in this manner.

2) Never mistreat our children. A *real* black mother will fight to the end to protect her babies. Have you ever witnessed a raging pit bull attack someone? Well, you will surely find out if you mistreat our children.

3) Men, especially black men, if you have a good woman at home, show your appreciation for her—often. If she is a good mother to your kids, a loving wife and supports you whole-heartedly, do not take her for granted. Because if she leaves you, you will spend the rest of your natural life singing, like Glen Jones, "I've been searching for so long, nobody like you, no where to be found".

4) If we disagree with you or show any disapproval of your opinion, do not perceive it as combative. We are entitled, just as anyone else, to express our opinions.

5) Never ask if we know how to "booty-clap". Seriously! Remember the white guy at the party asked my niece and her friends this degrading question. They were the only black women at the party. He did not ask white women, only black women. And they were dancing non-seductively. Therefore, I felt it appropriate to add this to my tips. Now if you are at a strip club, this question may be appropriate.

6) Never touch our body without an invitation. You risk getting the taste slapped out of your mouth if you try it.

7) Men, never ask a sister to make love on the same day of her hair appointment. Catch us *before* we go to the hair salon.

8) Fellas, the best gift you can give is time. We love spending time, quality time, with our man.

9) Now that I think about it, an occasional gift is not a bad idea. Flowers, diamonds, and chocolates are all great surprise gifts.

10) We never hear "I love you" enough. However, say it only if you really mean it and not because it sounds good.

11) You will never gain the attention of a classy, intelligent and sophisticated black woman by yelling "Hey", "Psssst", or "Hey lil momma". Approach us with class and dignity and we will return the love.

12) Black men, appreciate our beauty. Appreciate our full lips, curvy hips and beautiful brown skin. You ohh and ahh over the same features when other women pay for them. We are born with them. So drool over us in the same fashion.

13) Black men, when you see us walking behind, please be a gentleman and hold the door open; for the sake of common courtesy. If white men do it without even thinking about it, you should be slipping and sliding to the door for us.

14) Give us a helping hand at home. We always appreciate help, any help—doing the dishes, help with the kids, doing the laundry and cooking. Help a sister out sometimes!

15) "Club dancing" is not the only form of dance that we are skilled at performing. Some of us cannot dance a lick. And many of us love tap, ballet, even ballroom dancing. There are sisters who are as graceful as Cheryl from *Dancing with the Stars*. Last season, Laila Ali gracefully proved this to the world. She won third place in the competition. Booty shaking is not our expertise!

16) "Me time" is important—very important. Give us a little every now and then. Allow us time to hang out with the girls and enjoy life. Take

the kids for a day or maybe a weekend. Give us a break. Lord knows we deserve it.

17) As you are now aware, all black women do not have bad attitudes. Some are bitter and anger all of the time. But that's a personal choice.

18) Hollywood and the entertainment industry—stop portraying black women as negative characters in film, movies, and music videos. Stop it! Create more positive roles for us such as doctors, lawyers, great mothers and teachers. Not prostitutes, crack addicts and mothers who mistreat their children or mothers with twelve baby daddies. This only fuels the misconception of black women. Shame on you!

19) If we begin a sentence with one of these phrases—"Wait a minute", "Let me tell you something", or Tasha Mack's [from the popular television show *The Game*] favorite line, "Now what now?"—The words that follow may not be very *kind*.

20) Black women, appreciate one another. Celebrate each other. Women of other nationalities do it often. They compliment and encourage each other. We don't. We hate on each other every opportunity we get. We are all special and unique. Appreciate the uniqueness. Stop hating on each other because of our own insecurities and internal issues—we are too dark, our hair is not long and thick like such and such, we are too big. We are all beautiful in a unique way. Appreciate one another and stop the madness of jealousy and envy. If we want others to respect us, we must begin respecting *ourselves*.

21) God created black women as strong and beautiful creatures. Just as every other race of women, we are mothers, sisters, wives, and teachers who deserve to be treated with respect and dignity. I thank God for the millions who know the truth about *real* black women.

Okay, these were the frustrations associated with being unappreciated, misunderstood, and misrepresented. We are thought to have nasty attitudes and are promiscuous. But this is far from the truth. We are not "nappy-headed hoes" as Don Imus suggested referring to the black women of the Rutgers women basketball team. We are strong, loving and supportive women who care deeply for our families and friends. We give endlessly and effortlessly to our family, friends, co-workers, church members, you name it. We are hardworking women who can multi task twelve different things at once—work, attend school, raise productive and responsible children, chair two and three church committees, and still find time to attend each one of our children's extra-curricular activities.

Yes, we do all of these things and still look amazing in the process. Our physical beauty is often copied by others; but there is no other living creature more beautiful and stunning than the black woman.

CHAPTER 6

Black Women Who Conform to Stereotypical Behaviors

"We don't have to take our clothes off to have a good time."
Jermaine Stuart

"I will be a freak until the day; until the dawn!"
Adina Howard

Let me forewarn you, this chapter may rub some of you the wrong way. This was a very controversial topic online as well. Once again, I am not judging anyone. I leave that arduous task to the creator of the universe. Besides, that was not my job. My job was to listen to frustrated sisters online as they vented about these women.

But I will give my honest opinion—many times we, black women, poison our own image which cause others to disrespect, mistreat and misunderstand us. Some of us, and you know who you are, are as loose as a prostitute's panties. And I don't think this is what Bishop T. D. Jakes had in mind when he said, "Woman thou art loosed!"

I was not alone in my belief. Others—men and women—felt the same. Listen to the following online discussion: "Sistas we have got to do better!" It was written by a frustrated black man—"I may ruffle a few feathers, but I just got to get this off of my chest. The majority of black females (especially young from teens to mid thirties) will never have a good and decent man. While I think there are many attractive, intelligent, refined, classy, and open-minded black females out there, the ghetto hood rats, asymmetrical hair-do wearing, loud talking, neck and eye rolling, overweight, un-kept, rude, bad attitude, ebonic speaking females dominate the type of black females [that] I run into." He also said, "I think these are the primary factors that contribute to black men leaving black women for non-black women in DROVES!"

I agreed with him about the behaviors of some black women. But this is not the only reason black men date non-black women. (If you missed this information, see Chapter 2).

As you can imagine, he ruffled more than a few feathers. His thread ignited a heated debate that lasted for weeks. Many black women were offended and felt disrespected by his comments. While others agreed with him. Whether we agreed with him or not, there was truth in his comments. Sisters, we have got to do better! Many of us lack self-respect, self-love, and self-esteem which allow negative characteristics to surface. As young girls, these characteristics were not instilled and as the old folks say—"When you know better, you do better".

I addressed this issue online as well and received the same mixed response as the brother who began the discussion. My thread was titled, "Respect is earned." I talked about a conversation I had with a male friend. It stemmed from a weekend trip to Houston, TX. He and group of his friends went to a nightclub. He described it as a "nice, happening club". He also described the behavior of many of the sisters in the club. Pathetic! He noticed, in freezing temperatures, they wore "short, short, skirts, see through blouses, halters and tight, short a—shorts". He also said, "The ladies were "dancing like they were on a *BET Uncut* video".

Oh, he admitted that he enjoyed the show. But he also talked about them like dogs. Not to their faces, of course—with his boys behind their backs.

I laughed as he told his story and said, "Just because Lil John says 'bend over to the front, touch the floor bounce that a— up and down and get low' doesn't mean you have to do it *literally*!"

Everyone who read my thread cracked up laughing. But they agreed with me. I also asked "How are we (black women) going to gain the respect from men with this negative behavior?" This time, mostly men responded. Women did not have much to add regarding this question. Maybe they knew I spoke the truth.

In reality, many of us want respect from men; but fail to gain it because we do not demand it. Just as a guy online asked—"How can any man treat you like a queen if you act like a two dollar whore?" And he was right. Take groupies and gold-diggers for instance. They desire love, respect, and financial stability; but they do not fit the mold of a woman who can attract and *maintain* this man. Don't get it twisted, men will sleep around with these women and use them as sex toys until they get sick of dealing with them. But you will never see her on his arm at the *ESPY* or *Academy Awards*. You will only find her hidden in hotels and motels across the country.

I bet the wives of professional athletes and celebrities have a hard time keeping these women away from their men. Jackie Christie, who is married to former NBA player Doug Christie, often reflected on the strategies and actions of groupies. She was highly criticized for the tactics she used to keep potential groupies away from her husband. For instance, she did not allow Doug to interview with female reporters.

And Doug was criticized for being "too committed" to his wife. Can you believe that? Too Committed? Hearing some of the tactics Jackie used to protect her marriage, you would think she did not fully trust her husband. She proclaimed that she did not trust women. But who could blame her?

I understood exactly where she stood. Groupies understood it too. I am willing to bet they were aware of the beat-down they would have gotten if they approached Doug with any foolishness. I believe a Jackie Christie beat-down is worse than the beat-down that "Diamond" gave "Ronnie" in *The Players Club*. Ask Shaquille O'Neal, he knows a thing or two about a Jackie Christie beat-down.

Groupies were also aware that Doug had no intentions of cheating on his wife. It does not take a brain surgeon to know if Doug *wanted* to cheat; he would find an avenue to do it. Obviously, he loved his wife dearly and had no desire to be with another woman. If all married men, celebrity or not, had the mentality of Doug Christie, regardless of the other woman's pursuit, they would display self-control and simply reject the offer.

All of this faithful talk sounded really good online; but I am a realist. I know Doug Christie is a very rare breed. Many celebrity wives do not hold the luxury of security within their marriages. Many of them exchange happiness, faithfulness, and peace of mind for mansions, Mercedes Benzes, and even $4 million dollar diamond rings.

You know I am always open to give advice, whether solicited or not. And I have a suggestion for these very frustrated women. If relentless groupies constantly threaten the longevity of your marriage and your husband's actions only add to the problem instead of helping to solve it, don't fret. Here is what you can do: Don't beat the groupie down, curse her out, stalk and kidnap her; even though all of these sounds like pretty good ideas. Don't do any of this because this is what she expects you to do. Instead, take a lesson from the Bible. Follows God's instruction to *Joshua*. Joshua 6:4-5—Here is what you will need to carry out the plan: seven priests "with trumpets made of ram's horns", if priests are unavailable, Baptist preachers will work just fine; and a large group of people, preferably women—your mom, sisters, girlfriends, aunts and female co-workers. For six consecutive days, locate the groupie, march around her one full time without saying a word. Do not even glance at her. And please instruct your crew not to look at her. Because looking will lead to thinking; thinking will lead to reflecting on all of the pain she caused your family; and reflecting will lead to, you guessed it, a Jackie Christie beat-down in the center of the circle! You know that outcome is definitely not in the Bible. So once again, please do not look at her. Simply march around her one full time each day—for six days.

Now, the seventh day is a little different. This day, march around her seven times and allow the priest, or preachers, to blow their trumpets. As soon as you and your group of sister-friends hear the trumpets, "Shout with a great shout!" And witness as all of her faith in knowing that she snatched your husband from his family come tumbling down like the Walls of Jericho! I am telling you, this is the way to deal with groupies. Try it Ladies, it will work every time.

Groupies are not the only women who conform to stereotypical behaviors. Video girls also poison the images of black women. I love music videos. I have watched videos for the past twenty years. But recently they have become more raunchy and tasteless—women wearing little to nothing and doing things that should only be displayed privately in the bedroom.

Sisters online were disgusted with today's music videos. One concept arose during a conversation—darker skinned women are featured when the video has a negative message; but when the song has positive lyrics and expressing good qualities about women,—like Tyrese's song *One* and Fabulous' *You Make Me Better*—the women are usually non-black or so light-skin that they look white. I mentioned this concept to a close friend years ago. I was so glad the women online realized it too. And they did not place the blame on artists or producers. No. They placed blame on the character of the women who allowed themselves to be degraded for a few dollars, fame and recognition.

"No one put a gun to her head and made her tryout to be in the video", said one candid online sister.

I added, "If an artist holds a tryout session for dancers in his new video for a song entitled "Nasty Stank Ho" and the lines are five miles long and filled with half-naked black women who all want to be the nastiest stank ho, who's to blame? That is the purpose of holding tryouts—to find the nastiest one. Right?"

One young lady was very offended by my sarcastic remarks. "Why do you always have to be so sarcastic with your comments? We get your point!"

She was really upset with me. I figured she had just stepped off the set of one of those video shoots!

During one of the discussions, we came to the conclusion that some women use music videos as a stepping stone into the entertainment industry. This is understandable.

But, just as one guy stated, "There has got to be other music videos to audition for". Take Beyonce's video *Irreplaceable* for instance. She wore a bra and curlers in her hair and still looked amazing. In her other video, *Get Me Bodied*, she and her dancers dropped down low and swept the floor without looking like porn stars in the process. Basically, it all boiled down to the character of the female in the video. If she had any morals and values, her performance would reflect it.

Best selling author and former video girl Karrine Steffans was highly criticized for exposing the lifestyle of the music video industry with her tell all book "Confessions of a Video Vixen". Although I do not condemn her behaviors during her stint as a video girl, I admire her strength and courage in presenting her heart-breaking story. There were dozens of woman and men who judged Karrine for the things she did in the past; but everyone has made mistakes. It was obvious that she learned from her mistakes, and grew stronger in the process. I am certain that her story helped women who were involved in the music video industry and women who considered them. That was the purpose of her writing the book.

There was another group of women who were highly criticized online—strippers. Sisters griped and complained about their husbands and boyfriends who frequently visited strip clubs. Let's face it, men love strippers. They love the fantasies that strippers provide. Some men cannot stay away from strip clubs regardless of how hard they try—Former NFL cornerback Adam "Pacman" Jones for instance. Men are visual creatures. In order to maintain their attention, you must stimulate all five senses.

"If you can't beat'em, literally, beat'em at their own game", I advised frustrated online sisters. I suggested they secretly register for pole and lap dance classes. Hone the newly discovered seductive skills until they are confident enough to pull off a show in the privacy of their home. Yep, at home. Give that brother a show he will never forget. And the most fascinating part of it, he will never see it coming.

Here is the perfect plan to pull off your "home-made strip tease". With Montell Jordan's seductive song *Let's Ride* blaring from the stereo system, catch him as he steps out of the shower, still dripping wet. Sneak up behind him and snatch the towel from his waist. With your right hand, smack him on the butt and shove him onto the bed. Handcuff one of his wrists to the bedpost; stand over him like a police officer who just apprehended a hardened criminal. Then, let him have it! Display the moves that you'd been honing for the past few weeks. I mean, give it all to him at once—lap dance and all.

After Montel's slow song ends, speed things up a bit. Strip down to everything except that very sexy pair of thongs he has been trying to get you to wear for months. Play Sisqo's—*Thong Song*—and make him wish he had never purchased those panties. I must warn you, you'll have to be in good shape to perform at this pace; this song is very fast and it is 4:38 long!

After the show ends, you should be butt naked and still standing over him; and if he hasn't broken loose from the one handcuff, he should be handcuffed, buck-eyed, and holding his chest with his free hand.

If he survives this show without having a heart attack, stroke, or brain aneurysm, you will never have *any* more problems with him and strip clubs. You will probably have a harder time getting him to leave the house; even for work. Oh yeah, you will have to learn more creative routines to maintain his attention. But that is fine; learn them. If you don't, "Strawberry", from the local strip club, will be glad to entertain him. Just as I said before, if you can't beat'em, join'em!

The subject of groupies, video girls and gold-diggers was prevalent online. Black women are tagged more than any other demographic with these titles, even though women of all ethnicities can be included. Online sisters, and a few men, were quick to demean these women and categorize them as "home wreckers".

I had a few harsh words too; but I believed their lives lacked something—self-love, self-respect, joy, peace of mind, and attention.

I concluded, "Do a thorough internal examination of *you*. Find out what's lacking in your life. Determine what caused you to engage in these self destructive behaviors. And after that, fix it!"

In the end, we all agreed—your past does not determine your future. Learn from it and move forward. Just as the caterpillar during the molting process—it sheds his outer skin and forms a cocoon to hide inside until it gains enough strength to fly way. Allow God to act as your cocoon. Allow Him to mold and shape you into the woman He wants you to be. And please, do not live up to the stereotypical images that we as a race of people have fought so hard to dispel.

CHAPTER 7

The Constant Rise in Newly Diagnosed HIV Cases in Black Women

"If HIV-AIDS were the leading cause of death
of white women between the ages of 25 and 34 there
would be an outraged outcry in this country."
Secretary of State Hillary Clinton

"For I will restore health to you and heal you
of your wounds says the Lord."
Jeremiah 30:17a (KJV)

Fact: According to the Centers for Disease control, in 2006, 66% of new HIV cases were African-American women. I said it correctly, 66%! Come on ladies, what is going on with us? There has to be an explanation because these statistics are startling. HIV/AIDS was a very touchy subject online between black men and women. The women blamed the rise in HIV cases on men for their "lack of commitment" and the men blamed women for being "too promiscuous".

Of course I weighed in on the subject—"We look to God to restore our health when we should have listened as He warned us about the no-good man or other activities that led to the HIV diagnosis from the start", I said. "He reveals sign after sign, warning after warning, but we choose to ignore them and look the other way", I added.

Some agreed; while others did not. Whether they agreed or disagreed, the fact remains—black women are infected with this disease at a higher rate than any other group of women. And change begins with us. Not with men, not with the government; but with us. We must take a stand to protect ourselves from this deadly disease. We must make life saving changes that will slow our rate of infection.

Fact: This disease is the number one cause of death for African-American women ages 25-34 (Centers for Disease Control). Yes, black women are dying in record numbers from this disease—thousands each year. We are not dying because we are too promiscuous. No, we are dying because we are love starved. We are too desperate. Some of us are so love-starved that we will do any and everything just to hold onto a man; any man. We listen as men say condoms are "uncomfortable" or "sex doesn't feel right with a condom". Yes, we listen. And we accept it as a compliment because it makes us feel special; special because they love and trust us enough to have unprotected sex. But the thought never cross our minds that he could be feeding this lie to twelve other women. We do not think about the consequences of having unprotected sex. We constantly jeopardize our health, sanity, and lives for the love of a man. Maybe this is why we lead the nation in newly diagnosed HIV cases.

But sisters—just as everyone else—need love too. Many of us grew up fatherless; so we use men to fill this painful void in our lives. And many of us have no self-love. No self-worth. The absence of self love opens the door of desperation. The lack of self love leads to low self esteem. Low self esteem leads to emotional dependency. Emotional dependency leads to mistreatment. And mistreatment leads to another sister being added to the extensive list of newly diagnosed HIV cases.

While shopping in Wal-Mart about a month ago, I saw an Asian woman strolling through the produce section. The phrase on her t-shirt caught my eye—"Hard to get". I instantly thought of black women. "Huh, that should be out motto", I thought to myself. We should not only wear the t-shirt; but live by the phrase—hard to get. Maybe if we were *harder* to get, the number of HIV cases would decrease instead of increase. But this is not the case. So apparently, we are easy to get. So easy, that men can have three, four, maybe even five black women at once. And all five would be cool with the arrangement.

Hey, I told you, some of this information may be hard to digest; but it is the truth. Everyone online agreed with me—men and women. I am not saying this to be judgmental or critical. I am not pointing the finger at anyone. We are all in this together. But as I stated, it is the truth. We are our biggest problem. In relationships, we see warning signs of unfaithfulness which could easily jeopardize our health; but refuse to accept the truth. We even see signs of down low activity; but once again, refuse to accept the truth.

Fact: African-Americans make up 13% of the United States population; but account for 50% of newly diagnosed HIV cases. And remember, 66% of new cases are black women. Not sisters who are intravenous drug users. Not sisters on the street prostituting themselves for a fix. Not sisters contracting HIV through blood transfusions. No, most of them are black women who are involved in "committed relationships". These are beautiful black women who entrust their lives to men, selfish men, who only care about sticking and moving from woman to woman—and sometimes men. Men who refuse to take responsibility for their actions even if it means killing the women they claim to love and cherish.

I started this topic online several times not to start an argument; but to bring awareness to this epidemic. Black men were livid! They felt that I blamed them for the rapid rate of HIV infection in black women. Just as I explained to them, these were not my findings. Studies confirmed that heterosexual sexual contact with black men contributed to our rate of infection because they are more likely to have multiple sex partners at once. These are not statistics that I pulled from the air. A study conducted by the University of North Carolina revealed African-American men are more than twice as likely as white men to have multiple female partners simultaneously. Many online were skeptical about the statistics; but that was not my problem. I referred them to the university that conducted the study. I only reported the findings.

In June 2007, Secretary of State Hillary Clinton addressed this issue during the Democratic Primary Debate at Howard University which focused on African-American issues. "If HIV-AIDS were the leading cause of death of white women between the ages of 25 and 34 there would be an outraged outcry in this country", she said.

I agreed. Not just an outcry, there would be all sorts of congressional meetings, government sponsored programs and grants, executive orders from the president, and anything else one could think of to combat the fight against HIV/AIDS.

Yeah, this subject was heavily discussed online. And my advice was simple—stop being so easy! Easy women are like cheap liquor—any neighborhood wino can buy it. It is easy to locate because it's found on every street corner. And it is transparent; you can see *clear* through it; so there is nothing left to the imagination. Ladies, we should think of ourselves as fine bottles of wine. Fine wine has a distinct set of characteristics. It is sealed with a cork; which means it is hard to open. You have to search near and far to find it because it cannot be purchased at a corner store. Lastly, it is very expensive. Only a select few can indulge it. We should adopt this fine wine mentality in order to begin the process of lowering the number of new HIV cases among black women.

The method of infection was an interesting topic as well. How do we contract this deadly disease that devastates black communities worldwide? As mentioned earlier, heterosexual contact is the overwhelming method of infection. Man-sharing and overlapping relationships are notorious in the black community. And they are huge contributors in the spread of HIV/AIDS. Many believed black women are not worthy of long-term relationships and marriage. And online sisters believed there is a shortage of "good marriage-minded black men". This was stressed over and over. So, if they met someone who fit the profile of a good black man, they were more willing to share him with another woman rather than lose him completely. Men, especially the good catches, are aware of this mindset and use it to their advantage.

This brings me to a very interesting conversation with a distinguished brother who definitely fit the profile of a good catch. My sister and I were out for a night on the town with one of our close friends and her brother. I was aware that my friend's brother was attracted to me. She told me earlier in the day at a high school football game. She also informed me that he had a girlfriend. I knew instantly that he was off limits.

Later that evening, we went to a local club. As we sat at the table, we discussed relationships and dating.

"Yeah, I heard there is a shortage of good men for single women", he said.

I replied, "Yes, most of them are married or in a serious relationship; the good ones anyway. So what are we as single women to do? Share men?" I asked.

"Yeah, pretty much", he said surprisingly.

I turned and looked at him for a few seconds because I could not believe his response. "Well, I guess I'll be single forever because I'm not sharing anyone or anything!" I finally blurted out.

He looked at me very strangely as he sipped his drink. He did not respond. I guess my comment took him by surprise. And I was happy that it did. We had a great time the remainder of the night. But I guess he heard my message loud and clear—I refuse to be one of many.

Thinking back on our conversation, I started an online discussion the very next day. The subject was "Marriage and black women". I posted "White women marry early while black women marry in their late 30s or 40s. Why is this? Why did I do that? They went nuts! Especially the brothers.

"I don't think it's a matter of WW [white women] finding a soul mate. I think that is an expectation of WW to get married. WW and WM [white men] know the value of marriage because it builds wealth and keeps their families strong', said a sister in her 30's from New York. She continued, "It's drummed into their heads from an early age that marriage is a natural part of life." Oh, she went on and on.

"Unfortunately, many black men appear to take more pride in parading themselves around like stereotypical Mandingos [rather] than being husbands and fathers", said another frustrated sister.

A sister from Raleigh, NC believed that white women marry early "because there are numerous WM [to] marry and the WM [white men] want to get married". She also stated, "A WM [white men] will cherish his WW,[white women] but it is not the case for BW [black women] and BM [black men]."

As you can imagine, these comments infuriated brothers—once again. "Men like sex! It is hardwired into them [us]", said one brother from Vancouver, Canada. He continued, "Women, especially black women, seem to have a hard time getting this through their heads. If you are like the typical black woman and all you have to offer is a cheap f—, then men will not stay around."

Wow! If it were possible to get high fives through the computer screen, his palms would have been sore from the contact. "Amen" flew back and forth across the message boards like a Baptist congregation during Sunday morning worship; which, once again, demonstrated the common belief that black women are sex objects. Our value has diminished so low that it is difficult for men to take our hand in marriage; but easily creep down the hallway to room #105 at the nearest Motel 6 or Holiday Inn for a one night stand. This mentality is so sad.

Heterosexual contact is the source of many newly diagnosed HIV cases. But drug addiction is another crisis which fuels the increase. Drug addiction, just as choosing a sex partner, is a personal choice. And it has torn the black community apart. Many of us are hurting and using drugs to mask the hurt.

Needle sharing with other users who are infected with HIV/AIDS spreads the disease. Other countries employ needle exchange programs to combat the spread of HIV/AIDS among addicts. However, the United States failed to gain federal support for such programs. Needle exchange programs along with other rehabilitation treatment centers are needed to help those who are addicted to drugs and at risk of contracting HIV/AIDS.

This method of contraction is very dangerous because drugs addiction gives a false sense of invincibility. It makes one believe that he is invincible to everything—including HIV/AIDS and death. And some drugs are so powerful they'll make you believe you've just danced the electric slide naked with Tellitubbies! If you are so high and out of your mind that you believe you have danced with Tinky Winky, Dipsy, LaLa, or Poe, how can you remember who you've had sex with or if you used protection?

The down low phenomenon, which was recently exposed by author and HIV/STD prevention activist J.L. King in 2004, impacted the rise in HIV cases among black women. Men who use women to mask their homosexual activities with other men pose a big problem throughout our community. They have sex, most often unprotected sex, with other men, contract HIV, and pass it to their unsuspecting wives and girlfriends. Down low brothers live deceitful lives that endanger the health and lives of black women worldwide.

Honesty, acceptance, and communication are key factors that are missing in the black community which forces black men to live on the down low. Homosexuality and bisexually are taboo in the black community. They carry negative stigmas. Some men find it easier to hide their true feelings regarding bisexual tendencies. So they mask them. They are afraid of labels like fag and punk. They would rather live in denial than expose themselves as bisexual or homosexual. But the silence hurts us. Keeping their little secret jeopardize our health and put us at risk of contracting HIV/AIDS.

There were many online discussions regarding men on the down low and the negative effects within the black community. One day, the subject was "DL brothers: Are they the cause for HIV?"

"They [down low brothers] are a huge part of it; and certainly the main cause in the Black community", stated one sister from Atlanta, GA. She continued, "I call them nasty not because they are gay but because they are DOWN LOW and in relationships with unsuspecting and innocent women."

Another sister from North Carolina gave her view on the subject. She added, "Men who were incarcerated and having sex in jail get out and bring it [HIV/AIDS] home to their wives and girlfriends. I don't think that the total responsibility of how it got into the heterosexual population rests on JUST one community; but it rest on *all* of us to stop it."

There was no statistical evidence to show the exact number of new HIV cases in black women who were directly linked to down low brothers; but this phenomenon plays a significant role in the spread of the disease. The down low culture will be further discussed in Chapter eight.

So, how do we protect ourselves from this health crisis? Well, just as I advised online, we can start by using the brain that God gave us, listening to His little voice that he embedded deep inside, and stop believing the lies that men tell constantly. We are so quick to stay in unhealthy relationship in fear of being alone. We would rather risk contracting HIV/AIDS—a deadly disease—rather than be alone and content.

Unprotected heterosexual sex is our biggest problem. Each time we engage in unprotected sex, we play Russian roulette with our lives. Since many of you have never played Russian roulette, I will explain it in this fashion: it is a beautiful Friday afternoon; you are standing in line at the bank when four armed robbers burst into the building. You are terrified! But, would you risk your life by running *directly* in front of the armed suspects to escape through the front entrance? One or two may be crazy enough to try it; but the majority of us would not risk losing our lives. We would contemplate another option to save our lives. Most of us, the sane ones anyway, would analyze the situation, *use clear and rational thought* and proceed forward with a carefully planned course of action.

Okay, so why not take the same approach when it comes to the risk of contracting HIV/AIDS? Having unprotected sex is the same as running across the direct path of the armed bank robbers. Either approach, the results are tragic—death by a fatal gunshot wound or death by contracting HIV, the deadly disease that causes AIDS. It is that simple.

Earlier in the chapter, I mentioned low self-esteem and the manner in which it opens the door to mistreatment in our relationships. Women with low self-esteem are prone to remain in unhealthy relationships for security purposes. And once again, this is our problem. We must find ways to raise our confidence and self-esteem; which in turn allow us to feel good about ourselves. There are countless ways to boost self-esteem—strengthen spirituality, enhance appearance with exercise and proper diet, and seeking emotional or psychological support through therapy or counseling.

Raising our self-esteem and confidence enables us to eliminate these self destructive cries for help. If we are confident and love ourselves, we will not allow mistreatment from anyone and in turn demand respect from everyone; especially men.

We all agreed online, respect begins when a man approaches you. If we demand respect from the very beginning, they will respectfully give it. Men use inappropriate methods to gain our attention because they work. And judging the behavior of men today, they believe it is appropriate to yell and whistle at a lady to show interest. But as long as we continuously smile and grin at the whistles, they will continuously come our way.

Now, flip the script. If that same whistling fool approached enough women who ignored his disrespectful behavior, he would have to change his approach. Believe me, after three or four rejections, his next approach would sound similar to Luther Vandross' *Excuse Me Miss*—"Excuse me Miss, what's your name? Where are you from? Can I come? And possibly, can I take you out tonight?" Command respect from disrespectful brothers and change their behavior by changing our responses.

The number of newly diagnosed HIV/AIDS cases in black women has risen dramatically over the past few years. This deadly disease is not like cancer. We have control over contracting it with the daily choices we make. We, black women, must change our behavior and take responsibility for our lives. This disease should not be taken lightly and for this reason, I gathered a list of life saving tips because this disease has already taken too many of our lives.

Mikki's Staying Alive Tips:

1) Know your HIV status! Get tested if you have not done so already. Especially if you engage in risky behaviors such as unprotected sex, multiple sex partners, anal sex, etc.

2) Remove your underwear for two reasons only: to bathe/shower or make love to your *husband*. Keyword—HUSBAND. Sisters, we give it up too easily and too often. We are the last group of women to marry

and the first group abandoned. And why is this? It is simple-why buy the cow when you can get the milk free? I am not implying that we are the only women who engage in premarital sex; because we are not. Premarital sex gets us no where when it comes to men. It only prolongs our future wedding day. So, if you are fed up with being used, played, and abandoned after sex, please keep your panties on until the time is right. I don't care if they are granny panties or thongs; keep them on until *after* you are married.

3) When the choice is made to practice celibacy, don't be afraid or ashamed to share the news with guys you meet. Not in the initial meeting of course; but when the topic of "sex" arises. If he has good intentions, this will not frighten him. It will only confirm your character. If it does frighten him, happily let him go and thank God. He would have added more frustration to your life anyway.

4) If celibacy until marriage is totally out of the question, always use protection. Take responsibility for your health. Do not allow your partner to decide your HIV status. *Protect yourself.*

5) Limit the number of sexual partners. We all know that sex is wonderful! Especially when he knows how to put it down. But come on, it should not take five or six sex partners to satisfy your sexual desires. If this is the case, professional help is *always* available.

6) Build self-esteem and confidence. Self-esteem was discussed online a lot. Women with low self-esteem and confidence tend to engage in sex acts with several men to fill a void in their lives . . . to make them feel loved and worthy. This unhealthy practice opens the door to mistreatment in relationships and it increases your chances of contracting HIV/AIDS.

7) Trust intuition. Never go against the gut! If you have a gut feeling that something is not right in your relationship, you are probably right. Use your brain and not your heart, to make the appropriate choices for your future; even if it does not include your man. Make the right choices for *you.*

8) We all know the phrase "If it walks like a duck and quacks like a duck, it's a duck". This is not exactly true in the case of down low brothers. He walks like a man. He talks like a man. But he participates in behavior unbecoming of a real man; if you know what I mean. Sisters, we must be very careful with brothers in the 21st century. There are many brothers who walk the walk and talk the talk; but willingly find themselves in compromising positions with other men. We have got to pay close attention to our man's actions and behavior. It could be a life saver.

9) Communication is the glue that mends intimate relationships. Without it, they crumble like ten-day-old white bread. Engage in open communication with your man. Encourage him to share his innermost desires, fantasies, and fears with you. And you do the same. No subject should be off limits. Even if he shares startling news like stories of infidelity or bisexual tendencies. Listen without being critical or judgmental. Most often, this is the reason why many brothers hide their feelings and resort to the down low lifestyle because they feel that we will not understand. Always keep the lines of communication open.

10) If the lines of communication are closed, disconnect the relationship. I know this is easier said than done, especially if you are in love with him. But trust me; the results are less frustration, heartache, anxiety, worry, and less thoughts of committing felony assault.

11) Be like "B" (Beyonce)—"To the left; to the left!" Don't allow men to overlap relationships between his ex-girlfriend, new girlfriend, baby mama, and you. Remove yourself from this deadly equation. Think about it, if the four of you remove yourselves, who's left to overlap with?

12) Get the facts! HIV/AIDS is not a black disease. It is not a white disease. Nor is it a gay disease. HIV/AIDS is a deadly disease that attacks the human immune system. No one is exempt from contracting it. This is why we should fully educate ourselves about HIV/AIDS. Do not assume that you know everything about this disease. Know the real facts.

13) To reiterate, our response to men's negative behavior must change in order to change their actions. This reminds me of a friend who brilliantly executed this strategy while dancing with a guy she met at a nightclub. While dancing, he moved seductively toward her and slowly moved toward the floor. He got on his knees as if he was performing oral sex. She immediately stopped him. "Alright homeboy, you're not going to embarrass me out here. You better get up and dance with me right." He was confused. He looked at her with a puzzled look as if he did not understand why she asked him to stop. She said there were dozens of women on the dance floor who allowed this degrading behavior. And that explained his puzzled look. But her *reaction* changed his behavior. She demanded respect and received it in return.

14) My theory is this: If men encounter enough sisters who abstain from sex until after marriage, they'll have one of two choices to make—marry us or become gay. Bottom line. Online, there were many women who decided to abstain from sex until after marriage. Once again, we can change their mindset by altering our behavior.

15) Love yourself. If you do not love and respect yourself, no one else will. Without self-love, you'll allow mistreatment from anyone, especially men. Love the person you are—the woman God created.

16) Remember, marriage does not give an automatic pass from contracting HIV/AIDS. Maintain open communication with your spouse regarding sex. And if you are uncertain that he is faithful in the relationship, use precaution. *Protect yourself.*

17) Although HIV/AIDS is a deadly disease that kills millions worldwide annually, it is not an automatic death sentence. There are options to treat the disease and maintain a fulfilling life after an HIV diagnosis. But you must know the facts about the disease.

18) According to the Center for Disease control, injection is the second leading cause for HIV infection for African American women and the third leading cause of infection for African-American men. Needle sharing causes a higher risk for substance abusers because they are more likely to engage in riskier behavior. If you have fallen victim to substance abuse, please seek help. There are many programs designed to combat drug addiction and reduce the spread of HIV/AIDS through needle injection.

19) Ridicule and shame are two main reasons many choose to conceal their positive HIV status to family and friends. Others refused to get tested in fear of the backlash of a positive test result. Show more support and compassion towards individuals with HIV/AIDS.

20) Our community—the black community—must come together to conquer this health crisis. Let's stop HIV/AIDS from destroying us because at the increasing rate of African-American infection, it will eventually wipe us off of the map! We are dying in record numbers. And it has to come to an end. We have overcome numerous obstacles in our history—slavery, segregation, discrimination and poverty. If we are more honest with ourselves and love ones, we can win this battle too. We are stronger than HIV/AIDS!

21) Keep God in the center of relationships. Allow Him to guide your decisions and actions. Listen to that little voice within; the voice of reason. That's God! Never allow a man, any man, to overshadow God's voice.

The CDC reported black women accounted for 68% of new HIV infections between 2001 and 2004 and 78% of the new infections were contracted through unprotected heterosexual sex. After witnessing story after story of unfaithful partners, down low brothers, and unhealthy sex practices, I was prompted to write

---

this letter in hopes of inspiring a change in our behavior to stop the constant rise in new HIV/AIDS diagnosis in black women.

Dear Sisters,

What is wrong with us? There has to be something wrong because we are infected with HIV and dying in record numbers. Our situation is so bad that the American Red Cross developed an African American HIV Education and Prevention Instructions Course to teach us how to protect ourselves. This course is designed by African Americans for African Americans; but it is so sad that we have gotten to this point. This confirms the lack of self-control or the refusal to use protection we display when it comes to sex. We act as though we have no control over our minds or our bodies. We run around just as female dogs in heat who allow any stray male that comes along and have his way. Our behavior is ridiculous and it has to change.

The first step is healing—healing ourselves of old wounds from past relationships, closing the door to unhealthy relationships, and loving ourselves enough to avoid unhealthy relationships. The second step is changing our mindset. Changing our mindset and the manner in which we respond to men empowers us to turn our back on dysfunctional relationships. It empowers us to use our brains and make wiser decisions about sex. It empowers us to use our gut to seek the truth about our relationships and use our mouths to demand the use of condoms if we decide to have sex.

HIV/AIDS is a deadly disease. But it is not the same as cancer. Many forms of cancer are not preventable; but HIV/AIDS is preventable. It is preventable by sustaining from sexual activity and by protecting ourselves when engaging in sex. Sex is supposed to be a natural and exciting component within our relationship. In our case, Black women, it is not exciting at all. It is unsafe, unhealthy and kills us worldwide; one sister at a time.

Ladies, we have the power to send a strong dictum to the world and to stop the rapid spread of HIV/AIDS among black women. The responsibility falls on us. We hold the power in our hands. Actually, we hold the power in our legs and it starts by keeping them closed.

Your loving sister,
Mikki C. Zimmerman

Service Organizations and Community Activists who play a vital role in the fight against HIV/AIDS in the black community:

Dr. Helene D. Gayle (CARE USA)
The National Black Leadership Commission on AIDS
The United States Centers for Disease Control
The American Red Cross (African-American HIV/AIDS Program)
Dr. Shannon Hader (Director D.C. HIV/AIDs Administration)
Dr. Kimberly Smith (Infectious Disease Specialist)
Marie Saint Cyr (HIV/AIDS activist)
J.L. King (Author, HIV/AIDS activist)
Go Care, Inc. (Monroe, LA)
Dr. Bambi W. Gaddis (South Carolina HIV/AIDS Council

CHAPTER 8

Down Low Brothers

And ye shall know the truth, and the truth shall make you free."
John 8:32(KJV)

Either way you slice it, black women are doomed. If high blood pressure, Diabetes, and heart disease do not kill us, sleeping with down low brothers who sleep with other men will. Author and HIV/AIDS activist J.L. King exposed the twisted down low phenomenon in his bestselling book *On the Down Low* in 2004. In the book he revealed in-depth details of his life as a married down low brother and gave accounts on how his wife uncovered his dirty little secret. It was eye-opening to witness. The provocative book woke sisters up and forced us to carefully examine the men in our lives; and our past.

It is not a new concept. It has been happening for decades—undercover. J.L. King was brave enough to come forward with his story. But there are thousands of black men who relish in this lifestyle. Men who live on the down low dissimulate their true feelings to mask their sexuality—whether gay or bi-sexual. They cover themselves with different names like "freaky" and "metro sexual"; once again, to disguise their true feelings.

Truth is, these men are not really men at all. They are cowards. They use women as cover-ups to hide their homosexual feelings toward other men. They pretend to be strong heterosexual black men. But in reality, they are as sweet as the fruit punch flavored kool-aid they love to drink.

Men who live on the down low do not understand why black women are so frustrated with this idea. It is hard enough to meet a good black man. Just imagine how we feel when we discover that he is on the down low. Hell, that's an

---

added frustration! The funny thing about it is many of them actually believe they are straight men who "occasionally" have sex with other men. If you really think about this statement, it does not make a bit of sense. It is a twisted mentality that only down low brothers understand.

In 2003, the Centers for Disease Control reported 25% of men who had sex with men considered themselves heterosexual. Call yourselves what you'd like. I do not care for titles anyway. The fact remains, men who live on the down low have sexual relationships with other men and use women, most often black women, to cover up their little secrets.

I am not anti-gay or lesbian nor am I against bi-sexual individuals. But just as many of the online sisters stated, the actions of down low brothers not only affect them; they affect the unsuspecting women who they are involved with. If their actions only affected them, I say go as low as you care to go. But their actions span farther than the secret meeting places with other down low brothers. They devastate the lives of the black women who are used as decoys to obscure their deception. There may even be a link between the down low phenomenon and the devastating increase in HIV/AIDS diagnosis in black women.

How can we identify down low brothers? It is hard. They are not easily detected. Many are strong, athletic, Mandingo-type brothers; not the flimsy finger-snapping type. He is too obvious. The entire down low trend is rooted in secrecy. So it is hard to detect who is on the down low and who is not.

But the secrecy is the most frightening part of all. Listen, if you are a man who enjoys having sex with other men, that's your business. Sleep with them! Sleep with as many as your heart desires; but you have a moral and ethical responsibility to inform all partners of your lifestyle; not only the brother or brothers that are on the down low with you. Allow the female to make her own decision to get involved with a bi-sexual man. Do not allow your selfishness to decide for her. That is what's killing us!

The down low has changed the entire dating scene in the black community; especially among sisters. Many of us are suspicious of everyone and everything. We observed black men for any dubious activities—statements, homeboys, reactions, and body movements. Online sisters were terrified! They discussed it in great details. This question was asked online, "DL (down low) brothers: Are they the cause of HIV?"

A sister from Atlanta responded, "They are a huge part of it and certainly the main cause of it in the black community." She also stated, "These {are} nasty a—men, I call them nasty not because they are gay, but because they are down low and in relationships with unsuspecting and innocent women."

Another sister from New York added, "My take is that black women are going to get fed up with black men and let them sex each other to death!"

—

109

They were right. We are very frustrated with down low brothers. So frustrated, that I promised to invent a product that would assist in detecting down low brothers. And I was successful in my attempt. I cleverly envisioned a product that would throw a wrench in the down low game and turn it upside down. My invention—a small microchip with a hand held device that we control. Okay, here is how it works: place the microchip inside your man's butt cheek; don't worry, it is undetectable and waterproof. He will not discover it; not even in the shower. It is used as a GPS tracking device to his activities around the mouth and midsection. I named this ingenious invention the "Fag Finder".

Now if it works properly, it will beep or vibrate, just as your cell phone, in case of emergencies. Take this device everywhere—even to bed. If it beeps or vibrates while you are asleep and your man is not home, jump up, grab your keys and gun, and head for the door! It will give precise directions to his location . . . remember it's a tracking device. And with all of the high technology in the 21st century, you'll also be able to download appropriate songs like *Down Low* by R. Kelly, *Can't Be That Other Woman* by Changing Faces and *In My Bed* by Dru Hill. Do not worry about the price, I'll ask *Intel* to keep the price as low as possible because this device is a must-have for *all* sisters. I think they will agree.

Down low brothers exist and they endanger the lives of innocent black women each day. And it makes you wonder, where do down low brothers meet? Through research I found out—everywhere. They meet on the Internet, nightclubs, even church. Yes, in the Lawd's house! They also host "anonymous parties" to meet other down low brothers. Let me explain anonymous parties. They were described to me as "one big orgy". The location of the party is given but the names of the partygoers are not disclosed. You know that whole secrecy thing right? Well, they keep the place pitch black to protect the identity of the partygoers. So, the lights remain off during the entire party. This way, if he encounters the brother that he had sex with the night before on the street, he'll never recognize his face. In other words, they have sex with two, three, maybe four anonymous men in the dark so they won't feel ashamed or embarrassed if they run across him on the street. I told you they were cowards.

It sounds disgusting doesn't it? Well, it happens every day. What is even more disgusting, after sexing men all night, many times without condoms, they drive home, curl up with their wives or girlfriends, look her dead in the eyes and confess their undying love. Then have sex, unprotected sex, with her. This is how the down low brother operates.

Anonymous parties are just the tip of the iceberg. Cyberspace is loaded with down low men. Many of them are married or involved in "committed" relationships with women. For years their little freaky lifestyle went undetected. But thanks to J.L. King, the gig is up! Sisters everywhere are catching onto the down low brother's game. Ask "Sharon". She will tell you. I spoke with "Sharon's" best friend and she gave me the down low on how they busted "Sharon's" man. Listen to this:

"I'm Straight! No, Really, I Am!"

You know he lied to her? Oh yeah, he lied about everything—being faithful, their relationship status, and his sexuality. Over their two year relationship, he collected more secrets than a prolific hoarder collects junk and he did everything in his power to keep these secrets secret. But the painful truth was eventually uncovered by his soon-to-be bride in the most uncommon way. A three month scavenger hunt stained his squeaky clean image and revealed his true character—a lying, cheating, and double-life leading down low brother. This journey took her into frightening places that would even terrify the stripes from *Freddy Kruger*'s signature tight red sweater.

Gay chat rooms, anonymous parties, and even God's house were hot spots to hook up with other down low brothers. He was definitely a habitué of down low chat rooms. Throughout the day, he logged in and out disguised under different usernames. And the frightening thing about this brother is he was undetectable. He wasn't the flimsy, finger-snapping, "Ms. J." from *America's Next Top Model*. He was far from her, I mean, his type. He was the strong and athletic family man with a twenty year military career to protect his image from his twisted lifestyle.

His stunning looks were instrumental in the machinations of hiding his bisexuality. His six foot three inch frame and smooth clean-shaven face attracted single sisters with high hopes of snatching him as a potential mate. And this was perfect for him because the more women he surrounded himself with, the bigger his mack-daddy status grew; which, in his eyes, shattered any suspicions that anyone may have had regarding his sexuality.

She was no plain Jane herself. She was a beautiful sister with a genial personality. She was in her mid twenties, approximately eight years younger than he. She was a college senior majoring in education with high hopes of getting married and starting a family with "Mr. Right". And just as Waylon Jennings, she was "looking for love in all the wrong places".

Needless to say, they met online through a dating website. Both profiles identified their sexual orientation as "heterosexual". Too bad for her there was not a slot for "down low". But this brother was so far in denial, even if the slot existed, he would have never ever checked it. You see, hiding his bisexuality ensured his lifestyle of "having his cake and eating it too"—secretly having unprotected sex with other men which in turn endangered the health of unsuspecting sisters that he also slept with.

Deceiving her trust was easy because they resided in separate states. He lived on the east coast while she lived in the south. A month and a half of chatting, both online and via telephone, strengthened the chemistry between the pair. Soon after the initial meeting in a neutral location, they quickly developed a sexual relationship. And to let her tell it, the sex was like NBA action—FANTASTIC! He turned and flipped her as if she was his skating partner competing for a gold medal at the Olympics. The tranquilizing sex is what hooked and reeled her into his twisted lifestyle. And she was the perfect cover-up for him to disguise his life on the down low.

After two years, he began throwing around the "m" word—marriage. Of course, she welcomed the idea. This was right up her alley. She waited patiently for their relationship to shift in this direction. She even planned to move to the east coast after graduation. But there was one problem. She knew something was not quite right with this brother. She always knew. Don't get me wrong, she was madly in love with him; but she was always aware of his ability to disappear for days without an explanation of his whereabouts. You see, his strange ways were sort of the pink elephant in the room that neither of them wanted to discuss. She just accepted it without questioning, well, for two years anyway. She grew weary of the constant wondering and playing the what-if-this and what-if-that scenarios in her head.

At this point, she was sick and tired of pretending that everything was fine within their fragmented relationship because it was not. She needed to put her mind at ease if they were to successfully move to the next phase—marriage. So she did what any sane black woman would have done—sent a fraudulent email using all of his *personal* information to obtain every password to every email account that he owned and checked each and every folder. It worked too. She successfully retrieved his passwords and braced herself for the worst. Before going "Colombo", she convinced herself that he was cheating on her; but nothing could have prepared her for the lascivious images and details that she uncovered.

Web links to down low websites and chat rooms, pictures of naked men performing sexual acts on one another and video clips of him having sex with other men filled the inboxes of his email accounts. Oh, and he was a "top" too; which should be self explanatory. As you can probably imagine, she was devastated. Never in her freakiest dreams would she have thought that he was bisexual and possibly even gay. He didn't have a flick in his wrist or a switch in his hips; but he was bisexual. The same man who she thought would be a faithful husband and dedicated father was the same man who forced her into this sick and demented lifestyle.

As graphic as these images were, they were not enough for her. She had many questions like—"Why?" "Where?" "With whom?" and "What the hell?" Women are strange like that. Corroboratory evidence isn't convincing enough for us to dismantle an unhealthy relationship. No, we want our man to fess up to his lies and deceit. We want him to make like R&B superstar Usher and confess. And you know, getting a brother to confess to his dirt is like convincing Brittany Spears to act as a sane mother of two children. It's not going to happen!

She knew this was no easy task so she called for backup—her two best friends. Together they created online profiles with fake pictures and began what they called "Operation Find a Fag". They started a gay club on Yahoo! and it did not take long for this brother to join the new club. They learned through this operation that he had been living on the down low for three to four years and one by one they lured him into a conversation. I guess the fake pictures worked because he fell for it each time.

She chatted with him several times during this operation and was sickened with each conversation. Once she asked him, "U [you] got a girlfriend?"

He responded, "I have a couple of ex-girlfriends that pop in and out".

She then asked, "How often do you do this? [Meet men on the internet]"

His answer, "Sometimes I feel like a nut, sometimes I don't".

The conversations continued but grew more graphic in nature. During one chat, she curiously asked, "What made you do it? Have you always thought about it?"

He nonchalantly answered, "Nah, not really. I was tired of hitting females for some reason and I was like I wanted to try something different."

The conversations between him and her best friends were pretty much the same—graphic and disgusting. He unknowingly gave her all of the ammunition needed to end their moot relationship. It was obvious that he would not abandon his down low lifestyle to be in a committed relationship with her. And after witnessing all of this foolishness, she did not want to continue the relationship. Reflecting on the images that she had seen and the things he said made her want to puke with each thought of him. Besides, he made it perfectly clear that her sole purpose in his life was to serve as his "beautiful little cover up" and nothing more.

I don't have to tell you that this relationship ended right? She confronted him without ratting out her friends and letting him in on the little online escapades. He denied every bit of it. He swore that he had never had sex with *any* man, oral or anal. He denied having bisexual tendencies. He even denied, after she revealed a few of his online names, that he belonged to a gay club on the internet. He would never admit to anything. He was more interested in finding out how she obtained this "bogus information".

This man hurt her bad—to the core of her soul—and she wanted revenge. She contemplated spitefully sending the chat logs, graphic images and his profile information to "bust him out to his homeboys". She decided against it. She had to get him out of her system and try to move on with her life. And that's exactly what she did—moved on.

Months after the break, he called her still denying the fact that he's bisexual or gay and curious as to how she found out this information. Out of pure embarrassment and guilt, he concocted a conspiracy theory that someone posed as him online and joined gay clubs. Don't worry. She did not believe him. She eventually mailed copies of all of the online chat logs along with pictures from his email account. The return address included the user-names that they used to lure him into the online conversations. It has been one year since the break-up and he's still saying, "I'm straight! No, really, I am!"

Ladies, the time has come for us to take matters into our hands just as this sister and her friends. She found out the man she adored and cherished deceived and jeopardized her entire life while they were together. They even discussed getting married and starting a family. It was a good thing she found out before she bore children for this man. Starting a family with him would have made it harder to leave.

There is a valuable lesson to learn from "Sharon's" situation. Black women are suffering the consequences of the down low brother's actions. We are forced to live with their lies and deceit. But Ladies, I beg, please do not allow the down low brother to decide your HIV/AIDS status. Down low men are infecting us with this deadly disease and killing us just as an abusive man stalks and kills his wife with a 22 caliber pistol that he conceals on his waist. The down low brother's weapon of choice is also hidden below the belt—his penis.

If you think black women are not frustrated with the down low trend, think again. This is a plea to all brothers who are on the down low: Stop living a lie. Come up from the down low and out of hiding. You do not own the right to drag us, black women, into your twisted lifestyles. You do not have the right to choose when or how we should die. That task belongs to God. And you are not God. Down low brothers, please stop the madness. Your lies are killing us—literally! And sisters, we must protect ourselves from becoming another statistic . . . another victim of the game. The game is too risky—too deadly. Besides, we've already lost far too many.

CHAPTER 9

Racial Injustices

"Injustice anywhere is a threat to justice everywhere."
Dr. Martin Luther King, Jr.

"Justice is what love looks like in public."
Dr. Cornell West

"We aint meant to survive cause it's a set-up"—rapper Tupac Shakur said in his hit song *Keep Ya Head Up*—speaking on racism in America which is still alive and well today. Hatred is rampant in today's society. It is taught and practiced every day. Look at Jena, LA in the fall of 2006. Nooses were hung from a so-called "white tree" because black students sat under it. Are you kidding? And it all happened in the 21st century.

African-Americans, just as our initial arrival on slave ships, still catch the brunt of unfair treatment. Everything is slanted against us—education, the judicial system, wealth, everything. To get recognition on the job, we cannot only perform on a high level; we have to be *great* to receive the same recognition as our white counterparts.

The foundation of the United States was built from the blood, sweat, and tears of our enslaved ancestors. However, it is difficult for us to reap the benefits of their hard work. True enough, we live in a different era from 1607; when the first African slaves arrived in Jamestown, VA. But for some, it is hard to alter the 1607 mentality in regards to people of African decent. There are many people, young and old, who continue to treat us as second class citizens.

They believe we are inferior. Some still use derogatory terms to describe us like "nigger" or "spook".

Growing up in the mid 70's, I had never been called any of these terms; but I heard it for the first time in 2005. We were on a road trip. My sister, two nieces, and I were driving through Mississippi in route to Baton Rouge, LA. We were taking my niece to LSU for the fall semester. We stopped in Woodville, MS for a restroom break. Keep in mind; this was 2005, not 1805.

As we approached the door, a white couple walked up. "Is this Woodville or Niggerville?" she blurted out to her husband.

There were several African-Americans in the parking lot. I guess this is why she asked the stupid question. We all kinda looked at each other like "What the hell!" No one said anything directly to her. We just looked at her with a very puzzled look on our faces. I almost said, "I understand that you only have a middle school level education; but it's never too late to return to school and get a G.E.D." But I did not say a word.

My niece, Dominique, looked at me and asked, "Did you hear what she said?" We all burst into laughter. Her comments showed everyone how a *real* nigger behaves. Since no one entertained her ignorance, I guess she thought we did not hear her. She repeated it. Once again, we all laughed at her and continued into the store.

I had never experienced anything like that in my life. And to be honest, I was not angry with her. I felt sorry for her. It was obvious that she was miserable and wanted to make everyone, especially black folks, miserable with her. And the fact that we were in Mississippi, did not make the situation any better.

The clueless lady we encountered in Mississippi is not the only person who feels this way. There are thousands, maybe millions, across the country who share her mentality but are afraid to speak it in public as she did. They speak it among their family and friends privately.

Hatred is a very dangerous practice. Hate breeds stereotyping. Stereotyping breeds discrimination. Discrimination breeds racism. Racism breeds injustice. And injustice leads to the topic of this book—frustrated black people not able to find decent jobs to support their families. Frustrated black people not receiving fair treatment in the judiciary system. And Frustrated abandoned black folks crying and begging for help from the federal government for three long and hot days on roof tops after a category four hurricane floods their city. This is what stems from hate.

Racial injustice was constantly discussed online. Online sisters believed the so-called "scales of justice" which are proclaimed to be color blind, are not. In many cases, Lady Justice's vision is not 20/20. History proved that justice worked for some, not all. And if you need examples, I have plenty. Examine the crack cocaine epidemic for instance. Crack hit the inner city in the early 80's and devastated the black community for decades. Congress has yet to pass any legislation to slow or stop the production of crack. Their only solution—build more prisons and jails to house offenders with stiff drug sentences.

Now, examine the meth epidemic. It is a little different because meth devastated rural communities throughout the country—meaning more whites are affected than blacks. In 2005, Congress passed the Combat Methamphetamine Epidemic Act 2005 to stop the production of the illicit drug. This act allows consumers to purchase only three boxes of over-the-counter medication containing Sudafedrine—the main ingredient in meth—per month. Okay, Congress intervened to slow the production of meth. That was a good solution; but what about the production of crack cocaine?

I recall vividly when this act was implemented because it affected me directly. No, I have never used meth or any other illegal drugs; but I suffer from severe allergies. Late one night, I drove to Wal-Mart thinking, as usual, I would pick up a box of Sudafed because I was congested and could not breathe. I arrived at the store—still sneezing—walked around, and located the medicine aisle. I reached for the box and it was not there. Instead, a card that advised me to "take to the pharmacy". I almost burst into tears because the pharmacy was closed. I could not purchase the medication, meaning I would not get a good night's rest. I was totally disgusted! I returned to Wal-Mart the following morning and vented to the cashier.

"I couldn't breathe last night, so I couldn't get any sleep at all because of meth addicts!" I said to her.

She cracked up laughing. "I understand your frustration; but that is the new law", she replied.

Okay, two dangerous and highly addictive drugs—crack and meth. But two solutions to the problem. Why two methods? Why can't Congress pass the "Crack is Wack Act 2008" to stop the production of crack cocaine? Yeah, the Anti Drug Act of 1986 was passed, but this bill called for stiffer penalties for offenders. It was not designed to *stop* the production of crack. Only throw the offenders in prison for a longer period of time. For decades, crack devastated lives and destroyed the black community . . . just as meth. Similar problems; but different resolutions.

We discussed injustice within the judicial system online as well. One example—gun control laws. Black and brown children have been gunned down in the mean streets of Philadelphia, Chicago, Los Angeles, New Orleans and Baltimore for years without intervention from the federal government to protect them. But in June 2007, two months after the shootings on the very prestigious Virginia Tech University campus where thirty-two students and faculty members were murdered, the House of Representatives passed what many called "the first major federal gun control law in over a decade." This was a very rapid response by the federal government to this tragic event. But again, it makes you wonder about the thousands of inner city children who were murdered at the unjust hands of gun violence. Where is their justice? Same problem, different responses.

Need another example? Because I have plenty. This one deals with race and socioeconomic status just as the previous one. Two words—Hurricane Katrina. Being a Louisiana native and witnessing the destruction first hand, you know I had to discuss this tragedy. The world will never forget the human suffering that Katrina caused the state of Louisiana and the entire gulf coast region. The aftermath and the rescue efforts which exposed the incompetence of the Bush Administration were a national disgrace. I imagine terrorist took detailed notes of our response and stored the information for later use in plotting the United States' demise.

The aftermath of Hurricane Katrina was a constant topic online, as you can imagine. The blatant racial injustice broke the hearts and spirits of sisters worldwide.

"I believe God used the resilience of the citizens of New Orleans to uncover the truth behind the Bush Administration", one frustrated sister stated.

"If those were rich white people, do you actually think they would have taken three days to send help?" asked another. They went back and forth on this subject.

Of course I added my two senses. "God knew exactly what He was doing. And He was there with them—all 23,000. He was there at the Superdome. He was there on roof-tops. He was there in the Convention Center. He was there on I-10 as they walked around bewildered and confused. He was there as they waded through feces and other hazardous toxins. He was there for the three days the federal government hid. He was there through it all!"

I got several "Amens" for my comments. But everyone online, white and black agreed—social class and race played a major part in the turn around time for the federal government to send help to the people of New Orleans, LA. Some even believed that President Bush would have flown Air Force One himself to save the lives of wealthier citizens.

During a telethon on NBC, Rapper Kanye West made a comment in regards to President Bush and his slow response to the hurricane. "George Bush doesn't care about black people", Kanye blurted out as he veered from the provided script.

I knew exactly what Kanye meant; but I took it a step further. "President Bush doesn't care about *poor* people whether white, black, Hispanic, or Asian. He and the Republican Party cater to the wealth and powerful citizens of this country. Not the poor and less fortunate." My reason for saying it? It took the federal government three frustrating days to send help to the New Orleans residents who were hit hardest by the hurricane—9th Ward, East New Orleans, Gentily, Violet, St. Bernard, and Lakeshore. President Bush said nothing for three days; but it took only two HOURS after the Virginia Tech tragedy before he and Attorney General Alberto Gonzales personally called Virginia Tech's president and gave their condolences. Two hours!

Former Louisiana Governor, Kathleen Blanco, and New Orleans' Mayor, Ray Nagin, were highly criticized for their "lack of leadership skills" after the devastating hurricane hit on August 29, 2005. But what could they have done differently? They could not order any federal planes and Army tanks to wade into New Orleans to rescue citizens. Mayor Nagin's entire city was submerged under nine to ten feet of water. What could he have done differently? President Bush was well aware of the circumstances in New Orleans and the gulf coast. He had to have known. It was covered by every news network—CNN, Fox News, MSNBC, CBS, NBC, and ABC. How could the President of the United States be unaware of the suffering and demise of one of his American cities?

Mayor Nagin cried out for help, twice. After the first cry went unheard, he demanded help after days of waiting. He sent an S.O.S. demanding help to salvage his sinking city and rescue its starving and dying citizens. His cry was broadcasted over the television and he finally got the federal government's attention. He used profanity in his message; but who could blame him. Soon after, Army tanks, helicopters, buses, and everything else rolled into New Orleans.

It is a good thing I did not have to deliver the S.O.S. to the world. Mayor Nagin cursed, and I probably would have cursed too. But my message would have been delivered in English, Spanish, Portuguese, Russian, Ebonics and five African dialects! *Somebody* would have decoded it and relayed it to Mr. Bush. But it is such a shame that he had to beg for help from the federal government. One of their primary duties is to protect its citizens. Well, they failed tremendously and 971 people, mostly elderly, died as a result of Hurricane Katrina.

Yeah, we watched as they waited for three long days for help. But as I mentioned earlier, God was there with them. And He sent a savior along with the rescue team—Lt. General Russell Honore. He served as Commander of Relief Efforts after the storm. He calmed the chaotic city, restored order, and rescued thousands of helpless and forgotten people. He was truly God-sent and the great city of New Orleans would not have recovered without his guidance.

Throughout the course of my online research, black women agreed that racial injustices still exist; especially in the United States. African Americans have had a rough and rugged journey since our arrival. We have endured slavery, discrimination (outright and hidden), and racism. But we always manage to overcome. We are a strong and resilient race. We always overcome.

No, the scales of justice are not color blind. As a matter of fact, we should make Lady Justice an eye appointment because she may be Monochromic—sees things in black and white. And guess what, she favors the lighter shade.

—

When we speak of racial justice, we are not asking for special treatment. We are asking for *fair* treatment. A fair chance to succeed in life. We seek equality in every aspect of life—health care, education, the judicial system, and employment. We want to be treated equally; just as everyone else.

Dr. Martin Luther King, Jr. envisioned a dream where black people would be "measured by the content of their {our} character". We have not fully arrived at this point; but we are making progress toward it. Great progress. For the first time in our nation's history, African-Americans, Asian-American, Hispanic American, and Whites-have elected an African-American to the highest position, President of the United States. Not only black people, all Americans voted and elected a black president. On January 20, 2009, Senator Barack Obama was sworn in as the 44th President of the United States of America. On this day, it was as if white Americans finally accepted us-descendents of African slaves—as equals. You know, as if Dr. King's dream finally became reality. This historical day was divinely orchestrated by God. Nothing could have stopped it; not even the ugly face of racism. I believe He planned it all. And it could not have come at a better time.

In order to move towards total racial equality, we must begin first by understanding one another. Rapper Nas said, "People fear what they don't understand." This holds true in every aspect of life. We must understand one another in order to see each other as equals. As Americans, we should open our minds and hearts to learn more about each other rather than fight against one another. We have to live together so why not live as Paul McCarty and Stevie Wonder said—"Ebony and Ivory live together in perfect harmony".

CHAPTER 10

Unsatisfying Jobs

"Take this job and shove it! I aint working here no more!"
Johnny Paycheck

It is 5:40 A.M. Monday morning and your alarm clock sounds. You quickly hit the snooze button, moan, roll over and return to sleep. Nine minutes elapse, it is now 5:49 and your clock buzzes again. Immediately, you hit snooze, moan, roll over and return to sleep. Okay, it's now 5:58 and your alarm clock sounds once again. This time, you turn the alarm off, sit at the edge of the bed, scratch your left temple, look around for a minute or two, and burst into an uncontrollable cry! Sounds familiar?

This is reality for many of us every work day; not just Mondays. Unsatisfying jobs cause frustration for sisters worldwide. Unfair treatment, discrimination, sexism, racism, and every other "ism" one could possibly think of cause frustration daily in our work environments. Dead-end jobs are so bad for many of us that we feel like hostages without an escape plan. In the morning, we leave for work angry and frustrated only to return home in the same state of mind; sometimes, angrier and more frustrated.

Everyone and everything gets on our nerves at work—the constant flow of incoming email from supervisors, the phone that rings off the hook, the copier that works for everyone else except us, and that very noisy co-worker who sits directly across from your cubical. We are so frustrated with our jobs, that many of us are one print job away from resigning.

"I lasted a month", one fed-up sister revealed. "On Fridays, we worked like slaves!"

Another frustrated sister said, "I worked there {her previous job} until I graduated college. After college, I was out of there!"

I can attest to their frustrations. I know the feeling all too well. I have held positions where I felt trapped in a depressed pit and could not climb out. Actually, I have had several depressing pits. But thank God I was able to escape them all.

My first pit was horrible—a part-time cashier position for a national retail store. It was the Christmas holidays; so we were extremely busy. I worked six, sometimes seven hours each day without a break—restroom or water. Now, not getting a break was not a problem because there were always sales associates available to help. But one day, I worked with the store manager, who obviously felt that she was too important to jump on a register and give me a hand. My line of customers grew longer and longer; without any assistance. Eventually, it curved around the rear of the store. I followed store policy and rang the bell signaling for help. It took a while; but she finally made her way to the register. She logged on, helped a few customers and disappeared.

As I expected, more customers filled the store and the long lines developed once again. I ranged the bell, once again, for assistance. She re-emerged but did everything else besides help the customers—moved boxes, tagged merchandise, smiled and greeted the customers. She did everything but check out customers. I was so frustrated! I did not get a break. I was hungry. I needed a bathroom break. And I was sick of her nasty attitude. I looked at my watch and said to myself, "I'll give her thirty minutes. If she doesn't help me, I'm gone!"

I checked my watch periodically—every ten minutes. And sure enough, after thirty minutes, I grabbed my keys from the side pocket of the register, stepped out from the register, and headed for the door—with a long line full of customers. But instead of leaving, I made a u-turn back into the store. Keep in mind, I did not take a break, so I was starving. I proceeded to the candy aisle in search of a Snickers bar along with a cold refreshing coke to wash it down. I walked to the back, and stood at the end of the line that was now curved around the store.

The customers did not know what was going on. They turned around and looked in my direction and I turned around too . . to see who they were looking at. Needless to say, they were looking at me.

The manager was totally confused. But she quickly figured it out. She realized that I went from employee to customer and now stood in line waiting to be checked out. She was so upset! By the time I reached the register, her face was candy-apple red. But she had no other choice but to check me out. And she knew not to say anything to me. I probably, no, I would have cursed her out! I exited the store chewing my Snickers bar and drinking my coke—still wearing the black smock. Oh yeah, that was my last day.

—

I mentioned that I had worked in several pits, right? Well, the second one lasted longer than the first. Four years longer. I held on to this job because of the excellent pay and benefits. I worked as a customer service professional for one of the largest banking institutions in the country. I handled escrow accounts which paid the taxes and insurance for clients. I was attached to the phone system the entire day with hundreds of calls waiting in queue.

Calls were randomly monitored for "quality assurance". According to our job description, we were hired to answer the calls, assist the customer, fix all problems on the accounts, be courteous while they cursed us out, and do all of these things in less than five minutes. For most calls, this was nearly impossible. Sometimes calls lasted twenty to thirty minutes because the customer had so many questions about their account or they had multiple accounts. Although I was aware of my call time, I never rushed my clients off of the phone. I made certain that all of their issues were handled with one phone call to the call center. We also performed sales duties—soliciting credit cards and home equity loans to existing customers.

You talk about stressed and frustrated? Man, this job was very stressful. The morale of the customer service department was so low because the entire staff was disgusted with the added pressure from top management to meet our sales quota. Stress leaves were prevalent throughout this department. After one year, I immediately began to apply for other jobs within the company.

Over a three year period, I applied for more than twenty positions. I interviewed for several; but did not land any of the jobs. My performance as a CSP was never an issue because I received various awards for "customer service satisfaction" and "customer compliments". There was never a valid reason why I was not promoted; so I was led to believe that race was the common factor in getting a promotion. There were certain instances that proved my suspicions. I witnessed fairly new CSPs, who just so happened to be white, get promoted within six months ahead of seasoned reps who spent years in the position. And I was not the only African-American who recognized the discriminatory actions within the organization.

"Girl, unless we do like Michael Jackson—bleach our skin White—and wear a blonde wig, we will never get off of this phone", said one representative as we discussed promotions or lack of for African-Americans in the customer service department.

I hated this job. I was miserable everyday. It had gotten so bad that I began counting down the "minutes to go" in the last hour of each day. I could not wait to log off and go home. This job had such a negative affect on my mental state that I refused to talk on the phone at home. I had no desire to talk to anyone or to hear the phone ring.

In September of 2003, I was so depressed that I wrote a statement on a sticky note at my desk: "I will be so so so so happy when I am offered a job in accounting with any NBA team, WNBA team, NFL team or any other company! That will be a joyous day indeed." It may sound crazy; but I wrote the date and time on the note and kept it in a secret compartment of my handbag to remind myself of how much I hated this job. As a matter of fact, I still carry it today as a reminder to never return.

As the years passed, it became crystal clear to me that regardless of how well I performed, I would never "post out" of the customer service department. And I knew it was time for a career change. I was enrolled in school part-time at the local university; so switching to full-time was a great option for me to ponder. I was near the end of my curriculum; so evening classes were no longer available; only morning classes. This played a major factor in my decision. But maintaining mental stability was an even bigger determinant.

My answer came during a very frustrating escrow conversation with a client. Over the five years I had taken thousands of escrow calls. And I was great at explaining escrow. They even had me on a special "escrow call-gate". But this single call made it perfectly clear—it was time to let it go. I thoroughly explained the process of building up escrow funds to pay taxes and insurance twice. But regardless of how well I explained it, she could not understand. She was frustrated. I was frustrated. And after the third explanation, I finally went Ashford and Simpson on her. "Ma'am, we build it up, and build it up, and build it up until it's solid!" I yelled this out before I could stop myself. I quickly hit the mute button because everyone in the vicinity burst into a roaring laughter. My friend, who sat in the cubical directly across from me, laughed so hard that she slid out of her chair onto the floor.

Apparently, she finally understood. "Oh, I see", she replied.

I wasn't sure if she really understood or if she thought that I had lost my mind. Either way, I knew and all of my co-workers knew—it was time for me to get out of there. My team was a joy to work with and I loved my supervisor. But I could not take anymore explaining nor the yelling and cursing from customers.

Less than a month later, I turned in my resignation letter. Sheer joy and elation filled my soul as I handed it to my supervisor. My departure saddened my team. But they understood. They threw a big going-away party for me on my last day. But I missed it because I called in sick. They really talked about me—badly. Not behind my back though. They caught me on the day I cleaned out my desk.

After I quit, I returned to school full-time the following semester as a happy full-time student and graduated one year later with a Bachelor Degree in Business Administration with concentrations in accounting and marketing.

Those were just a few of my horror stories. Thousands of sisters have witnessed the frustration of unsatisfying jobs. They not only affect your life, they affect the lives of everyone around you—family, friends, and co-workers. Many of the women that I spoke with were not as fortunate as I. They could not just quit their jobs and go back to school or find a more satisfying job. No, they were "stuck in a hole with no way out", as they put it, and very frustrated about it.

Everyone deserves to be happy; especially in our careers. We spend a large portion of the day at work. There are so many who are frustrated and disgusted that we force ourselves to smile and make friendly conversation with colleagues. And we should not feel this way. We should be excited and enthusiastic about work—just as the Seven Dwarf singing "Hi ho, hi ho, it's off to work we go!" But many of us sing a different tune. We are miserable because we settle for a job rather than pursue our passion. We are unhappy because we do not explore opportunities that fulfill our purpose in life.

Just as I advised to the Ladies online, discover your passion and purpose in life and pursue it. Regardless of how long it takes to figure it out, once you find it, you will spend the rest of your life loving it!

CHAPTER 11

Pursuing a Good Education

"I gotta go to school! I gotta go to school!"
Nettie

Black women worldwide knew the significance of a good education—especially a college education. You cannot make it far in life without it. Many of us felt like Nettie—"I gotta go to school!" With so many single sisters heading households, we realized receiving a college education raises our economic capabilities and allows us to take better care of our families.

I spoke with hundreds of college students online—male and female—and they all felt the same. Years ago, a high school diploma was sufficient to secure a decent paying job. But today, a high school diploma cannot secure a groundkeeper position at a car wash. It has so little merit, that it is almost equivalent to your kindergarten certificate. Not to downplay the fact of graduating from high school. Getting a high school diploma is a great accomplishment; but in today's competitive job market, it is not enough. A good college education is needed to compete for high-paying jobs in the 21st Century.

Age was irrelevant online. Women of all ages attend colleges and universities across the country. There were older women returning to college after years of absents, like myself. Of course, there were young women who were fresh out of high school. Some were on the verge of giving up; while others proclaimed they were "sick and tired of school". Of course, these comments were made by upper classmen—juniors and seniors—who progressed further along in their curriculum. Freshmen and sophomores were too busy with other things like "partying and hanging out" to feel the pressure of very demanding professors or research project deadlines. Their only concern was finding a ride to the next Alpha, Kappa, or Que-Dog party.

Just as many of the frustrated women, I have witnessed and also heard horror stories of being a full-time student. The spring semester of 2007, my niece described what she called "a total meltdown" while working on a project that accounted for 20% of her final grade. She was a senior majoring in fashion design at Louisiana State University—Baton Rouge. The project consisted of constructing a garment from scratch . . . literally—make the pattern, cut it, and sew it to make the final garment.

She designed an elegant cocktail dress. She estimated two days to sew and one day to hand stitch. But there was a problem. On the final night, she mistakenly sewed the bottom layer backwards. When she discovered the mistake, she was beside herself! She burst into tears and began to throw things all over her room.

After about 45 minutes into the tantrum, she "prayed and asked God to help calm me [her] down". He did. She regained her composure, removed the bottom layer, and sewed it on the correct way. It took hours and she did not get any sleep. When she finished the final stitch, it was time to get dressed for class. Apparently, all of the trouble paid off in the end. She did not get any sleep that night; but she got an "A" on her dress.

One of my best friends also experienced a meltdown while working on a master's degree. It was toward the end of the semester—and you know finals heighten your stress level. Well, while typing a fifteen page research paper, which was due the following morning, she accidentally unplugged her computer and lost all of her unsaved information. But get this; her unsaved information was the *entire* paper. She did not prepare the report in longhand, she "free-styled it"—thought of it as she typed—all night. It was all gone. She turned her dorm room upside down! She "flipped things over" as she cried in total disgust.

Just as my niece, after a few hours she gathered her composure. She started over from the very beginning—page one. She stayed awake all night long too; and was able to reproduce a fifteen page report for her eight o'clock class the very next morning. Oh, and this time, she saved her work as she typed.

I also know the struggles of pursuing a college degree. And you know me, always got a story to tell. Just as I explained to the women online, I love sharing my life experiences; especially, if my story encourages someone. Or if it makes them smile; I love to make people smile. I guess my ADHD is kicking in because I am straying from the topic at hand . . . Let me get to the story—my struggle in pursuit of a college degree spanned over many, many years—fifteen to be exact. Here's my story:

My fifteen year bachelor degree

I graduated from high school in May 1991 and began college soon after. Before the fall quarter, I attended freshman orientation during the summer. Reflecting back, orientation should have been an indication of things to come in the fall. I had a blast! I took placement tests, registered for fall classes, learned the campus and most importantly partied like a rock star. I met an amazing group of young ladies who, of course, partied with me. After summer orientation, I could not wait to return for the fall quarter.

Fall quarter arrived. My parents and I drove thirty-five miles west to Louisiana Tech University's campus. But before they dropped me off, we stopped by the supermarket to pick up a few items. I moved all of my belongings into my new dorm room. My parents helped me organize things and get my room in order. They stayed a few hours. My mom hates traveling at night; so they left before night. As my mom walked out of the door, she handed over an envelope filled with cash, gave me a hug, and exited the building. I was so sad. I cried as they drove away. But the sadness did not last long. My roommate arrived after they left. Boy was I glad to see her. I helped her settle into our new home. We both were so excited to be on campus.

Now that I think about it, my roommate Connie—who was my best friend from high school—and I should not have attended the same school. Maybe I should have gone to school out-of-state to get away from high school friends and concentrate on my school work. But I did not. As a matter of fact, I moved into a dorm with ten, maybe eleven of my high school friends. And to make matters worse, twelve other students from my graduating class were only six miles west at Grambling State University. Can you say "Reunited and it feel so good?" That's what happened—often. We reunited and threw mega parties night after night.

The night before classes began; my roommate and I were on track to become model students. Our backpacks were filled with loose leaf paper, pens, and pencils. Our schedules were taped to the front of our binder so we would not get lost in our new and unfamiliar surroundings. Our clothes were pressed and prepared for class. We were in the bed before 10:00 P.M. A knock on the door changed everything. Three of our friends—Katina, Anita and Tonya—were at the door. My roommate opened the door. They barged in, flipped on the light switch, jumped onto our beds and screamed, "Waaaaaake up! Waaaaaaake up!" You know that we did not get much sleep that night right? We were up all night long talking, eating, and playing around.

We arose the following morning tired and sleepy. We still managed to make it to class on time. Needless to say, the entire quarter was reminiscent to this particular night. Constant partying, late night visiting, playing games like

Pictionary, Gin, Jacks, and having cook-outs like it was the Fourth of July was common among us.

I should not have to tell you—I had a ball the first quarter at Louisiana Tech. And my grades reflected it too. I made two Ds and one F. I was placed on academic probation for the following quarter. I had to get my act together quickly—before I was kicked out of the university permanently. Fortunately, I rebounded. The next quarter I passed all of my classes.

I adjusted my study habits. But I did not stop partying. My friends and I were the socialites of the campus. We made friends with various student organizations—sororities, fraternities, football and basketball players (male and female). I mean, we were the click! We were invited to all parties on and off campus. And we gladly accepted the invitations.

We were also popular in the dorm. Everyone knew us. Unfortunately, the resident assistants and the hall director knew us too. All too well I might add. We were written up several times for stupid stuff—ironing in the rooms, making too much noise, and having too many visitors at once. It had gotten so bad the hall director threatened to kick us out of the dorm. Imagine that.

After one full year of partying and having a marvelous time on campus, we returned for our sophomore year a more responsible and mature group of young ladies. My roommate did not return for fall semester; so I moved in with another roommate—Kim. We hit it off instantly and she became a part of our click.

Yes, we still partied; often. But we did not party as much as we did our "foolish freshman year". We continued the tradition of attending football and basketball games. We still had cookouts. But they were not as extensive as before.

During my sophomore year, I began my first relationship. I was introduced to him by my roommate. She did not actually meet him at first. She dated his brother and collectively they decided to hook us up.

We talked over the phone several times before we actually met. I was captivated by his conversation. But when I laid eyes on him, I instantly fell for him. He was tall—six feet and two inches. He was light-skinned with light brown eyes. And you know light skin was in back in the 90's. He was athletic and definitely "my type". We became a couple and dated for the remainder of the year. I traded in weekend parties to spend time with him back home. As time passed, we grew closer and closer.

I returned to campus the next year but; not for long. I was three months pregnant with my son. I knew this news would devastate my crew; but I had to tell them. I gathered them in the room and broke the news to them. As I suspected, they were devastated. We all cried. My roommate even left the room to collect her thoughts.

Although I promised to return after my son was born, I did not. My mom gave me the option to return to Tech. But I did not want to leave my son at home while I attended school out-of-town. After he was born in April 1994, I transferred to Northeast Louisiana University, now the University of Louisiana—Monroe, in the fall.

For the next eleven years, I was in school one semester and out of the school the next. Sometimes I scheduled only one class, while other semesters I was full-time. There were also periods that I did not attend school. One time I was out for nearly three years. Another time, I was out two years.

Hey, I was no dummy. In high school, I took honors classes in Math, English, and Science. And I made Bs without even studying. But during this uncertain time in my life, I was doing too much at once. I worked several unsatisfying jobs; which only added to my frustrations.

I was young and unsure of my future. I knew that I wanted to return to school and finish my bachelor's degree in business; but I also knew that I would have to make lots of changes. So I did.

In life, everyone experiences what I call a "transition period"—a time when everything sort of comes together and falls into place. Mine arrived in 2005. Since birth, I have always attended the same church. But I never joined the church to become an official member. So the first Sunday in 2005, I made it official. My son and I accepted Christ as the head of our lives together and we were baptized the following Sunday.

After I turned my life over to God, everything lined up in accordance to *His* will. Not mine. Thankfully, during this time, I lived with my parents; so I did not have any real bills to worry about. I finally quit my stressful job and returned to school full-time. I attended both summer sessions and the fall semester. I passed all of my classes. After years of partying and going back and forth to school, I knew my time had arrived.

The spring of 2006 was supposed to be my graduating semester. I had only one class left in my curriculum. I registered for Managerial Economics, the hardest class in the program. And to make matters worse, there was only one professor teaching this class. He was the professor from hell! Taking his class alone did not help me or several other students in his class. We all failed. I was forced to take the class again during the summer. And thank God, a different professor taught the class—Dr. Nelson. I understood his teaching method clearly. I successfully passed the course.

Graduation day was finally here! After fifteen years of going back and forth, in and out of college, I was finally going to receive my degree. I was so excited! The night before graduation, I pressed my robe that hung from my closet door. My cap, with the tassel dangling on the side, sat on my dresser. I stared at it most of the night. Even got out of bed a few times trying it on to make sure it was a perfect fit. I was ready to take that long awaited walk across the stage at the ULM Coliseum.

My whole family was present; except my sister-in-law. She was unable to take the day off from work. My parents, sisters, and brother were there. My son was so happy and my nieces and nephew were there as well. Everyone was extremely happy for me.

As I waited to step up on the stage, I said a short prayer—"Thank you Lord for this day". My name was called. I stepped onto the stage. I almost fell out! I shook Dr. Cofer's hand—once again praying; but this time praying for the strength to make it across—took my picture, and received my degree. I had made it.

With all of the partying that I did on Tech's campus, you would think that I would not want to ever party again. Wrong! It was time to party. I celebrated with my family. We took lots of pictures and dined at a local restaurant. The day progressed just as I imagined it all of those years. It was truly one of the happiest days of my life. I will never forget the experience. Nor will I forget the fifteen year journey that led to this day. "Overjoyed!" is the word one of my classmates used to describe the feeling.

The women online agreed, "It takes determination and drive to finish college". Whether it takes less than four years or fifteen years, the results are overwhelming. Patience, persistence, and perseverance are necessities in pursuing a college education.

Yes, pursuing a college education is very frustrating. And there will be times when you feel like giving up. There will be times when graduation day seems too far away. There will be times when you are forced to sit out a semester or longer. But don't give up. Somehow, some way, keep fighting. Keep pursuing. Keep pushing. Believe in yourself and have faith in God. Remember, I had plenty of reasons to give up—fifteen to be exact.

Even today, I have not given up my quest for knowledge. This upcoming summer, I will apply for the graduate program at Liberty University to major in the Master of Business Administration with a concentration in International Business. I am pretty confident that I will be successful in the program. Oh, and if you are wondering—this degree will not take *another* fifteen years. Only two.

CHAPTER 12

Backstabbing Friends and Co-Workers

"True friends stab you in the front."
Oscar Wilde

The O'Jays said it best—"Smile in your face, all the time they want to take your place, backstabbers, backstabbers". We expect this type of behavior from enemies or haters for that matter. But what if your friend or trusted co-worker displayed this behavior? How would you handle it? What if one day you receive the devastating news of your husband's affair with your best friend who is also your trusted co-worker? How would you handle this situation?

I have never been in this predicament, but I suppose one would go through the four questions that anyone would ask themselves—when, why, how and where? Next, one would probably reflect on all of the in-depth details of your personal life—especially your great and satisfying sex life—that you shared with her. While the very depressing lyrics to a popular blues song plays over and over through your head,—"You should have kept it in the bedroom"—your next reaction might be to pay an unexpected visit to your husband and best friend's office. And after you show up and show out, both employers would be forced to close the office for the remainder of the day! But even if you blew off enough stem to pollute all five Great Lakes, your heart will still have an enormous hole in it.

Sounds like an episode of "Cheaters" doesn't it? Backstabbing, especially from close friends and family, is extremely devastating. When the news of the betrayal comes your way, you immediately blame yourself for their indiscretions and think of everything that you could have done differently to prevent this travesty from occurring. And it was constantly mentioned online. The truth is, it is not your fault. You did nothing accept trust someone who you thought could be trusted. You opened your heart to this person only to have them turn around and stab you through it.

Many of the women that spoke with me online were betrayed by backstabbers in many areas of their lives. Some of them were betrayed by friends, some were betrayed by family members, and others were betrayed by co-workers and even church members. They had jobs and husbands/boyfriends stolen from them without ever having a clue as to what was happening until it was too late.

One sister in particular shared her story of betrayal. The title of her message was "My husband cheated and it hurts". She begin by saying, "For the past three years I have continued to live with my husband even though I found out he had an affair and had another child". She explained how "chaotic" her household was and how she spoke "to him with HATE". She was frustrated with the fact that her husband "has another family to discuss personal issues with".

It seemed that many other sisters shared this same frustration because she received an overwhelming response to her thread. One response began, "My dear sister, I know your pain. I too am in the predicament so I know all too well what you are going through." Some women stated they abandoned their broken relationships while; others remained and regained the trust of their cheating spouses.

I have been disappointed by people who I considered acquaintances; but I have never been burned by family or close friends. I consider myself to be a very personable and approachable individual; however I'm cautious, very caution, about who I allow to penetrate my close circle of friends. It takes months, years in some cases, for me to get close to someone and share personal information about myself with them. I make acquaintances easily, but it takes time to build *true* friendships.

I have a small circle of friends who have been a part of my life for almost twenty years. I met one in middle school. I met four my freshman year of high school and the last two during my freshman year of college. Their names are Connie, Kim, Denita, Tonya, Tara, Sandra and Tiffany. These seven women have been with me through thick and thin. Some would say that we are almost as close as the Joseph sisters of the hit series *Soul Food.* We have shared great times together as well as horrible times.

Over the past twenty years, we have argued, celebrated, congratulated, separated, and reunited. We have supported each other through good and bad relationships and marriages, meaningful and meaningless jobs, baby showers and graduations. Although many of us reside in different parts of the country—Fort Worth and Dallas, TX; Bastrop and Monroe, LA; Sacramento, CA; and Norfolk, VA—we are well aware that one phone call is all it takes to bring us together.

A true friend is someone who relishes in your successes and offers support through your failures and heartaches. A true friend is not jealous or envious of you. She is one who willingly listens without judging or criticizing you. She is always honest even if the truth hurts your feelings. The bottom line is, friends are easy to meet and forget; but *true* friends are just the opposite.

CHAPTER 13

PMS (Pre Mad-Woman Syndrome)

"Baby, PMS is REAL!
Denita J. Nash

Ever laughed and joked with your boyfriend or husband one minute only to unjustifiably curse him out in the next? How about feeling so stressed at work that you exited the building without notifying a soul; not even you immediate supervisor? Ever been so agitated that the slightest sound of a particular voice sends you into a total meltdown? Check the calendar. You could be experiencing PMS or pre-menstrual syndrome without realizing it.

PMS was another hot topic online. While most men think it is an excuse for women to act like "bitches", many women are unable to identify PMS symptoms; so most often they are misdiagnosed. According to my research, black women are not only talking about PMS, we are learning more and more about it and its symptoms.

It is almost a monthly topic between my friend Denita, and I. She'd say, "Mekee, I think it's [PMS] kicking in!" And the conversation goes from there for several minutes.

PMS is defined by WebMD.com as "a medical condition that has symptoms that affect many women of childbearing age." It also states, "PMS can cause a variety of physical and psychological symptoms that occur just before your menstrual period." If only men could understand that PMS is a medical condition and not an excuse.

I tried explaining this to one brother online; but he would not bulge. "You know I'm not buying that right?" he asked.

We went back and forth on this subject; but my attempt to explain PMS was hopeless.

I began experiencing the physical symptoms of PMS in my late 20's—backaches, cramps, headaches and bloating. I knew they were attributed to my monthly menstrual period. But I did not worry because they were mild in nature. A few years ago, I began experiencing the emotional symptoms of PMS. Irritability, mood swings, and fatigue are frustrating problems for me about two weeks before my period.

Thankfully, they do not interrupt my daily routine. But there are women whose symptoms are so severe that medications are prescribed to alleviate them. Some women even experience a more severe condition called Premenstrual Dysphoric Disorder or PMDD. Other psychological symptoms of PMDD are depression, anxiety, confusion, social withdrawal, and mood swings.

The cause of PMS has not been discovered, it is attributed to fluctuating levels of the hormones estrogen and progesterone before the menstrual cycle begins. PMS is also hard to detect due to lack of testing. However, a Thyroid test can be given to evaluate the thyroid to assure it is functioning properly. Women of childbearing age may also be asked by their physician to keep a diary to monitor their symptoms each month. If a trend is present, they could most likely be attributed to PMS; if all other conditions are ruled out.

Although there is no cure for PMS, there are several ways to treat its symptoms. Eating a healthy diet is one. Eliminate foods that are high in salt, sugar, and caffeine. Exercise, especially walking and aerobics, is another method to relieve symptoms. Medication is another form of treatment. Non-prescription medicines such as Aleve, Advil, and aspirin can be purchased over-the-counter to treat the physical symptoms like backache, cramps, and headache. In the case of severe emotional symptoms, anti-depressants can be taken as well. Non-traditional treatments such as message therapy, spa and Jacuzzi visits, and pain relieving creams, like *Icyhot*, are great treatments as well.

According to the American College of Obstetrics and Gynecology, up to 85% of women of child bearing age experience symptoms related to their menstrual cycle. But, only 2-10% experience severe symptoms. Many of the women that I spoke with during research stated they also experience some of the symptoms at least two weeks before their period.

Knowing that many black women experience PMS each month, it is important that we educate ourselves about this very frustrating condition. We can start by developing a close relationship with our gynecologist or health care provider. They can assist in understanding the menstrual cycle and the frustrations that come along with it. The more we understand about PMS, the less frustration it will cause in our lives—period!

—

CHAPTER 14

Misogynistic Lyrics That Degrade Women

"Anything that is too stupid to be spoken is sung."
Voltaire

*"I can't even turn on my radio for somebody hollering
about a bitch or a hoe!"*
Leela James

I have two passions in life. Music is undoubtedly one of them. Sports is the other. I fell in love with music as a young child. I not only listen to music; I have an emotional connection with artist through their music. I remember at the tender age of eight or maybe nine, standing in the hallway outside of my sister's door listening as she played her albums. I would not dare attempt to enter the room. I just stood outside the door and listened as she and her best friend, Nell, played her records. Old mind and soul soothing songs that I love so much like, *Let's Do it Again, Don't Ask My Neighbor,* and *Close the Door;* you know that heart-felt music that you feel deep down in your soul. I'd just stand there and listen to each record play. The sound took me to a beautiful place that is difficult to describe.

I remember her extensive album collection too. I skimmed through it when she was not home. She stored them in a large cardboard box that she kept close to her bed—something like those old milk crates back in the day. It included great artist like Stevie Wonder, Diana Ross, Teddy P., Earth, Wind and Fire and many, many more. I loved them back then and I still love them today.

I was raised in a Baptist church; so of course gospel was one of my favorite genres of music as a child. Sitting in the congregation on Sunday mornings listening to the Tabernacle Baptist Church choir was always a treat. I watched as they wore long burgundy robes with white embroidery, swayed back and forth and clapped their hands. I learned quickly—"He's an on-time God"—because Mother James made certain that everyone realized it after she sung. Another former choir director, the late Freddy Davis, sung with great conviction—"My Soul's Been Anchored". Every time he sung it, he shut the church down!

Being a small child with no worries, I did not quite understand why this song touched my heart as it did; but I knew there was power behind those words. And after Freddie sung it, the women in the congregation shouted and stomp their feet. The men were no better; they stood and waved their hands. I knew back then this was a special song from everyone's reaction.

When hip-hop was introduced in the late 1970's, I thought I had discovered music heaven. The sound and delivery of the lyrics were so unique. I instantly fell in love with it. Artist like The Sugar Hill Gang, Curtis Blow, Grand Master Flash and the Furious Five, Run DMC, Whodini, and Doug E. Fresh introduced us to a genre of music that we had never heard before. Lyrics like "Don't push me 'cause I'm close to the edge. I'm trying not to lose my head" explained the hard times that black folks in the inner city faced during a stagnate economy. We understood the lyrics, "It's like a jungle sometimes it makes me wonder how I keep from going under." We even understood the "huh, huh huh, huh, huh".

Early hip-hop made sense, actually it made perfect sense. It was very creative and had artistic integrity. It carried positive messages to back up the lyrics too. Songs like Queen Latifah's *Ladies First*, and *UNITY*. Great artist like Public Enemy delivered positive messages such as "Fight the power". One could say that early hip-hop stirred us in the right direction. The artists dropped knowledge with each and every hit they wrote, produced, and performed.

Speaking of mind stimulating hip-hop lyrics, how could I not discuss the greatest lyricist of my time—Tupac Shakur. His songs *Keep Ya Head Up, Dear Mama, and So Many Tears* spoke to the hearts of many who related to him. *Anyone* could listen to Tupac; but understanding his lyrics was another thing. Tupac was real; a little too real for many people. He removed the rose-colored blinders and took you to a place that you never knew existed.

His critics labeled him a thug. And yes, he had issues. I would be the first to admit it. But who doesn't? He wrestled with demons that haunted him and tragically lost his life because of them. But he left us with lyrics that I still use today—"They say the blacker the berry the sweeter the juice; I say the darker the flesh then the deeper the roots"; "We aint meant to survive cause it's a set-up"; and "Will the real men get up, I know you fed up ladies, keep your head up!" I know Tupac had problems; but I would defend him, despite his faults, to anyone.

You see, Tupac did not rhyme just to hear himself on the radio. He spoke on issues that were critical to inner city youth—gang violence, drugs, and teen pregnancy. He brought these problems to the forefront through his music. He was, and in my book, still is the greatest rapper ever.

Where, oh where has all of the good music gone? What in Heaven's name has happened to it? In the past, artist collaborated on songs like *We are the World* and the East/West coast collaboration—*We're All in the Same Gang*. I understand music evolves with time, but if music is a sign of today's time, this world is going straight to hell with a couple of suicide bombers attached. Sex, strippers, grillzs, making it rain, and chains that hang low are the only items up for discussion. It's the same non-sense over and over again. And most of it sounds the same; only with different beats.

Long ago, when a young man gave a compliment to a lady, he borrowed lines from music. He used Stevie Wonder's lyrics—"Isn't she lovely? Isn't she wonderful?"

Or he used Johnny Gill's lyrics—"My, my my, my, my, my, my, you sure look good tonight!"

To confirm his intense feelings, he used Freddie Jackson—"You are my lady. You're everything I need and more."

And to let her know that he was in the mood, he drew from Teddy P and commanded, "Turn out the lights and light a candle." Panties and bras flew all over the place before he finished the word "candle"!

And if clubbing was your thing, you danced to Montell Jordan's *This is How We Do It*, or listened to MC Hammer—"Just put on the Hammer and you will be rewarded. My beat is ever booming and you know I'll get it started!"

Now fast-forward to today's music. How did we allow music to go downhill? In the 21st century, what type of music is made? T-Pain's "Girl I been shaking, sticking and moving trying to get to you and that booty". No artistic value at all—Me and my booty? Who says this to a lady? A crack head could write many of the lyrics we hear today. Me and my booty?

Online sisters noticed another aspect of today's music. It has too many stupid instructions to follow: close your eyes, bend over, shut-up, don't say anything, and clap your hands. One song in particular, D4L's *Shake Your Laffy Taffy*, included a verse that stated, "I got a hundred ones [dollar bills] I wanna pour on you." I'm listening to this foolishness and thinking, "Okay, instead of pouring them on me, log onto *www.MCI.com*, pull up account number 52698741 and "pour" seventy-five of them onto my account and pay my telephone bill. Afterwards, I could "pour" the remaining twenty-five into my gas tank. And if he still wanted me to shake something, I could shake that MCI bill across his face all night long! Now that's what he could do with all of those one dollar bills.

Anyone can sing and rap. Like I said before, a drug addict, if he can sit still long enough, can write and perform a song. It does not mean it should be recorded and played over the airwaves for the world to hear. I sing all of the time. I sing throughout the day while bathing, driving, and even writing. As a matter of fact, I'm singing at this very moment in the midst of typing. I can even spit a few rhymes if someone is brave enough to listen. Believe me, I am the sing-along-to-every-song queen. But Lord knows I do not belong in anyone's recording studio.

It takes a musically gifted person to deliver great music. Many entertainers mislabel themselves as artist when they are only singers. Aretha Franklin is a gifted artist. Whitney Houston, Patti LaBelle, Mary J. Blige are gifted artists. Luther Van Dross, rest his melodic soul, was a gifted artist. There are so many others who are truly talented—Anita Baker, Mariah Carey, Prince, and Stevie Wonder. The list goes on and on. But every singer is not an artist.

True enough, I am a huge hip-hop supporter; but I almost gave up on it a few years ago. The lyrics have become so disgusting and almost unbearable. I believe Nas and Busta Rhymes agreed on this issue. In January 2007, Nas released his album entitled *Hip-hop is Dead.*

While promoting the album, he was asked, "Who killed hip-hop?"

"Fans, DJ's, and artists", he answered.

At the 2006 BET Hip-Hop Awards, Busta Rhymes went on a tirade after he accepted his award. He criticized the performance of certain artists; but failed to reveal any names. He criticized them for wearing their pants hanging below their butts and grabbing their crouches as they ran "back and forth across the stage". He was disgusted by some of the performances he witnessed. And who could blame him.

Hip-hop has become so negative. And the negative connotations in music videos—violence, derogatory images of women (mostly black women), and mismanagement of money—are constantly thrown at children who aspire to be like the artists—who fail to practice what they preach. They send messages glorifying the thug life; but live in gated communities and send their kids to private Catholic schools.

If this new sound in music did not negatively affect our youth and community, I and many of the women that I spoke with, would not care what they sang and rapped about. We would simply ignore them and listen to the new inspirational music and the oldies-but-goodies that we love so much. But it is hard to ignore lyrics that encourage violence and misogynistic views of women. That is why we have a problem with it.

Our kids are not the only group who listen to hip-hop music. According to researchers, 80% of rap music is purchased by suburban white kids. They love rap music! The only difference is rap music does not negatively affect white communities as it does black communities. Suburban white kids cannot relate to the hard core lyrics in the music. They hear the rough and raw lyrics and think the words are "cool". But that's just it—they know they are just *words.* They don't live in the poor and drug ridden neighborhoods that artists rap about. They don't see half-naked white women degraded and sexually exploited in rap videos. They have never witnessed a drive-by shooting. So no, they cannot relate to these lyrics. That is not reality to them. It is *entertainment*.

It's different in the hood. Black kids not only listen to hip-hop, many of them live it. African-American kids who live in impoverished neighborhoods interpret the lyrics differently. In their households, there is no voice of reason to steer them in the right direction. The negative lyrics they hear mimic the turmoil they see on a daily basis. And they think it is okay. It must be; if the artists they idolize say it is okay to be ignorant, degrade women, grab your crouch, smoke weed, curse, and just act a plum fool!

But it is not okay. And this is why we, parents, must step into the picture and intervene. We are our children's voice of reason. If we are not; then who will they look to for guidance? We cannot leave the responsibility of raising our kids to hip-hop artists. That is not included in their job description. Their job is to entertain. That's it—entertain. Whether you view their performance as entertainment or not. And our primary role as parents is to monitor everything that affects our children's lives—music, television programs, friends—everything. We must shield our children—from elementary school into adulthood—from the negativity in today's music.

There was a time in music history when artists were concerned about the integrity of their music. You know, the image and the message it portrayed; especially if it affected children. And many of them still do. But for some, the dollar-dollar bill is their only concern. The driving force behind their music is money. They do not care about images. They do not care about the messages. Their only concern is "making their money stack". Ethics and morals don't mean a thing to them. Baby, just show me the money! Who cares about the millions of children who look up to them . . . as long as they roll in the dough, nothing else matters.

Yes, the twenty first century entertainers are hard-noised businessmen. They will do and say anything to sell their music. And I'm not knocking their hustle. I am simply making a comparison of the past and present artists; just as we discussed online.

Many of today's artists are in the business not for the love of music, but for the love of money. However, the sad reality is the fact that we actually buy the music. The more they curse, call women b—, discuss murder plots and drug sells, the more we buy. Apparently, they say exactly what we want to hear because we buy it. It is the simple rule of supply and demand. As long as there is a marketplace for it, they gladly supply it.

In a sense, they remind me of the neighborhood drug dealer who sells crack and other illicit drugs in their community. He does not care if he kills his fellow brother or sister. His attempt is to make as much money as possible regardless of the lives lost or the consequences. Forget about all of the lives he destroys! To hell with all of the young men who watch him in the neighborhood and aspire to be like him. Damn all of that! As long as there are addicts asking for his product, he gladly supplies it for them.

Rap music sales were down by 30% in 2007; but we still buy it in large quantities. It is a tell-tell sign that we as a society have lost our morals, dignity and sanity. And sometimes we allow our children, even babies, to listen to this junk. I am not boycotting hip-hop music. I listen to hip-hop too. That is not my point.

Just as one sister online suggested, "If you allow your children to listen to hip-hop, be prepared to explain the difference in the negative and positive lyrics".

She raised a very good point. It is pertinent that we instill high morals in our kids so they are able to recognize and appreciate quality music. So, if they happen to hear a booty-clapping song, they will recognize it as just that and simply ignore the lyrics rather than follow the disgusting instructions.

Take my son for instance. He is 14-years-old. And he loves rap music. He knows the difference between a Kanye West and a not so Kanye West rapper. He can distinguish between the two. He hears the lyrics of stupid songs; but he does not obey them. To be honest, he just began listening to it about two years ago. When he was in elementary school, he wanted to listen to rap; but there was only one rapper that I would allow him to listen to—Bow-Wow. He wanted to watch rap videos too. But again, I did not let him. I am sure he may have gotten a sneak peak while at his friend's house. But he knew the words in the lyrics were only words.

Making quality music is a difficult task for many entertainers to grasp. Music is a beautiful form of expression. Each genre has its own distinctive style. Hip-hop is jam-packed with colorful and interesting personalities. Some are cool and laid back while others are outrageous and in-your-face. I expect this from hip-hop; it lies on the opposite spectrum of music from gospel and R&B. Often times, hip-hop contains rough and raw lyrics that are hard for many to stomach. Some of the lyrics are based on one's own interpretation. I get this. And I also understand free enterprise, freedom of speech and making your money stack, for that matter. But some things are better left unsaid.

As I said earlier in the chapter, integrity is the missing component in today's music. If producers and entertainers lack integrity, it shows through their music. Classy entertainers like Beyonce, Mariah Carey, and Mary J Blige for example, produce quality music; even when the demand for stupidity is great.

Another entertainer who I love, as I mentioned before, is rapper Bow Wow. I have followed Bow-Bow's career since the release of his first album—*Beware of Dog*—in 2000. His first single *Bounce With Me*, was a treat for all hip-hop fans—young and old—to enjoy. In this song, he declared that he "was brought up with respect" and has proven this throughout his career.

Bow Wow released his fifth album *The Price of Fame* in December 2006 which featured the hit *Shortie Like Mine*. Under the mentorship of super producer Jermaine Dupri, he continues to deliver hit after hit with each new album.

In an industry that is driven by the slogan "Sex sales", there are many artists who entertain by a different motto. According to these artists—talent sales. They are the true artists whose music sells; not sexually explicit lyrics. They do not compromise their integrity and character regardless of the industry's image. Aretha Franklin, Anita Baker, Whitney Houston, Patti LaBelle, and Mary J. Blige have produced decades of beautiful music. The soulful melodies they write, produce, and perform enlighten our hearts and soothe our souls time after time. They exude class and elegance through their music.

I have loved music my entire life. I am only 35-years-old; so of course I consider myself a young lady. But a road trip in the summer of 2006 to Houston, TX, with two of my nieces who are in their early 20's almost tripled my age. My two sisters—who are older than I—accompanied me as well. We had a great time. But there was one constant conflict—music selection. We were there for four days and after two days of smooth mellow jams, my nieces almost had old school meltdowns. They were sick and tired of "listening to slow and droopy music".

Each day, we loaded into the truck, turned the radio to Magic 102.9, and listened to oldies like *Casonova, Mr. Big Stuff, Cool it Now,* and *P.Y.T.* My sisters and I were jamming! But my nieces were frustrated. They suggested that we "play cds instead of listening to the radio". Why did they suggest this? Just our luck, there was brand spanking new Gerald LeVert cd in the truck. We popped it in, stopped at track #6, and played *It's Written All Over Your Face* not once, not twice, about six times in a row!

"Go to number seven!" Tasha said each time the song ended.

We ignored her. Over and over she heard, "Kick it! Sugaaaar, sugaaaar, sho do do; Sugaaaaar, sho do do do".

They were disgusted and almost in tears. They left their MP3s in our hotel room. And they sat on the back seat; so it was nothing they could do. My sister and I were in total control of the music. Eventually, we allowed them to select the music for the remainder of the trip. I did not mention it to them; but I sympathized with them because there was no way in hell that I could have listened to today's rap music for three or four consecutive days. I would have been stone crazy!

After we made the switch, I climbed into the back seat and Tasha selected the music. During this time, I listened carefully to the lyrics of a few songs. But my brain could not take it! I retrieved a pen from my handbag and began a list of the most stupid songs that were played. And there were plenty. I even compiled a list to include in this chapter; but I realized this would be an impossible task—the list would be too long. Instead of 21 songs, I would have 2,221. So that idea was thrown out of the window. Besides, those songs were not worth my time nor the pen and paper to jot them down. Instead, I envisioned a special award show dedicated to entertainers who write, produce and perform stupid music. I called it "The American Music-Less Award Show". Yeah, my ADHD kicked in again and I began to daydream about this show. Oh, it would be fierce and filled with entertainers who really think they have talent; you know, sort of like *The American Idol*.

I carefully planned this show. The first award—"The Most Disgusting Song Ever Recorded". The nominees were: *The Whisper Song* by The Ying Yang Twins, *Neck and Back* by Khia, *Shake That Laffy Taffy* by D4L, *I Was Getting Some* by Shawna and *Ms. New Booty* by Bubba Sparxxx featuring the Ying Yang Twins. The winner was a five-way tie because they were all equally disgusting. They have nice beats; but the lyrics are so sickening that you cannot enjoy it.

The next category was "The Artist You Cannot Understand" and the nominees were: The Ying Yang Twins, Trick Daddy, Young Drough, and Lil John. The winner by a landslide was the Ying Yang Twins! I told you, this show would have been off the chain and the competition got better and better; or should I say worse and worse.

Other categories were: "The Dumbest Producer"; "The Artist in Desperate Need of an Intervention"; and "The Artist Most Likely Mistaken for a Street Prostitute. As you can imagine, those songs drove me out of my mind on the back seat of the truck. My imagination was totally out of control!

But if you think about it, this fictional award show is needed in today's music industry. Contacting BET's president Debra Lee to get this show off the ground may not be such a bad idea. But, the sad thing about it is "The American Music-Less Awards" would be filled with artists who have zero talent but believe in their musical abilities.

One thing is for sure, Mary J. Blige will be absent from this show. Alicia Keys, Mariah Carey, Chris Brown, Common, Jay-Z, Jermaine Dupree and Ne-Yo would also be absent. The truth is, there is an infinite number of truly gifted artists who would not receive an invite to this worthless award show. And these are the entertainers I will pay homage to—the truly talented artist of my lifetime. They deserve recognition. And I will begin with Gospel. Through the years, Gospel music has inspired me and strengthened my relationship and faith in God. Here are 21 of my most inspirational songs.

1) *My Soul Has Been Anchored in the Lord*—Moses Hogan
2) *I'll Hasten to His Throne*—Whitney Houston
3) *Don't Give Up*, and *Open My Heart*—Yolanda Adams
4) *Lean On Me, Silver and Gold, Down By the Riverside and Looking For You*—Kirk Franklin
5) *Don't Give Up, I Believe, Be Optimistic, and Hold On*—The Sounds of Blackness.
6) *Stand and Speak to My Heart*—Donnie McClurkin

7) *He's an On Time God*—Dottie Peoples
8) *Jesus is Love*—The Commodores
9) *I Don't Believe He Brought Me This Far, Yesterday and Shackels*—Mary Mary
10) *I Believe*—Fantasia
11) *I Want to Thank You God*—Howard Hewitt
12) *I'll Take You There, It's Okay, Heaven, and Addictive Love*—Bebe and CeCe Winans.
13) *You Will Know*—Black Men United
14) *I Won't Complain*—Rev. Clay Evans
15) *Wash Me Lord, and Thank You Lord (He Did it All)*—John P. Kee.
16) *Amazing Grace*—Aretha Franklin
17) *So Satisfied*—Luther Barnes
18) *It'll Be All Over in the Morning*—Bebe Winans and Anita Baker
19) *The Lord Will Make a Way Somehow*—Al Green
20) *Jesus Will Pick You Up*—Pastor Shirley Ceasar
21) *Restoration*—Ruben Studdard

The next genre of music is Rhythm and Blues/Soul. R&B is one of my favorite types of music. I listen to it every day. Here are my top 21 artists and a few of their hits:

1) Aretha Franklin—This "Queen of Soul" is the first woman inducted into the Rock and Roll Hall of Fame. And believe me, she gets her respect in the music industry. She deserves it! Her hits include: *Respect, Chain of Fools, You Better Think, Natural Woman, Freedom, Pink Cadillac, Willing to Forgive, Til You Come Back to Me, and Never Gone Break My Faith.*

2) Anita Baker—This eight time Grammy winning songstress is my favorite entertainer. I love all her music—old and new. My favorite songs are: *Body and Soul, Caught Up in the Rapture, I Apologize, Sweet Love, No One in the World, Angel, Fairy Tales, Good Love, You Bring Me Joy, You're My Everything* . . . I could go on and on.

3) Whitney Houston—Say what you may about Whitney; but the truth remains, she is a musical genius! She even brought tears to my eyes as she sang the national anthem in Super Bowl XXV. She tore the stadium down! And no one has topped her version yet. Her hits include: *You Give Good Love, I'm Your Baby Tonight, Saving All My Love For You, Greatest Love of All, All At Once, Didn't We Almost Have it All, Where Do Broken Hearts Go, All the Man I Need, I Have Nothing, I Will Always Love You, I Believe in You and Me* . . . Somebody please stop me!

145

4) Mary J. Blige—Sisters across the world adore Mary. She inspires us. Over the years, we've grown and matured with her. With all of her relationship drama, she managed to find true love. This gives us—single women—hope that we too will find Mr. Right some day. And sisters, we will do anything Mary tells us to do; won't we? In February 2007 during a Super Bowl XLI advertisement for Chevrolet, she advised viewers to "Buy you a Chevrolet". Come on y'all, you know there were thousands of sisters riding around in brand new Impalas after that commercial aired! I would have purchased a Chevy too; but I already owned a Cavalier. Yes, Mary is very influential—worldwide. And we adore her. My favorite Mary J. Blige hits include: *Real Love, You Remind Me (remix), Reminisce, Sweet Thing, Love No Limit, Deep Inside* (my theme song), *My Life, Mary Jane (All Night Long), Enough Cryin, Be Happy, I Can Love You Better, Dance For Me, Be Without You* and *Take Me As I Am, Just Fine, Work That, Fade Away, and Stay Down.*

5) The late great Luther Van Dross—Rest his melodic soul! He was the greatest balladeer of my lifetime. Even though he is not here, his music remains in the hearts of millions worldwide. A few of his hits are: *Never Too Much, Don't Want to Be a Fool, Here and Now, Any Love, Superstar (Until You Come Back to Me), A House is Not a Home, There's Nothing Better Than Love, So Amazing, Wait For Love, If This World Were Mine, Creepin', Since I Lost My Baby, If Only For One Night, and Dance With My Father.* Rest in peace Luther Van Dross.

6) Pattie LaBelle—This legendary songstress is known for her flashy hairstyles and electrifying performances. Her powerful voice has brought many couples together and helped a few of us get through bad break-ups as well. Her hits include: *Kiss Away the Pain, Lady Marmalade, If Only You Knew, The Right Kind of Lover, If You Ask Me To, New Attitude, On My Own, Somebody Loves You Baby (You Know Who it Is), It's a New Day, Love, Need, and Want You, and When You Talk About Love.*

7) Michael Jackson—This international icon is loved and adored around the world. He is truly the "King of Pop". I still listen to his record-breaking album *Thriller* several times a week. I have loved his music my entire life. His hits include: *Got To Be There, Billy Jean, Rock With You, Lady in My Life, Beat It, Thriller, I'm Bad, Black or White, Something About You, Remember the Time, Man in the Mirror, P.T.Y., Don't Stop Til You Get Enough, The Way You Make Me Feel, Wanna Be Startin Somthin, Human Nature, You Rock My World, and Butterflies.*

8) Stevie Wonder—This multi-talented Grammy-winning entertainer revealed his dancing skills to the world at the 2005 BET Awards. Stevie not only performs music, he writes, produces, and plays

the instruments as well. I have loved Stevie's music since early childhood. And I still love it today. My favorite Stevie hits are: *Living For the City, Lately, Happy Birthday, That Girl, Ebony And Ivory, Ribbon in the Sky, I Just Called to say I Love You, Part-Time Lover, That's What Friends are For,* and *For Your Love.*

9) Gerald LeVert—It doesn't matter what you called him—"Gerald", "G", or "Teddy Bear", he was certainly one of the best male performers of our time. We were numbed by his untimely death in November 2006; but his music keeps his memory alive and well today. My favorite Gerald hits are: *Baby Hold On, Private Line, That's What Love Is (with Mikki Howard), Can't Help Myself, I'd Give Anything, Answering Service, Already Missing You, What About Me?,* and *In My Songs.* Rest in peace Gerald LeVert.

10) Prince—He is the ultimate entertainer. Prince captured our hearts with his wide variety of musical talents and unique sense of style. This soft-spoken musical genius's career spans over decades and he is one of my favorite performers. His hits include: *Do Me Baby, Pink Cashmere, Still Waiting, Purple Rain, 1999, I Would Die for You, Scandalous, Controversy, Little Red Corvette, When Doves Cry, Let's Go Crazy, Insatiable, Adore You,* and *I Want to Be Your Lover.* Prince proved he still has the golden flare when he performed *Purple Rain* at the half-time show of Super Bowl XLI.

11) R. Kelly—Although this masked Piped-Piper of R&B often finds himself in *compromising* circumstances—"trapped in the closet" or cheating with Mr. Biggs' wife—his is still known to make us "Step in the name of love". His hits include: *Slow Dance, Your Body's Calling, You Remind Me of Something, I Wish, When a Woman's Fed Up, Ignition (Remix), Bump and Grind, Home Alone, Twelve Play,* and of course, *Step in the Name of Love.*

12) Chaka Kahn—This soulful Diva is known for her irreplaceable voice and unique sound. Her music is the most sampled throughout the music industry from artist such as Mary J. Blige, Busta Rhymes, and Kayne West. She is truly one of my favorite performers. Her hits include: *Aint Nobody, I Feel For You, I'm Every Woman, Through the Fire,* and *What Cha' Gonna Do For Me.*

13) New Edition—This boy band has been around forever and they are one of my favorite groups of all time. Although they experienced adversity within the group, they have survived and still make beautiful music together today. Their hits include: *Mr. Telephone, Cool it Now, Is this The End, I'm Leaving You Again, Count Me Out, If It Isn't Love, N E Heartbreak, Can You Stand the Rain,* and *Boys to Men.*

—

14) Maxwell—I would love to do a little something, something with this sexy and soulful brother! I love Maxwell's sound—smooth and mellow. His hits include: *Get to Know Ya, Lifetime, This Woman's Work, Now, Ascension (Don't Ever Wonder), Sumthin' Sumthin'. Til the Cops Come Knockin, and Whenever, Wherever, Whatever.*

15) Lauryn Hill—I am still waiting for her and the Fugees to grace us with their presence and record a new album. I think we should begin a petition. What do you guys think? Her hits include: *Ex-Factor (my favorite), Doo Wop (That Thing), Nothing Even Matters, and Everything is Everything.*

16) Mariah Carey—We fell in love with this beautiful butterfly in the summer of 1990 with her first album *Mariah Carey* which featured ballads *Vision of Love and I Don't Wanna Cry.* She has entertained us for years with her inspiring hits: *Love Takes Time, Make it Happen, Dream Lover, I'll Be There, Hero, One Sweet Day, Butterfly, Shake it Off, Fly Like a Bird and We Belong Together.*

17) Usher—Whether keeping secrets or telling "confessions", he entertains us with his mellow voice and smooth moves. We've watched as he developed into the fine entertainer he is today. And I do mean *fine.* A few of Usher's hits are: *You Make Me Wanna, Nice and Slow, My Way, U Remind Me, You Got it Bad, U Don't Have to Call, Confessions Part II, Burn,* and *Yeah* featuring Lil John.

18) Toni Braxton—Toni's captivating lyrics helped me through difficulties in my life. I still listen to *Let it Flow* when I feel down and out and need a little encouragement to move forward. A few of her other hits are: *Love Shoulda Brought You Home, How Many Ways, I Love Me Some Him, Breathe Again, You Mean the World to Me, He Wasn't Man Enough, and You're Making Me High.*

19) Bobby Brown—He was labeled the "King of R&B" by his ex-wife Whitney Houston. Over the years, many of us have witnessed Bobby at his worst; but the fact remains, this brother can jam! It's his "prerogative" to do things his way and I aint mad at him for it. His hits include: *Tenderoni, Don't Be Cruel, Humpin Around, Every Little Step I Take, If It Aint Good Enough, and My Prerogative.*

20) Janet Jackson—Mike's little sister, Jermaine's main squeeze and one of my favorite entertainers of all time. She's a classic beauty with great musical talent that led to a career which spans over two decades. Her hits: *What Have You Done For Me Lately, Nasty, When I Think of You, Miss You Much, Love Will Never Do (Without You), Control, The Pleasure Principle, That's the Way Love Goes, I Get Lonely, and So Exicted.*

21) Monica—"Miss Thang" reminds me of myself. She is so down-to-earth and she's also a fellow Scorpio. God has truly blessed this young lady's life and she is not afraid or ashamed to speak of His goodness. She's also not afraid to tell you where to go if you step to her the wrong way. I told you, she is a Scorpio! After a brief hiatus, she returned with the new album *The Makings of Me* in October 2006. My favorite Monica hits are: The entire *Miss Thang* cd, *Angel of Mine, The First Night, The Boy is Mine featuring Brandy, and Every Time tha Beat Drop featuring Dem Franchize Boyz.*

Compiling this covenant list was so hard that I could not stop at 21. I added one more spot. And to make matters worse, I have two artists in this spot. Man, I really love music! Kem and Anthony Hamilton.

Kem is one of my favorite new artists. I fell in love with his smooth and unique sound the first time I heard it. I swear this brother is going to sing at my wedding—as soon as I find a groom. His hits are: *Matter of Time, Love Calls, Brotha Man, Find Your Way (Back in My Life), Heaven, Set You Free, I'm In Love and I Can't Stop Loving You.*

Anthony Hamilton—this singing sensation from the South has a down home persona and his music touches your soul. His hits include: *Charlene, Comin' From Where I'm From, My First Love, Sista Big Bones, and Can't Let Go.*

Hold on! How did I forget about the man—Teddy P! I must have temporarily lost my mind. Ladies, when you hear Teddy playing softly in the background as you enter your man's place, tell the truth, your heart beats faster and faster, doesn't it? Some of us immediately begin sweating too. I know, I have been there too!

Yes, he is the man. Teddy Pendergrass' hits include: *It's Time For Love, Love T.K.O., When Somebody Loves You Back, Close the Door, You're My Latest, My Greatest Inspiration, Turn Off the Lights, If You Don't Know Me By Now, Wake Up Everybody, and It Should've Been You.*

Although I have a love-hate relationship with today's hip-hop music, it remains one of my favorite genres. Here are 21 of my fondest rappers:

1) Tupac Shakur—*Dear Mama, Keep Ya Head Up, So Many Tears, California Love, I Aint Mad At Cha, Brenda's Got a Baby, and Me Against the World.*
2) Run DMC—*King of Rock, Walk This Way, You Talk Too Much, It's Tricky, Run's House, Hard Times, You Be Illin', and It's Like That.*
3) Notorious Big—*Hypnotize, Big Pappa (remix), and Going Back to Cali.*
4) LL Cool J—*Mama Said Knock You Out, I Need Love, I'm Bad, Rock the Bells, Around the Way Girl, Going Back to Cali, Who Do You Love featuring Total, Jingling Baby, Doin It, and Hey Lover.*

5) Public Enemy—*Can't Truss It, Shut 'Em Down, Don't Believe the Hype, 911 is a Joke, He Got Game, and Fight the Power.*

6) KRS-1—*KRS One Attacks, Sound of Da Police, Brown Skin Woman, and Stop Frontin.*

7) Sugar Hill Gang—*Rapper's Delight*

8) Grand Master Flash and the Furious Five—*Internationally Known, Sign of the Times, and The Message.*

9) Eric B & Rakim—*I Aint No Joke, Move the Crowd, You Gots to Chill, Follow the Leader and Paid in Full.*

10) Queen Latifah—*Ladies First, U.N.I.T.Y, Just Another Day, Set it Off, and Latifah's Had it Up 2 Here.*

11) Jay-Z—*Can I Get A, Money Aint a Thang, Big Pimpin', Excuse Me Miss, Dirt Off Your Shoulders, and Lost One featuring Chrisette Michele.*

12) MC Lyte—*Cha Cha Cha, Stop, Look, Listen, Ruff Neck, Poor Georgie, and Cold Rock the Party.*

13) Doug E. Fresh—*Keep Risin' to the Top, All the Way to Heaven, The Show, Lottie Dottie and Excuse me Doug E. Fresh.*

14) Salt N Peppa—*Do You Want Me?, Push It, Independent, Shake Your Thang, Let's Talk about Sex, Whatta Man and Shoop.*

15) Da Brat—*Funkdafied, Give It 2 You, Fa All of Y'all, That's What I'm Looking For, and Sittin' on Top of the World.*

16) Common—*All Night Long, Book of Life, Back to Basics, and The People.*

17) Whodin—*Funky Beat, Friends, One Love, Five Minutes of Funk, The Freaks Come Out at Night, and You Got a Big Mouth*

18) Bow Wow—*Bounce Wit Me, Where My Dogs At, My Name is Bow Wow, Let Me Hold You, Fresh Azimiz, Like You, and Shortie Like Mine.*

19) Kanye West—*Through the Wire, All Falls Down, Jesus Walks, Gold Digger, Touch the Sky, Can't Tell Me Nothing, The Good Life, and Flashing Lights*

20) Nas—*It Ain't Hard to Tell, One Love, Hate Me Now, Made You Look, and Hip hop is Dead.*

21) Outkast—*So Fresh, So clean, Ms. Jackson, Southernplayalisticaillackmuzik, Roses, and Hey Ya!*

I don't know what would happen to me if music suddenly disappeared. I would probably fade away along with it. Many believe today's artists have chased *good* music into a dark and gloomy place; unable to break free; while others believe music has been kidnapped and held captive by street thugs camouflaging themselves as entertainers. I spoke with several sisters who felt the same way.

One sister from Chicago, IL stated, "I've totally gotten away from R&B altogether."

Another sister from Louisville, KY explained, "I don't buy this new junk [music] out there now. I have been buying o'skool {old school} for quite some time now."

One by one, they agreed. The quality of music is not the same as long ago. I spoke with a sister from New York who felt "today's artists as a group can't hold a candle to old school music."

Although the fate of music looks pretty grime, I have faith in the new and upcoming artists such as the breath taking Academy Award winning Jennifer Hudson, the lovely Beyonce', American Idols Fantasia Barrino, Taylor Hicks, Kelly Clarkson, Jordin Sparks, and Rubben Studdard; Anthony Hamilton, Ryan Leslie, the soulful Melanie Fiona, Raheem DeVaughn, Omarion, Marvin Sapp, John Legend, Justin Timberlake, Heather Headley, Marques Huston, Mario, Jamie Foxx, Robin Thicke, Chris Brown, Ne-Yo, Cheris, T. I., Keri Hilson, Jimmie Cozier, Alicia Keys, Trey Songs, Joss Stone, Kanye West, Musiq Soulchild, Rihanna, Shakira, Chrisette Michele, Raphael Saadiq, Kelly Rowland, Day 26, Lupe Fiasco, Amy Winehouse, Eminem, Tank, J. Holiday, Bobby Valentino, Kem, Adele, Jazmine Sullivan, Leona Lewis, Lyfe Jennings, Charlie Wilson, Ledisi, Laura Izibor, Estelle, Noel Gourdin, Amerie, Floetry, Fergie, LaToya Luckett, Solange, Fabolous, Leela James, Twista, Keisha Cole, Carrine Bailey Rae, Gnarles Barkley, the Pussycat Dolls, Vivian Green, and Ciara. I believe the next generation of *good* music lies safely within the vocal cords of these great talents.

The artists who are named throughout the chapter are not the only ones I have listened to and adored over my lifetime. There are dozens of other bands and groups, R&B and rap artists that I love. Of course, I cannot list all of them; but I would be remiss if I did not pay homage to them. They are: super producers Quincy Jones, Jermaine Dupree, Diddy, Pharrell, Timberland and Dr. Dre; the late James Brown (Godfather of Soul), James Ingram, Ron Isley and the Isley Brothers, Stacy Lattisaw, Confunktion, Ginuwine, Ziggy Marley, Phil Collins, George Clinton and Parliament, Earth, Wind and Fire, the late Ray Charles, Jermaine Jackson, J. Moss, the late Aaliyah, Brian McKnight, Cameo, L.A. Reid and Babyface, Black Eyed Peas, Paula Abdul, Jon B, Mint Condition, Phil Collins, Seal, Zhane', Jennifer Holiday, Jon B, Dave Hollister, Cherrelle, Hall and Oates, Naughty by Nature, Def Leppard,

Kindred the Family Soul, Color Me Badd, H-Town, Beastie Boys, Mos Def, The Staple Singers, The Gap Band, Freddie Jackson, Tracie Spencer, Howard Hewitt, Vanessa Williams, Teddy Riley, Destiny's Child, Jodeci, Dru Hill, Rob Base and DJ E-Z Rock, Bone Thugs n Harmony, Chubb Rock, Biz Markie, Yo-Yo, J. J. Fad, the jazzy Maysa Leak, Jill Scott, Angie Stone, India Arie, Michael McDonald, Zapp and Roger Troutman, Ready for the World, Lil Romeo, Changing Faces, Low Key, Club Nouveau, The Deal, After 7, Boys II Men, Mya, Carl Thomas, EnVogue, Guy, TLC, Joe, the late Lou Rawls, Lisa Lisa and Cult Jam, Smokie Norvel, Johnny Gill, Tracy Chapman, Nancy Wilson, Lenny Kravitz, Rebe Jackson, Keith Sweat, Silk, Wyclef Jean, Rome, Total, Take 6, SWV, LSG, Brand New Heavies, Blackstreet, Jagged Edge, Brownstone, Deborah Cox, Ice Cube, Nate Dogg, Tony', Toni', Tone', Teena Marie, Snoop Dogg, El Debarge, Debarge, Ruff Endz, Al Jarreau, Erykah Badu, Donnell Jones, the legendary Tina Turner, Young MC, Kelly Price, Shai, Sheila E, The Roots, Arrested Development, Groove Theory, X-Clan, Soul to Soul, Basic Black, Mase, Shanice, The Backstreet Boys, New Kids on the Block, Atlantic Starr, Betty White, Starpoint, Sunshine Anderson, Avant, 112, Jodid Watley, Pebbles, Mya, Eve, Howard Hewitt, Q-Tip, A Tribe Called Quest, Mikki Howard, BBD, Tweet, Ashanti, Syleena Johnson, X-Scape, Keith Murray, Hip-hop mogul Russell Simmons, B2K, Smokie Robinson, Natalie Cole, the late Marvin Gaye, Clive Davis, Sade, Regina Bell, Karen White, Stephanie Mills, Chante Moore, Frankie Beverly and Maze, Angela Winbush, Lionel Richard, Pebbles, the great Al Green, Brandy, Curtis Blow, the Fat Boys, Heavy D and the Boys, DeLaSoul, Phyllis Hyman, EPMD, Jaheim, Slick Rick, Eric Benet, Gwen Stefani, DMX, Kool Moe Dee, Full Force, The Fugees, Najee, Coolio, A Few Good Men, Force MD's, No Doubt, Angela Bofill, Phyllis Hyman, Donna Summer, Midnight Star, Skyy, Aaron Neville, Big Daddy Kane, Wu Tang Klan, The Bar-Kays, Busta Rhymes, Digital Underground, Al B Sure, Donnie Hathaway, Patti Austin, Lalah Hathaway, 'N Sync, Troop, Surface, Christina Agulliar, Missy Elliot, Montell Jordan, Pink, MC Hammer, DJ Jazzy Jeff and the Fresh Prince, Roberta Flack, Donnell, Jones, The Commodores, The O'Jays, Gladys Knight and the Pips, Hi-Five, Meli'sa Morgan, Faith Evans, Morris Day and the Time, Tyrese, the late Rick James, the legendary Diana Ross, the late Barry White, Kenny G, Dionne Warrick, Winston Marsalis, Tevin Campbell, Glen Jones, Tamia, D'Angelo, the Temptations, and MeShell Ndegeocello.
—

CHAPTER 15

Online Dating

"I was looking for love in all the wrong places."
Waylon Jennings

Searching for love? Well, you do not have to look very far; it's just a click away! Feel free to log on any online dating site to find your knight in shining armor. But if it was that easy, I would have found him years ago. The truth is your online knight in shining armor is more likely a thug with shining gold teeth in his Cadillac sitting on 22's.

Women worldwide agreed—"This brother is prevalent online". And there were hundreds of dating sites online—Yahoo Personals, EHarmony, BlackPeopleMeet, and Match.com—just to name a few. It seems that everyone, single or involved, is looking for their "computer love".

Online dating is so frustrating for many reasons. The primary reason behind the frustration of online dating was the fact that nearly everyone lied about everything—weight, height, and especially age. Many people used online profiles to create a false persona of someone they wish they were. Not who they actually are. This alter ego was their "impersonator". The impersonator represented them physically by using fake profile pictures. He represented them emotionally by painting a picture of a mentally stable person who was well put together. But after time passed, his true colors came shining through. And you discovered his story-book life was one big lie!

One not so frustrated sister disagreed with me. "Online relationships are not a joke!" she stated. "You have to keep in mind that there are real people behind the words you read on your computer screen."

I replied, "Yeah, real people who lied constantly."

Researchers at Cornell University's department of communication found that of 80 online daters from New York City, which consisted of men and women, 81% lied in their online profiles in reference to height, weight, and age. The daters lied to make themselves sound like ideals mates. Men were prevalent on these online dating sites—lying, scheming, and looking for unsuspecting women for all the wrong reasons.

There was one big difference between men and women who dated online; women browsed dating sites seeking "love". Men, on the other had, browsed the sites looking for "a good time" or "sex with no strings attached".

The caliber of online daters was another big problem with dating sites. I cannot count the number of times I have heard men and women proclaim that "everyone online is unattractive or ugly". I did not agree with them. There were times that I witnessed profiles which required a double-take because the brother was *fine*. But there were also profiles that made me wish I had never logged onto the site. Believe me, I am a witness! I witnessed men online who resemble the crack-head "Tyrome Biggums" from *The Chappelle Show* or the *un—rehabilitated* "Eddie Cane" of BET's movie *The Five Heartbeats*. And to let them tell it, they were Denzel look-a-likes!

Yes, there were a variety of characters online—down low suspects, brothers in need of green-cards to remain in the United States and married men looking for extra poom-poom on the side. Heck, there may have been a few on the FBI's *Most Wanted List*. And they were all searching for love.

For all of the bad profiles, there were a few good ones too. I actually met one. He was from Buffalo, NY and resided in Dallas, TX. He was a pretty cool guy. Fine too. But sadly, we lost contact after a few months of chatting. Honestly, he was the only sane brother I met online.

According to my research, sisters online were also discouraged because online relationships do not last.

"They seem to die out easily", said one frustrated sister.

Another stated, "They are unfulfilling and they don't last long".

The process usually followed this pattern: meet a nice guy, chat for a few days before exchanging numbers, talk over the phone for a few days, either he or you lose interest because of something stupid—you cannot tolerate his voice or he does not call back as promised—the calls stop and there you are, back online looking for a new computer love. The process was tiresome and it got old after a while. For this reason, many online daters became frustrated and ditched dating sites altogether because finding a lifetime mate online seemed hopeless.

I understood their frustration. I experienced it too. But Ladies, there is hope. I spoke with dozens of women who actually found mates online and remain happy today. They explained to me how they found love; so of course, I will share their online dating tips with you.

1) Be honest! I cannot express this tip enough. Dishonesty was the number one problem with online dating. Be honest about everything—appearance, marital status and children, if any. Don't be ashamed, be honest and be yourself. If you resemble the drug addicted character "Wanda Dean" from *Holiday Heart*, claim it! And if you struggle with self-esteem issues, deal with them before you decide to date online. Hey, if you truly love yourself, you would not have a reason to lie.

2) Respect yourself and demand respect online—For example, if a guy is disrespectful towards you, ignore him. You do not have to respond to every message or comment received; especially if he is disrespectful. I had an online profile once. Actually, I have had a few. And one day I received a message from a guy who asked this disgusting question: "I have one???? [question]. If I sat upon the edge of the table, pulled up a chair and open them [your] legs because I love spicy food, would I have a full course meal or an appetizer? Do you think I'll get my prize fruit filling?"

   I wanted to ask him—"Are you serious?" But as you can imagine, I did not respond. I quickly forwarded his message to the trash folder.

   Four days later, I received another message from him; but its context was *totally* different.

   "Hey, sorry about before. [I] didn't mean to scare you. How are you?"

   See the difference? I responded to the second message by saying, "I'm fine. Thanks for asking." If you demand respect online, you will receive it.

3) Never give personal information during the initial meeting—Your full name, address, not even your phone or cell number until you are certain that he is not a serial killer or a psycho stalker. You know there are plenty of online nuts.

4) Face-to-face meetings are a no-no! Not until you are absolutely certain this individual can be trusted. Do your homework. Perform research and background checks on the guys you meet online. Do not take his word on everything he tells you. Remember, he's a stranger behind a computer screen. He will tell you anything and pretend to be whoever you want him to be. You can listen to him if you wish. But don't cry after he kidnaps and holds you against your will. You'd be bound and gagged like *Dr. Hannibal Lector* in *The Silence of the Lamb*. Take time to really find out about him before you meet him. It could mean life or death.

---

5) Remember, God has a mate for everyone. Online dating is sometimes fun and exciting; but God has the "Perfect Match" for us and He will send "Harmony" that cannot be found on any social website. Wait and allow Him to lead us to the lifetime partner that He prepared. With this being said, happy online dating!

CHAPTER 16

Unsuccessful Yo-Yo Dieting

"Back then they didn't want me. Now I'm hot, they're all on me."
Mike Jones

Ask any black woman how she perceives her looks and 95% will quickly respond, "Oh I look good!" Or ask her what size is too big. She would probably say, "Size doesn't matter". From a size 2-26, online sisters' responses to these questions remained constant.

Historically, black women have always had healthy body images. We embrace our curves more than any other demographic because we understand real women have curves. Our obsession with image is not to be pencil thin like many of the women in Hollywood. No. Our obsession is to be "thick and curvy like Beyonce". Not to say that black women do not suffer from eating disorders; because some do. They are present within the black community. But they are not as prevalent as in the white community; especially among teens and young women.

Black women also struggle with weight loss issues. Most times, we do not resort to eating disorders as a means of solving the problem. Yo-yo dieting is our problem. We have tried all sorts of diets—water, grapefruit, low-carb and cabbage soup. You name it, and we've tried it. Getting in shape is no easy task and it is not temporary. It is a lifestyle overhaul. Changing the types of food we eat and changing what we do with our bodies—meaning exercise and conditioning—are key in the weight loss process. These two components are critical in losing weight. One can exercise all day long, but if your calorie intake remains the same, you will not lose mass or inches. You will only maintain your present body weight.

Yo-yo dieting is a constant struggle for black women. Just as the women online, I too have struggled with yo-yo dieting. Over the past ten years, I have packed on more than 55lbs that is so hard to lose. It is not the diets that failed. I have failed at dieting.

According to online sisters, consistency was the biggest problem. I am no different. I get siked and pumped up to start a new diet. The excitement usually last about two to three weeks. During the first week, I am like Taebo instructor Billy Blanks . . . all over the place. I eat a healthy diet and workout religiously everyday. And the weight comes off fast too. One time, I lost ten pounds in one week.

Now the second weeks is a different story. I continue to eat healthy; but I include a "free day" to treat myself for a job well done in week one. And during my free day, I eat whatever my little heart desires.

Week three is hopeless. The workouts cease and the healthy diet is almost non-existent. I usually convince myself to take a "quick break" from dieting. The break lingers for weeks, sometimes months. This cycle continuously repeated itself and I found myself back at the very exciting first week.

Ten years of yo-yo dieting which produced the same results each time—no permanent weight loss. Nothing helped me, not even advice from Oprah Winfrey and her world-renown trainer Bob Greene. After watching an episode of *The Oprah Winfrey Show* with my mom in February 2007, I was convinced that it was time for a total body overhaul. During the show, Oprah advised viewers to "stop lying to yourself" when it comes to making the long-term commitment to lose weight. I realized I had been lying to myself for years. Of course, I wanted to lose weight; but I was not willing to make the commitment to lose it forever.

The very next day, I logged on to Bob Greene's website, thebestlife.com, to receive a free diet profile. Just as the past ten years, I began *another* weight loss regime. Again, I started walking 30-45 minutes each day and changed my diet. Same results. After two and a half weeks, I was back to my old routine—eating whatever I craved in large amounts and not exercising.

After this failed attempt, I thought to myself "If Oprah can't inspire me to lose weight; I must be a hopeless case!" But, I was not. This time, God had a different plan for me. He intervened and gave me a second opportunity to use the words that sprung me into action—"Stop lying to yourself!"

Three months later, on May 23, 2007, Oprah aired a follow-up show to reveal the results of the dieters who took the challenge, along with me, to change their lifestyles, lose weight and keep it off. All of them lost weight and they looked amazing! Witnessing the results of these ordinary people who did not have the luxury of expensive diet supplements or trainers reignited my fire to lose weight permanently. I knew that my time had arrived to regain the body that God intended for me. How did I know? I received a shipment of meal replacement shakes that I ordered the same day the second show aired. It was as if God himself spoke to me and said, "It's time!"

I hastily sprung into action. And I have not looked back since that day. No more week ones for me. Not ever. It has been six weeks since the second show aired and I have lost eight pounds the healthy way. I slowly altered my diet and I exercise—walking 30 minutes a day. During this weight loss process, I learned that there were two obstacles to overcome in order to lose weight permanently. The first obstacle is consistency. The second is patience. I was consistent alright; consistent at starting diets. And patience was non-existent. But losing weight is a process. It takes time to lose weight—lots of time. As I mentioned, I lost eight and I have 54 more pounds to lose in order to reach my goal. Regardless of how long it takes, I am sure God will help me succeed!

For the past six weeks, I have slowly made lifestyle changes that are critical in losing weight. These changes helped me lose weight permanently and I am certain they will be beneficial to you as well.

Mikki's Quick Dieting Tips:

1) **Think positive!** If you do not believe in yourself, no one else will.

2) **Think "water is my best friend".** I went from drinking 6-8 glasses of water a week to 8 glasses per day.

3) **Get moving!** Exercise is so important in losing weight. It's almost impossible to burn fat without moving and exercising. Walk 30—45 minutes per day. If the idea of walking is boring, spice it up a little. Dance *The Cupid Shuffle* six times in a row! That'll give you a 30-minute workout for sure.

4) **Don't supersize it, kids size it!** Order from the kid's menu. You will be surprised at how much food comes on a kid's plate. Some restaurants have a "Big Kids" plate. Order it instead of an adult meal. It works for me each time.

5) **Find healthy meal replacements.** My meal replacements consist of protein shakes. They come in all flavors—chocolate, vanilla, and my favorite Pina Colada. I substitute at least one meal, mainly lunch, with a shake. I also eat a bowl of Bran Flakes or Raisin Bran cereal as meal replacements.

6) **Never deprive yourself of food.** Eat the foods you love in moderation. Slowly eliminate sugary foods like desserts, white bread, rice, sugary sodas and drinks from your diet. Eat them in moderation; but don't go cold turkey. It never works.

7) **Eat more fruits and vegetables.** If you do not eat fruits and vegetables, slowly build up your intake of these foods. Try to eat an apple or an orange each day and build up from there.

---

8) *Use smaller plates*. Smaller plates help to control portion sizes. Don't return for seconds and thirds just because the plate is smaller. Chew your food slowly and enjoy the meal the first time around. If you are still hungry, get seconds; but don't pile a large amount of food onto your plate. Remember the old saying, "Your eyes are bigger than your belly".

9) *Find a support group*. Get support from family and friends who will support you with your weight loss efforts and not discourage you from losing it.

10) *Do it for you*! Many of us have the wrong agenda when it comes to losing weight. We do it for all the wrong reasons—to show our ex what he could have had if he stayed, to look better than our best friend who recently lost weight, or to prance around the co-worker who turned us down three months ago because he thought we were too big. Lose weight for you. Do it so you will feel great about yourself; not for everyone else to be proud of you.

For ten years, the word "diet" did not work for me. Each time I started a new diet, I always failed. I had no positive results. But the words "lifestyle change" have. I have learned the three key factors in losing weight—motivation, consistency, and patience. Women online agreed, without these three components you are doomed to get trapped in a vicious cycle of yo-yo dieting. The weight you accumulated over years will not disappear in four or five weeks. It takes time to lose it and a *lifetime* to maintain.

CHAPTER 17

Non-Voting Black Folks Who Complain About Everything

"If American women would increase their voting turnout by ten percent, I think we would see an end to all of the budget cuts in programs benefiting women and children."
Coretta Scott King

Voting, or lack thereof, was another hot topic throughout cyberspace. The 2008 Presidential election was a constant debate. "Who are you voting for—Barack or Hillary?" This question was asked frequently. And many had similar answers—"I'm undecided". The presidential election was not the only election discussed. Some discussed voting for their favorite contestant on *American Idol* or favorite celebrity on *Dancing with the Stars*. I joined the discussions too because I love both shows.

There were others who did not join the conversation because they refused to vote for anything. This group concerned me the most because they complained about everything; but did not vote. They complained about George W. Bush and his administration. They complained about the war in Iraq. They complained about the rising cost of health care and the problems with the public school system. They even complained because Lala Ali did not win the *Dancing with the Stars* competition. They complained about nearly every subject that arose; but they refused to participate in the electoral process. They simply refused to vote.

"My one vote will not change anything" and "My vote will not count" were two excuses that were used to justify their absent votes. After witnessing the

Republican Party steal the Presidential election in 2000, I understand why they felt this way. But just imagine one million people making this same statement. That's one million votes gone down the drain. One million! Some agreed with me, but I still could not convince them to vote.

African-Americans won the right to vote with the 15th Amendment to the United States Constitution on February 3, 1870. Our grand-parents and many of our parents endured beatings, police dogs, water hoses, club sticks and unjust "literacy test" to gain the right to cast a vote. In knowing this, we should be the first to arrive at the voting polls.

The process is much simpler today—get into your car, drive to the voting site, present valid identification and cast a vote. No beatings, water hoses to dodge, and police dogs attacks. It is a very simple process. But many African-Americans still refuse to exercise their hard fought right to vote.

There was nothing worst than listening to someone whine and complain about everything; but refused to take the necessary steps to change the outcome. During my research, I heard dozens of reasons; I mean excuses, why black folks refused to vote. The five most common reasons that I witnessed were:

1) "My vote doesn't count"—This is the number one excuse that was used. With 12 million registered black voters in the United States, there is no reason why we, as a united force, cannot change the outcome of major elections. There are millions of African and African-American women and men who died to allow us a voice to make a difference in this country. We should not allow their deaths for justice to be in vain.

2) "I don't have time to vote"—This excuse really got under my skin because we find the time or make time to do any and everything else—shop, party, cheat on our spouses—but we cannot take ten to fifteen minutes of our "busy" schedules to vote.

3) "I don't know anything about the candidates or their platforms"—Many registered voters have no clue about some of the candidates or their platforms. But we research and learn more about them, their past, what they stand for and have stood for in the past. Voting for a candidate only because the two of you share race, gender or political party is an unhealthy practice in politics. You may as well not cast a vote because you still know very little about the person you voted for. Please, do your homework, learn the individuals and their platforms, and exercise your right to vote!

4) "I cannot find transportation to the voting poll"—This excuse is just ridiculous! In many parts of the country, transportation is provided to those who do not have access. So basically, someone will pick you up and take you back home in order for you to voice your opinion by

voting. Please don't offer this as an excuse for your absent vote because it's really not an excuse. It is called being *lazy*!

5) "I don't want to vote"—People who threw this excuse around traded their right to vote for the right to be stupid. How could anyone, especially black people, fix their lips to mumble the words—"I don't want to vote"? We live in a country which allows every citizen 18-years and older the freedom to cast a vote and elect officials who make critical decisions regarding issues that affect our lives and the manner in which we live. And some people "just don't want to vote". No, these people are not stupid. They are ignorant of the facts of the democratic system in which we live. They are not aware of the power of their one vote. They do not realize that one vote can make a difference in the manner in which our country is governed.

Yes, I have witnessed many excuses why some refuse to vote. Just as millions of other sisters. But I will never fully understand why African-Americans and women, who were deprived of this right for hundreds of years, refuse to exercise their right to vote; but still find reasons to complain about everything. The two don't go hand-in-hand. And just as the old saying goes—"If you are going to pray, don't worry. And if you are going to worry, don't pray". The same applies to non-voters. If you are going to complain, vote. And if you vote, don't complain!

CHAPTER 18

Bad Hair Days

"No matter what I have on, I always feel good if my hair is done."
The Fabulous Toccara Jones

"Where is my beautician?"
Aunt Loretha Wright

There are many common factors among all women regardless of race, but there is one distinct characteristic among sisters—we love our hair! Whether long, short, thick or thin, we love our hair. Out of sheer curiosity, which is the reason I wrote the book, I polled hundreds of online sisters and asked, "Would a bad hair day tempt you to call in sick and miss work?" Many of them quickly answered with an emphatic, "Yes!" There were a few "No's" and some who answered "Maybe"; but the majority of them would have paid a visit to the beauty shop before going to work. An overwhelming 85% confessed that they would be tempted to call in sick to work all because of a bad hair day.

The bottom line is we love our hair. We cherish it. If our hair is not at its best, we are not at our best. There were many days that I felt like calling in sick because my hair was sick. Let's not speak of social gatherings on a bad hair day—they are totally out of the question.

Speaking of hair, I have worn dozens of styles, just as many women, throughout my life—curl, wave neauve, braids and a perm. My hair has changed just about as many times as my job. When I feel the need for a change in my appearance, my hair is usually the first change I make. For sisters, going to the beauty shop is therapeutic. That's it—therapy! Getting your hair done is so rejuvenating. You feel renewed exiting the doors of the beauty shop. The scent of Organic Root hair spray and oil sheen soothes your soul just as a Vanilla and Lavender scented candle.

Yes, my hair has changed over the years. But my stylist has not. Her name—Tara; but she is known to most of her clients as "Twinkle". She has been my stylist for nearly twenty years. I remember the first miracle she performed on me. It was the fall of 1991, my freshman year in college. She permed, wrapped, and swooped my hair up at the center with a big full angle bang. I thought I was the stuff! I was headed to Louisiana Tech's campus with my hair just right.

Everyone, male and female, gave compliments on how "nice" my hair looked. I knew from that day forward, Twinkle and I would have a very long relationship. And plus, she dated my brother during this time. She instantly became a part of the family.

It is really hard to put into words. Black women have special relationships, more like bonds, with their hairstylist. We keep their phone numbers on stand-by, just in case of an emergency . . . listed below mama's number and sometimes before hubby's. We have long histories with our stylist and Twinkle was no exception to this unwritten hair rule.

I introduced her to all of my friends and they loved her too. Twinkle has a God-given talent as a stylist. We consider her a styling Goddess! For more than fifteen years, she curled, flat-ironed, and tapered her way into our hearts. She does an array of styles and all types of hair. But short and sassy cuts are her specialty because she is so creative—not ghetto creative; but classy creative. She's also visual which makes her an even better stylist.

Take any picture to her salon and she works her magic. Miniature pictures, large pictures, pictures cut from an Essence magazine, you name it and I have carried it to Twinkle. She examines it for a while, and a few minutes later, I walk out looking like the model on the picture. Well, my hair resembles the model's hair; if nothing else.

Having a stylist like Twinkle, it is hard to have a bad hair day. But sometimes I do. Every woman experiences bad hair days. But there is a select group of women who seem to never have bad hair days. Like the beautiful actress Malinda Williams. Her hair is *always* gorgeous! Whether she rocks a chic short cut or a long bob, her hair is always put together nicely. I have worn several of her hair styles. Malinda's hair is always a constant topic in Twinkle's salon.

For example, here is one of many "Jocking Malinda Williams' hair" stories. Okay, in the summer of 2006, I saw an advertisement for a new television series called *Wind Fall* which was scheduled to air on CBS. I saw Malinda and only a glimpse of her hair cut. But a glimpse is all I needed to see. I nearly flipped off of the sofa trying to get to the computer to surf the internet for close up pictures of her new do. Fortunately, I found several pictures. I saved and printed them to show to you know who—Twinkle.

"I have some pictures to show you", I said during a phone conversation. She did not ask any questions at the time because she was busy with another client. She advised me to "bring them to your {my} next appointment"; which was the following day.

When I walked through the door, with a sheepish grin she asked, "Where are the pictures?"

I went into the story of how I saw this advertisement; but I never mentioned Malinda Williams' name.

With the same grin on her face she asked, "Which picture?"

I looked at her for a short while. She looked at me. Soon after, we burst into a roaring laughter. Everyone else in the salon was totally confused. But Twinkle and I were on the same page. I knew that she had seen the same commercial and concocted the same idea.

Later that night, I talked with my friend Denita. I told her about the advertisement and the incident that took place at the salon with Twinkle.

As I explained, she replied, "Hmmm".

I knew right away that she too had seen Malinda Williams' hair and planned to get the same cut. Well, she saw the advertisement and already made an appointment with Twinkle too. Boy I tell you! I did not get angry with her or Twinkle.

I laughed and said, "Women all over the world probably did the same thing that we did."

She agreed. And if you are wondering, we all got the same hair cut.

During our lifetime, every woman experience bad hair days. But as I mentioned before, there are a few women who seem to have every strand of hair in place at all times. Many of these women have "glam squads" to keep them looking fresh and fly at all times, especially in the public's eye. But their hair always looks great. And just as many of the chapters in the book, I have compiled a list of 21 women who, in my opinion, never seem to experience bad hair days. They are:

1) **Malinda Williams (of course she is #1 on my list)**
2) **Nia Long**
3) **Halle Berry**
4) **Oprah Winfrey**
5) **Jacque Reid**
6) **Queen Latifah**
7) **Regina King**
8) **Pink**

9) Kimberly Elise
10) Monica
11) Alicia Keys
12) Anita Baker (I still love her classic cut in the *I Apologize* video)
13) The First Lady, Michelle Obama
14) India Arie
15) The fabulous Toccorra Jones
16) Tracee Ellis Ross
17) Terri J. Vauhn
18) Camille Cosby
19) Wendy Raquel Robinson
20) Rihanna
21) Angela Burt-Murray

Okay, I must admit. I am *slightly* biased towards shorter hair. Regardless, bad hair days have nightmarish effects on women. I spoke with dozens of sisters who gave the perfect solutions for bad hair days—"Wear a hat" or "Stay at home".

I have several hats—mainly caps and visors—stored in my closet specifically for bad hair days. When getting a quick hair appointment with Twinkle is virtually impossible, I'll throw a Saints cap on and head for the front door.

Bad hair days, in a sense, are like unexpected thunderstorms. They ruin your plans and dampen your spirit just as an ominous forecast. They are universal not only with black women, but women from all walks of life. True enough, "Your hair is your Glory"; but there is nothing glorious in experiencing a bad hair day.

CHAPTER 19

Ridiculous Stereotypes

"If a million people say a foolish thing, it is still a foolish thing."
Anatole France

What are stereotypes and exactly how are they formed? According to the online reference site *Dictionary.com*, a stereotype is "a simplified and standardized conception or image invested with special meaning and held in common by members of a group." Great definition. But it still does not answer the question of how they began. Regardless of how they are formed, they are only a perception and far from the truth.

Some stereotypes are pointless and can easily be ignored; while others are demeaning and hurtful. African-Americans and people of African decent have been stereotyped for centuries. Over four hundred years ago as our African ancestors were captured, shackled, chained, and brought to a foreign country against their will, they were treated as worthless property to be bought and sold. Their capturers were unfamiliar with their darker skin complexion, tightly curled hair, and what they perceived as a strange method of communication. Many stereotypes were born and bred from the ignorance of these capturers due to a lack of information about African people and their culture.

Even today, in the 21st century, black people are still branded with negative stereotypes—bad credit, broken English. If it is perceived as negative, it is associated with black people. There are many today who still believe these ridiculous stereotypes—especially regarding black women. And I, along with many other frustrated sisters, was sick and tired of the negativity.

"Stop branding us!" one online sister begged.

—

Ignorance is a contributing factor in stereotyping. When we do not fully understand something or someone, we tend to draw our own conclusions about the situation. Even if it's not true. Hopefully, this chapter will dispel negative beliefs about African-Americans and set the record straight. Listed below are 21 of the most ridiculous stereotypes about black people:

1) Black people have rhythm—not true! I know a few who cannot dance in rhythm to save their lives.

2) Black people eat fried chicken and watermelon—Former professional golfer Fuzzy Zoeller definitely believes this stereotype. His comments after Tiger Woods won the Masters Tournament in 1997 confirmed his belief. Not true! One of my best friends, who is black, is allergic to chicken. Oh, and my son hates watermelon.

3) *All* Black men are well endowed—Regardless of how we wish this stereotype was true, it is not. I've heard dozens of horror stories about brothers and their small "pee-pees".

4) Black people cannot swim—Just because we would rather sit *around* the swimming pool at a pool party instead of diving in does not mean that we cannot swim. In 2006, Republican Senator Tramm Hudson stated, "Blacks aren't the greatest swimmers or may not even know [how] to swim." Black gold medalist and world record holder Cullen Jones shattered this stereotype in the Pan Pacific Championships in 2006. He is the first black to hold a swimming world record.

5) Black people are lazy—There are thousands of hardworking successful black people throughout the world—Black doctors, attorneys, television personalities, athletes, and entrepreneurs. A quick check-list of them: President Barack Obama, Bob Johnson, Michael Jordan, the late Johnny Cochran, Magic Johnson, Oprah Winfrey, Condoleezza Rice, and Bill Cosby—just to name a few.

6) Black people are always late—I know this one is hard to believe; but no we are not always late. My pastor makes it a point to begin all services and meetings on time to dispel this age old stereotype.

7) Black people are not articulate—I cannot understand why it is so hard to believe that all black people do not speak Ebonics. We use proper English—conjugate nouns and verbs or have an extended vocabulary. No, it is not called "talking white". It is called speaking English! We are very capable of speaking articulately and using correct English.

8) Black people are defiant and hostile—It's evident that California Governor, Arnold Schwarzenegger believes this stereotype. He said it himself in a closed-door meeting with his advisors in March 2006. The mixture of black and Hispanic blood gives Puerto Ricans "very

hot personalities". Very hot personalities? He later apologized for his comments saying they were not "meant to be in any negative way". I have one question, do hostile black people exist? Yes, they do; but there are also hostile white, Hispanic and Asian people as well. Hostility is based on a combination of qualities—personality, genetics. Not race. If black people are categorized based on the actions of a few, maybe we should follow suit. Let's see, based on Gov. Schwarzenegger's past of groping women and smoking pot, we could label all Austrian men as womanizing pot smokers who speaks broken English. But this would be an unfair stereotype, wouldn't it?

9) All black women are promiscuous—Please refer to Chapter 5.

10) Now this one kills me—our favorite thirst quencher is "red kool-aid"—I understand there are some, well, many of us, who love kool-aid . . . okay, a lot of us, but we also indulge in others drinks like water, sports drinks, fruit juice, and sodas. Red kool-aid? Come on now . . .

11) Black people run faster that any other race—There is no scientific evidence to prove this stereotype. We'll label this one as just plain stupid!

12) Black women cannot grow long hair—Oh, don't laugh. There are some who believe this stereotype. Case in point: while in college, I participated in a marketing study group which consisted of four white females and two black females; including myself. The subject, somehow, switched from marketing our product to grooming hair. One of the white females made this comment as if it was common knowledge—"You guys' hair can't grow long, right?" In fear of what I might have said to her, I did not respond to her dumb statement. I simply turned and looked at the other sister in the group who kindly proceeded to explain the proper procedure to treat African-American hair and allow it to grow long. All four of them listened tentatively and replied "Ohh, okay" throughout the black hair lesson. So it was obvious that they really believed sisters cannot grow long hair. I added, "I wear my hair short by choice; but if I want long hair, I *can* grow it. I have worn it long before".

13) Black people have bad credit—Okay, I do know a few black people whose credit is shot to hell; but I also know black people with excellent credit ratings. Once again, this depends on the individual and the financial choices he/she makes, not race.

14) Light-skinned blacks are more attractive than darker skinned blacks—I call this "Massaih's mentality". There are actually some black folks who believe this as well. Whether you are pitch black or pale white, "Beauty is in the eyes of the beholder". I tested this stereotype in March 2007 with

a group of student that I tutored in an after-school program with my church. There were about 16 students in my class, my son included.

One of the light-skinned students told another dark-skinned student to "shut up with your ugly black self".

"Why did you call her black? Everyone in here is black; including you." I said.

He did not answer.

That prompted me to ask the question, "How many of you think that lighter skin black people are more attractive than dark-skin blacks?" I was shocked at the results. About 11 or 12 raised their hands. Even the kids with darker complexions raised their hands too. Some looked away, like they were embarrassed at their answers, as they raised their hands. The student who made the comment and the little girl who the comment was directed towards both raised their hands too. My son did not raise his hand. I asked the girl why she felt light skin was more attractive, but she could not answer the question. I asked her several times, but she did not have an answer. She just shrugged her shoulders each time.

15) Blacks are inferior to whites—Many believe this stereotype was formed to brainwash black people into actually thinking that we are inferior. Truth is, we have the ability to do almost anything—mentally, emotionally, and physically—that we set our minds to do.

16) All Black women wear the same shade of foundation—I often wonder why certain cosmetics companies develop products for African-American women when they dump us all in the same category—dark or deep. Our skin complexion ranges from the fairest fair to the darkest dark. We do not fall into "dark and deep". That just kills me! Please, just leave it to MAC, Fashion Fair, Cover Girl, Iman, or Bobbie Brown to develop our products.

17) Black people are not politically informed—Not true. African-Americans turned out in record numbers to help elect the first black president in November 2008—Barack Obama. Not only African-Americans voted for President Obama, white, Asian, Hispanic, young, and old voted for him as well. Although there are some who refuse to participate in the political process, for the most part, we are politically informed.

18) Black people cannot watch movies at the theater without talking back to the screen—Yes, we are very expressive and emotional people; but it is possible for us to enjoy movies without saying a word. I have yet to witness it myself. But I am almost certain that it is possible.

19) Black church services begin at 10:00 AM and end at 4:00 PM—Everyone knows how black folks love the Lord, but our services do not last six hours long; unless of course, you are Baptist.

—

20) The electric slide or any type of shuffle is performed at *all* black weddings or parties—Although we are known for getting our slide on, I have been to a few black weddings and parties where the electric slide was not performed; I said a *few*.

21) Black people love Bill and Hillary Clinton—Now I must confess, this is not a stereotype. This is a fact! We love Bill and Hillary Clinton. I know a few black people who think Bill Clinton is their daddy without any resemblance to him. The Clintons have done a wonderful job of gaining the respect of African-Americans and black people throughout the world. I will never forget when Bill Clinton, who was president at the time, addressed Grambling State University's class of 1999. I did not attend the ceremony, but I viewed clips on the evening news.

President Clinton was charming and charismatic as usual. He wowed the graduates with his proclamation, "I came from a place where everybody thinks they're somebody; but I wanted to come to the place where everybody is somebody."

The slogan, "The place where everybody is somebody", is Grambling's motto. He received a standing ovation. I will say it again; we love Bill and Hillary Clinton!

These are only 21 ridiculous stereotypes that black people constantly face. There are many others. Once again, stereotypes are born of ignorance and lack of understanding. But it is our responsibility in the black community to dispel negative stereotypes with our actions.

CHAPTER 20

Not Recognized as True Sports Fans

"Hello!" You play to win the game!"
Coach Herman Edwards

"Both teams played hard. God Bless and good night!"
Rasheed Wallace

"The Bears are who we thought they were!"
Coach Dennis Green

"Playoffs? Are you kidding me? Playoffs?
Don't talk to me about playoffs!"
Coach Jim Mora

Exactly what defines a "sports fan"? Is he someone who loses his voice after cheering for his beloved team after *every* game? Is he someone who paints his face and dresses in team colors for each and every home game? Maybe, he is someone who rattles the names of the University of Michigan's "Fab Five" off of his tongue as if he's being quizzed the very next day? Well, magnify this one hundred times and you have me—the self proclaimed "Diva of Sports".

For me, sports is not just recreational. It is a way of life. I arise in the morning with my television on ESPN and fall asleep with it on ESPN. For me, a typical TV line-up on an off day goes as such: 10:00 A.M—a repeat of last night's *SportsCenter*; 11:00 A.M.—*First Take*, formerly *Cold Pizza*; 3:00 P.M.—*NFL LIVE*; 4:00 P.M.—*Around the Horn*; 4:30 P.M.—*Pardon the Interruption*; and

5:00 P.M.—*SportsCenter* once again, and depending on the season, maybe catch a Monday night football game or NBA action. I suppose it sounds like an obsession; especially for a female. But this is not my fault at all. It was totally premeditated!

My entire life has been centered around sports. For years, I thought Super Bowl Sunday was a national holiday. We gathered around the television and watched the two remaining teams—representing the AFC and NFC—grind it out to the win the covenant Vince Lombardy Trophy.

Over my lifetime, I have witnessed a lot in sports history. As a child, I witnessed Tom Landry's Cowboys—Roger Staubach, Toney Dorset, and Randy White—win Super Bowls. I watched wide-receiver Jerry Rice complete one-hand catches from QBs Joe Montana and Steve Young; set 38 NFL records; and win championships in the 80's. I also witnessed Emmitt Smith, Michael Irving, and Troy Aikman win three championships within four years in the early 90's. And this was only football season!

Basketball season was reminiscent of football. My dad, brother, and I were all "Showtime" Laker fans. I witnessed as Magic Johnson constantly confused defenders with his sick no-look passes. I witnessed as Michael Cooper, long white socks and all, reign threes from the arch. I watched classic match-ups between the Los Angles Lakers and three of their rivals—Chicago Bulls, Detroit Pistons, and Boston Celtics. Even today, I close my eyes and envision the locker room atmosphere after the back-to-back championship wins in 1987 and 1988: Magic's ear to ear grin, Pat Riley's hair slicked back from the champagne baths, and Kareem sporting his signature goggles.

I watched games along with my sister who was a huge 76ers fan. She loved them all—Julius "Dr. J." Ervin who transformed the dunk into an art form, Maurice Cheeks, and Mosses Malone. That was in the 80's. In the 90's, she became a "Bad Boys" Piston fan. She still teases me and my brother with John Salley's "back to back" gesture (after they upset the Lakers in 1990 winning consecutive titles in two years).

My mom was a Chicago Bulls, correction, a Michael Jordan fan. She knew the entire team; but Michael was the only player she constantly praised. Michael Jordan this and Michael Jordan that.

"He [Michael Jordan] can't win the game all by himself Geneva", my dad always told her.

My dad was right. Mike had help. Plenty of it. MJ and his supporting cast—Coach Phil Jackson, Scottie Pippen, Horace Grant, three point specialists John Paxton and Craig Hodges, and who could ever forget the colorful rebound king Dennis Rodman—dominated the NBA winning three consecutive championships twice within eight years.

Sports has been a constant factor throughout my life. Many of my childhood friends, male and female, were involved in sports. I never played for an organized

—

team, except neighborhood teams; but I was always in the middle of the action. Everyone who knew me understood the importance of sports in my life. Still today, my family, friends, and even co-workers know that I am an ultra sports fan. They have also heard many of my sports stories. I have hundreds—*literally!* Here are a few of them:

While working as a library assistant in a local elementary school, the principal—Mr. Brown—greeted me at the door each morning with sports page of the *News Star* to begin my work day.

"Here ya go Ms. Z", he said as he handed the paper to me.

The school only received one paper daily; so I shared the sports page with three other men in the school. They quickly learned that I was a sports nut too. We shared the sports page for two years. Mr. Brown retired a year later.

During football and basketball season, I am the sports information desk—so to speak—for my father, sister, and brother. Key match-ups, game times, and statistical facts are my specialty.

"What time does the game start?" My father asked.

"Who's winning?" My brother asked.

"Mekee, who plays tonight?" My sister asked.

Of course, I confidently answered their questions each time.

In 1998, I was selected by *The News Star* to participate in the Annual Pigskin Picks contest. Each week during football season, a guest was asked to choose the winner of key high school, college and professional games. There were thirty games to predict and I did pretty well—20/30 was correct.

Here is another great story: With the NCAA tournament in full swing, I found myself dreaming of basketball while preparing for the birth of my son in March 1994. My son was delivered by cesarean section; so I was fully sedated. During the surgery and awaiting the arrival of my bundle of joy, instead of dreams of bottles, rattles, or baby formula, I dreamt of playing one-on-one with a really tall man. I cannot remember his face; but I thought it was Magic Johnson.

"Well, you got your baby boy!" said Dr. Williams in the recovery room.

Either the pain meds had kicked in or my mind was totally on the game going on in my head because I responded, "My baby who?"

Of course I was excited about the birth of my son. He was my first born. But I was also excited about the NCAA tournament. My stay in the hospital lasted longer than expected. So my boyfriend and best friend, Connie, watched the remainder of the tournament from my hospital room. Oh, and if you are wondering—The Arkansas Razorback won the championship.

There are dozens of other stories that I could share to display my passion for sports. Decades of sports data are permanently embedded in my brain. Names of players and the colleges they played for, even their coaches' names. True enough,

I watched sports for more that twenty years of my life; but I have also listened to various analysts who give their perspective on sports and sports figures. Shows like *SportsCenter, Up Close With Roy Firestone, NBA Today,* which is now called *NBA Fastbreak, SportsCentury,* and *Beyond the Glory* just to name a few.

Over the years, I have agreed and disagreed with sports analysts as they praised and criticized athletes like Magic Johnson, Serena Williams, Michael Vick, Peyton Manning, Michael Irving, Dennis Rodman, and Tiger Woods. I have witnessed Roy Firestone of *Upclose with Roy Firestone,* make athletes cry as if they just exited their mama's funeral. I watched *SportCenter's* Chris Berman and Dan Patrick share the camera as anchors. Heck, I even shed a few tears when Dan Patrick and Keith Olbermann parted ways in 1997 as Keith left *SportsCenter* to pursue other career opportunities.

I still love to hear "The Swam" {Chris Berman} say "He could go all the way!" after a long touchdown run. And describe a high flying hit as it goes "Back, back, back, back, back!" Graig Kilborne, Chris Meyers, Robin Roberts and Kevin Frazier are other former anchors that I really enjoyed to watch.

I love *SportsCenter*—even today. My evenings are not fully complete until I hear Stuart Scott describe a fantastic play "As cool as the other side of the pillow" or Scott Van Pelt warn defenders "Don't bring that kool-aid to a grown man's party".

John Saunders, Suzy Kolber, Mike Hill, Linda Cohn, Steve Berthiaume, John Anderson, Steve Levy, and the very sarcastic Kenny Maine are all great to watch for pre and post game analysis. Their fun and sometimes cynical delivery of sports highlights entertain and amuse everyone night after night.

Oh, and football season would not make any sense without *Sunday NFL Countdown*—an hour long show which analyzes each match-up during football season. I must admit, I have missed a few church services to watch this preview show. Don't worry; I have already repented for it. But if you have seen the show, you understand what I mean. Who can resist watching Chris Berman, Tom Jackson, Coach Mike Ditka, and Ron Jarwarski lose intense football debates with the very outspoken Hall of Famer Michael Irving?

For my daily fix of NFL coverage I watch *NFL Live* hosted by Tre Wingo along with the very sexy duo—Darren Woodson and Mark Schlereth. It also features my favorite analyst Sean Salisbury whose presentation is candid and straight forward—the way I like it! Merrill Hodge, Eric Allen, Michael Smith, Chris Mortenson, and Hall of Fame sports writer John Clayton also appear on the show. They are all great sports analysts.

Believe it or not, ESPN is not the only sports network that I tune in to watch. Fox Sport Network is another one of my favorites. *The Best Damn Sport Show Period* hosted by Chris Rose and Bad Boy John Salley, who constantly criticizes football players by calling them "salvages" and always shows of his "fresh new pair of Jordan's" during the show.

Beyond the Glory is great too. It airs on the Fox Sport Network. This in-depth hour long program dissects the lives of athletes in all area of sports. Only God knows how many episodes I've seen—Chris Webber, Deion Sanders, Pete Rose, Terry Bradshaw, Ray Lewis, the late Reggie White, Michael Irving, Karl Malone, Reggie Miller, and Donavan McNabb—the list goes on and on.

And if you're an NBA fan, how can you not tune in to *Inside the NBA* which is hosted by Ernie Johnson along with Kenny Smith and Hall of Famers Charles Barkley and Earvin "Magic" Johnson? You simply cannot resist! I look forward to the NBA season partly because of the colorful characters on this show. Their antics—Magic's insightful perspective, Charles' on-set demonstrations, and Ernie and Kenny taking jabs at Charles every chance they get—keep basketball fans tuned in.

I will never forget the funniest moment ever on the show. In September 2006, the crew played a hilarious joke on Kenny Smith by setting up a "retirement ceremony" for his jersey. They showed old footage of Magic Johnson, Reggie Miller, and Charles Barkley's jersey being raised to the rafters at the arenas where they spent years playing professionally. All of a sudden, a fake Kenny Smith jersey came strolling by on a clothes line with socks, underwear, and T-shirts. Kenny actually caught on to the joke early, but when he saw his jersey on the line, he immediately snatched it down. They cracked up! And so did I. I loved it! I even have this *Youtube* clip embedded on *MySpace*. I still crack up when I watch it.

With sports being such a huge part of my life, how could I not pass the love to my son, just as it was passed to me? Actually, he got a double dose because his father loves sports too. He played every sport in high school—football, basketball, baseball, and track and field. But his passion was football; just as my son. DeAndre', my son, has a God given talent for football. I know all mothers may feel this way, but my son was born to play this game. At only ten months old, he carried his father's miniature football everywhere as he strolled throughout the house in his walker. And he was eight when he joined his first organized football team. It was flag football with the YMCA. He hasn't looked back since.

Baseball is another sport that my son has played since the age of five. Tee-ball was lots of fun. Watching four and five year olds hit the ball and run to third base rather than first base always entertained the crowd of parents. I must admit, I am not a big baseball fan. But I enjoy watching my son hit a line drive past third base.

Yes, I have witnessed some spectacular plays during my son's sports career. I have seen him shake a defender twice his size on the playground so badly that the guy slid clear across the court. I have seen him spin around a defender in open field to score his first touchdown in flag football.

This juke was so amazing that my brother ran up and down the sideline and screamed "He's going to Florida State! He's going to Florida State!"

He also earned the nickname "Mr. Excitement" from one of his baseball coaches because he "always does something exciting during the game".

These plays along with many others are forever sketched in my sports memory bank. They are included in the long list of spectacular moments in sports that span over twenty-five years. Of course, I cannot include the whole list in this chapter. So, I narrowed them down to ten. It was not an easy task; but I managed to pull it off. Here are my ten most memorable moments in sports:

10) Charlotte Smith's three pointer—with .07 seconds remaining in the 1994 Women's NCAA Championship game between Louisiana Tech's Lady Techsters and the University of North Carolina. Charlotte Smith hit a three pointer and snatched the title from the Techsters. I was on the phone, three-way, with friends who lived on campus. We planned the victory party which would have taken place in Harper Hall. Charlotte's amazing shot shattered our party plans. Boo hoo hoo!

9) Michael Jordan's push off—That's right! He pushed Bryon Russell to get a clear shot and won the playoff series and the NBA championship against the Utah Jazz in 1998. His push was the biggest no-call in NBA history. My mom swears it was not an offensive foul. I won't repeat what my dad called it . . . the word begins with a "b" and ends with a "t". Michael Jordan and the Chicago Bulls should have lost this game—period! There should have been a game seven to play for the title. But there was not. I thought cheaters never win? Apparently, the Chicago Bulls did not get this memo.

8) Tiger Woods first major golf victory (1997 Masters)—I am not a big golf fan, but this moment is special to me because it is extra special to my dad. He is the sole reason why I witnessed this win. Tiger won by a record margin of 12 and became the youngest and the first of African descent to win. I recall watching the large crowd of spectators who followed him to the 18th hole and the great big bear hug he gave his father, the late James Earl Woods.

7) The Motown Mayhem—Now, I have witnessed many NBA fights—Magic Johnson and Isaiah Thomas, Larry Johnson and Alonzo Mourning, Bill Laimbeer and damn near everybody in the NBA—but none of these compare to the disaster in Detroit between the Indiana Pacers and Detroit Pistons in November 2004. Fist, chairs, cups, and fans were flying all over the place! It all began with a Ron Artest foul on Ben Wallace as he drove to the basket. A shoving match began on the court, but it seemed to be under control. They managed to get Ron

Artest away from the floor and on the sidelines. Suddenly, a fan threw a cup at Ron Artest and hit him in the chest. He snapped Ron, along with other Indiana Pacers, ran clear into the stands and all hell broke loose! The players were removed from the floor and sent to the locker room. The game was cancelled. Huge fines and long suspensions followed. This brawl sparked NBA Commissioner David Stern to impose new policies to improve the NBA's image. It was a definite low point in NBA history.

6) Super Bowl XLI—This was a Super Bowl to remember; especially for African-Americans fans. Not one, but two very soft spoken African-American coaches took the field to compete for the NFL championship title. Of course, I cheered for the New England Patriots because the Chicago Bears upset my beloved New Orleans Saints in the NFC title game one week prior; ending our Cinderella 2006 season.

5) Super Bowl XXII—This was another great moment for African-American fans. Doug Williams, who hails from Grambling State University under the keen leadership of the late Eddie G. Robinson, was the first black quarterback to play in a Super Bowl game. He was also the first black starting quarterback to win MVP. I was a freshman in high school during this season (1987-1988). My entire family witnessed this moment. I remember my dad went on and on about Doug, Grambling, and Coach Robinson. And I do mean on and on.

4) Chasing OJ—I remember exactly when this drama began. It interrupted the NBA playoffs between the New York Knicks and the Houston Rockets in June 1994. NBC showed split coverage of the "low speed bronco chase" and game five at Madison Square Garden. "Why are they interrupting the playoffs for this foolishness?" I asked my sister. I was disgusted.

3) "Timeout!"—It still hurts me today to discuss this moment; but I will try. Chris Webber's timeout in the 1993 NCAA championship game against Dean Smith's Tar Heels remains one of my saddest moments in sports history. Picture this: my roommate and I, who are big Michigan fans, surrounded by nine or ten Fab Five haters. I am sporting a blue Michigan cap—worn to the back—and screaming from start to finish. With nineteen seconds left in the game, Chris Webber rebounded the ball, traveled (which the refs did not call), continued in the direction of his bench, and called a timeout that his team did not have. A technical foul was called and Michigan turned the ball over to Carolina which resulted in Michigan losing the national championship. I felt so bad for Chris Webber. My roommate and I were in "depress mode" the entire week following the game.

2) Dome Sweet Dome—(The New Orleans Saints first home game after the devastation of Hurricane Katrina) I have witnessed hundreds of Saints games live and on TV, but I have never witnessed a team play with such pride and passion as the Saints on this emotional return to the Super Dome. After the devastating effects of Hurricane Katrina forced the Saints to play their 2005 home games in San Antonio, TX, they returned home with a vengeance in the presence of a sold-out crowd of 70,003 fans on September 25, 2006. The Saints man-handled the Atlanta Falcons beating them 23-3. The Falcons never had a chance. Pro bowl wide receiver Joe Horn led the Saints onto the field and to victory. This was truly an amazing game. I will never forget this one as long as I live.

1) Magic Johnson's retirement and HIV announcement—This was the saddest day in sports history for me—November 7, 1991. My roommate and I were in our dorm room on Louisiana Tech's campus when our friend Shelia, a former high school point guard, burst into the room and screamed "Magic has AIDS! Magic has AIDS!"

She motioned for us to come to her room. We took off! We ran to her room, three doors down the hall, to watch the press conference. I only remember hearing "HIV" and "I will have to retire from the Lakers". I almost fell out. I sat on her bed in total disbelief. Dead silence fell upon the packed room. I just sat there and began to cry. Everyone thought that Earvin "Magic" Johnson, the greatest point guard to play the game, was going to die.

My roommate advised me to call my brother, who was the biggest Lakers fan, to see if he had heard the news. As I suspected, he heard the news and was devastated too. Thank God, our greatest fear did not come to pass. Magic Johnson is alive and healthy today. It has been seventeen years since his announcement. And thank God for those seventeen years.

Over my lifetime, there have been many other memorable moments in sports, as you can imagine. These moments would not have been born without the coaches, athletes, and sporting events that made them possible. I would be remiss if I did not mention the 21 that continue to shape and mold my sports world.

1) Earvin "Magic" Johnson—He was truly a magician on the basketball court. From 1979 to 1991, he led the Los Angeles Lakers to five NBA championship titles, won three MVP awards, and won three finals MVP awards. He also earned three additional championship rings as a Lakers executive from 2000-2003. This flashy point guard with the wide smile was a specialist at finding the open man; whether Kareem Abdul Jabbar, Michael Cooper, A.C. Green, or Kurt Rambis. And his no-look passes were amazing! He constantly confused defenders. Magic

—

could have been waving to his beautiful wife Cookie in the stands and still complete a pass to a cutting James Worthy for two points. That's how special he was.

Magic was a joy to watch. And he's still creating magic off the court with his charitable works as an HIV/AIDS activist throughout the black community. In my opinion, he was truly the best point guard to play the game of basketball. I know, I know, I've said this before.

2) The late Coach Eddie Robinson—This Louisiana sports legend had "one job and one wife" for over 50 years. In 56 seasons, he led Grambling State University to 408 victories and coached over 4,000 players which 80% of whom received college degrees. On October 5, 1985, he accomplished one of his greatest feats. He won his 324th game and passed the legendary coach—Paul "Bear" Bryant—as the coach with the most wins in college football. Coach Robinson's record was subsequently broken by Saint John's coach John Gagliardi in 2003.

Coach Rob, as he was called by many of his players, was an excellent mentor on and off of the football field. I spoke with former Tigers Doug Williams—Super Bowl XXII MVP—and Monroe, LA native James "Shack" Harris about their experiences with Coach Robinson.

"My mom agreed for me to go to Grambling", Doug Williams said. He also said that he was "sleep when Coach {Robinson} called" and his mom "answered the call". He later admitted "It was the best decision of my {his} life."

Quarterback James Harris, who was the first black quarterback to start in an NFL playoff game, also weighed in on playing for Coach Robinson. "Coach Robinson prepared his players for football and life after football", he added. "Coach Robinson never made excuses for us {his players} being black", he also said of the legend.

The Zimmerman family has a history with Grambling State football as well. Three of my cousins—Dale Zimmerman, Sr. Dale Jr., and Robert Zimmerman—played quarterback for Coach Rob.

To his players Coach Robinson was more than a coach; he was a father figure and role model. Sadly, Coach Robinson lost his long battle with Alzheimer on April 4, 2007. The nation mourned the lost of the football legend. He was given the highest honor by former Louisiana governor Kathleen Blanco. Coach Robinson's body laid in state in the Louisiana State Capital Rotunda on April 9, 2007. I was honored to be in attendance at his funeral on April 11, 2007. I even excused my son from school to accompany me and witness this historic occasion. Thousands were in attendance to say good-bye to Coach Eddie Robinson—Rev. Jessie Jackson, Sen. Mary Landrieu, former players,

Grambling State faculty, students, and fans. Rest in peace Coach Rob. You've definitely earned it!

3) The New Orleans Saints—Now, the Zimmerman family is a very diverse group when it comes to sports; but there is one constant among us—our unwavering love for the New Orleans Saints! Through the good, bad, and the down right ridiculous late fourth quarter losses, we have been right there screaming, "Who dat, who dat? Who dat say they gonna beat them Saints!" From the "Cha-ching" years, being called the New Orleans Aints, wearing paper bags on our heads, and burying voodoo dolls, we have been right there. Honestly, in Louisiana it is almost impossible not to support the black and gold.

During the home opener of the 2008 season after Hurricane Gustav hit Louisiana, a fan held a sign that read" We may not have our lights, but we have our Saints!" Yeah, that is how much we love our Saints. And If you know absolutely nothing about the Saints, here's a brief history—they have had two owners : John W. Mecom and Tom Benson who is known for dancing and twirling his Saints umbrella on the Superdome turf after a big win; outspoken coaches—Jim Mora {Playoffs? Don't even talk to me about playoffs!}; bad quarterbacks—Bobby Hebert and Aaron Brooks; a running back gone wild—Ricky Williams; great offensive tackle Willie Roaf, and one "savior" who managed to kick us out of some very sticky situations—kicker Morten Anderson.

But through it all, we have had some great coaches, Hall of Famer Mike Ditka, defensive specialist Jim Haslett, and our present Coach, who I deemed "The Wizard" for his great offensive schemes, Sean Peyton. After a devastating season following Hurricane Katrina in 2005, which forced the Saints to play all of their home games in the Alamo Dome in San Antonio, TX; they resurrected in 2006 to win the NFC South Division and reach the NFC title game which they lost to the Chicago Bears. In reward of his successful 2006 season, Coach Peyton won Coach of the Year.

Although we have lost the heart and soul of our team and fan favorite—wide receiver Joe Horn—to free agency, we are in position to become a very good team in the upcoming years. If running backs Deuce McAlister and Reggie Bush continue to run the ball marvelously, wide receiver Marques Colston continues to catch everything that's thrown in his direction, and offensive genius Coach Sean Peyton continues his magical play calling, the New Orleans Saints will remain a force in the NFC division. Geaux Saints!

—

4)   The National Football League—Football is the most popular sport in the United States. Pass action fakes, blitzes, sacks, interceptions, and kickoff returns for TDs are aspects of the game that just sends chills up the spines of football fans young and old. Thirty-two teams compete for five grueling months to perform in "The greatest show on turf" to determine the last team standing—the Super Bowl champs.

Dozens of great players laid the foundation for today's NFL stars to carry on the great tradition—Jim Brown, Dick Butkus, Mike Singletary, the late Walter Payton, Joe Montana, Dan Marino, Jerry Rice, and Emmitt Smith, and Lawrence Taylor, just to name a few.

Due to the lack of dedication, self respect, and love for the game of football, the NFL's image has been slightly tarnished with off-the-field mishaps and run-ins with law enforcement; which sparked NFL Commissioner Roger Goodell to implement a stricter conduct policy in 2007.

"It is important that the NFL be represented consistently by outstanding people as well as great football players, coaches, and staff", Goodell said.

I guess the saying "One bad apple spoils the bunch" does not apply in the NFL. True enough, there are a few players who are in need of an intervention, but they do not represent the hearts and souls of this covenant fraternity of men.

5)   The National Basketball Association—I believe Dr. James Naismith, basketball founder, envisioned the NBA when he invented basketball in 1891 (Springfield, MA). High flying dunks, long-range threes, no-look passes, and "get that shot outta here" blocks are great aspects of the NBA. These elements keep NBA stadiums packed throughout North America from season to season.

From the legends I have witnessed through vintage footage—Bill Russell, Wilt Chamberlin, Pete Maravich, Elgin Baylor, Walt Frazier, Bob Cousy, and George Gervin—to the legends that I had the pleasure of watching as a kid—Magic Johnson, Michael Jordan, Charles Barkley, John Stockton, Karl Malone, and Patrick Ewing—these tremendous athletes have entertained basketball fans for decades.

I have witnessed clutch shooters Larry Bird, Reggie Miller, Robert Horry, and Chauncey Billups spoil opponent's early victory celebrations with only a few seconds left on the clock. Another element of the NBA that I love is the players nicknames: Dr. J., The Dream, Magic, Run TMC, Zeke, The Microwave, Big Shot Rob, The Iceman, The Glide, The Worm, C-Webb, Vinsanity, CP3, The Mailman, The Jet, The Human Highlight Reel, Plastic Man, Flash, The King, The Big Ticket,

---

The Answer, Air Jordan, and how many nicknames does Shaquille O'Neal have—Shaq Daddy, The Big Aristotle, The Diesel, Shaq Fu, and his latest, The Big Shaqtus. I love it!

All Star Weekend is another one of my favorite pieces of the NBA. It gives the players a break from the 81 regular season game schedule and adds excitement for the fans. Some of my fondest NBA memories stem from All Star Weekend—the 1986 slam dunk champ Spud Webb capturing the title in front of his hometown crowd in Dallas, TX; the rematch between Michael Jordan and Dominique Wilkens in Chicago, IL before Michael's home crowd and Tracy McGrady's off the backboard to himself dunk in the 2002 All Star game.

If you think regular season and All Star break are intense, wait until post season. It really gets heated. Ballplayers live to play in the post season. This is when it *really* counts. They raise their level of play because they know either you "win or go home".

Recently the playoffs were extended to a seven game series for each round which is great because it gives fans more games to enjoy. I am certain that NBA fans agree, throughout the pre-season, regular season, All Star break, and post season—"NBA action is fantastic!"

6) The NCAA basketball tournament—For college basketball fans, "Selection Sunday" is equivalent to any national holiday; well except Christmas and Easter of course. Brackets, upsets, sweet 16s, Elite Eights, and Final Fours are important factors of the tournament. For the past fifteen years, I have witnessed top seeded teams crumble during the first and second rounds. I have witnessed devastated teams who were "on the bubble" have their post-season dreams shattered.

Each year, I fill in my brackets, men and women, and enter at least one of the many online NCAA contest. Millions of college basketball fans participate to showcase their expertise of college basketball knowledge. I have not won yet, but I have come pretty close. In 2007, my final percentage was 99.3% correct for the men's tournament. Not to toot my own horn, I even predicted the two teams that would make it to the championship and also predicted the final score correctly. Yeah, I guess I am tooting my horn!

7) Michael Jordan—Whether you call him "MJ" or simply "Mike", he is the greatest shooting guard to step onto a basketball court—period! Please believe that it kills me to say this because I have always cheered against him and the Chicago Bulls. But I have never been a hater; so I must give him his props. I still remember his 1991 playoff performance against my Los Angeles Lakers. He changed hands in the air while going to the hole for a lay-up. I had never seen anything like it in my

life. The Chicago Bulls won six titles in eight years with Michael Jordan leading the way.

He did not accomplish it alone, he had plenty of weapons in his arsenal—Coach Phil Jackson, Scottie Pippen, John Paxton, Dennis Rodman, and Ron Harper to name a few. Michael Jordan never hesitated to entertain his fans either. He was unstoppable! Or should I say "unstopa-Bull". "Some people want it to happen, some wish it would happen, others make is happen"—this is one of my favorite Michael Jordan quotes. And make it happen he did. I think everyone should strive to "Be like Mike".

8) Venus and Serena Williams—The Women Tennis Association was not prepared for what the Williams sisters brought to the tennis world. No one was ready; except the Williams' of course. We weren't ready for the beads, braces, cat suits, or the back-to-back aces that came along with Venus and Serena. Their powerful serves added brilliance to their unbeatable game. For four consecutive years, they swapped Wimbledon title from 2000-2003.

And after years of dominating the tennis world, critics—who I classified as haters—doubted their commitment to the game. They also felt the sisters had too many extra activities distracting their attention from tennis. Serena proved them wrong in the 2007 Australian Open. She entered the tournament ranked No. 81 in the world, but quickly soared to No. 14. Not only did she win the tournament, she dominated opponent after opponent, including No. 1 seed Maria Sharapova in the final. After the win, her critics sung a different song. Their opinions of Serena went from "Serena is not fit" to "Serena is here to stay!" Oh, how quickly they forget.

This Olympic gold medalist, Wimbledon, Australian Open, French Open, and US Open winning duo are here to stay! They continue to dominate opponents—making them dizzy and woozy—as they face off on the tennis court. They entertain the tennis world in both style and grace.

9) Coach Leon Barmore—A Ruston, LA native, built the Louisiana Tech program into one of the fiercest dynasties in women's college basketball. In twenty seasons, he accumulated 576 wins and only 87 losses giving him the best winning percentage—.869—at the time of his retirement in 2002.

I became a Lady Techster fan instantly after moving into Mitchell Hall my freshman year in 1991. My roommate and all of my friends regularly attended home games. We even became friends with many of the players. One of my best friends and I still joke about Coach Barmore's "game face" and how he rarely showed his teeth during games; not even after a win. Apparently, not smiling or showing teeth worked well for him. He

—

had a great career at Louisiana Tech. He was inducted into the Women Basketball Hall of Fame in May 2003 and the Naismith Memorial Basketball Hall of Fame in August 2003. I was not present for either ceremony; but I am almost sure that he showed his teeth at one of them.

10) The Fab Five—This team, in my opinion, was the greatest college basketball team every assembled. They single handedly changed the culture of college basketball in the early 90's with their baggy shorts, black socks, bald heads, trash talk, glares, and stares. They alley-opped and slammed their way into the hearts of basketball fans across the country. Chris Webber, Jalen Rose, Juwan Howard, Jimmy King, and Ray Jackson frustrated opponents with their flashy plays and trash talking. Although they were unable to win a national title, they were the first team of starting freshman to play for a championship in 1992.

Three of the players—Chris Webber, Jalen Rose, and Juwan Howard—were drafted in the NBA and enjoyed great careers in the league. But due to a money laundering scandal involving Chris Webber and a Michigan booster, the late Ed Martin, the University of Michigan attempted to erase the memory of the Fab Five. They forfeited all of the Fab Five wins and removed banners reflecting the wins from their stadium in 2003. The Fab Five may have been erased from the record books; but they will never be erased from the minds and hearts of the millions of fans who adored them. Go Big Blue!

11) The Houston Comets—the WNBA's first dynasty. From the very beginning, the Comets dominated the WNBA by winning the first four championship titles from 1997-2000 under the leadership of Hall of Fame coach Van Chancelor. Led by "The big three" Cynthia Cooper, Sheryl Swoops, and Tina Thompson, they were a strong force in the newly formed basketball league.

12) NCAA football—Whether regular season games or Bowl Championship Series, college football is electrifying! College football is known for its fierce rivalries—Miami vs. Florida State (me and my brother's favorite); Michigan vs. Ohio State; and Texas vs. Oklahoma. There are many great college teams, but LSU and Florida State are the two that I root for each year. LSU has participated in scores of nail-biting games over the years. One SEC match-up in particular featured LSU and Kentucky; LSU quarterback Marcus Randall threw a 75 yard "Hail Mary" pass as time expired to win 33-30 on Kentucky's home turf. Another LSU highlight game was the 2005 Peach Bowl. The Tigers manhandled the Miami Hurricanes by a final score of 40-10. And who can forget the

BCS Championship game in 2004 under the leadership of Coach Nick Saban and again in 2007 under the leadership of Coach Les Miles.

Yes, college football has offered some memorable moments . . . remember QB Vince Young and the Texas Longhorns against Reggie Bush and USC Trojans in the 2006 Rose Bowl? What about the 2007 Fiesta Bowl? I f you are a college football fan, I know you remember this one. Boise State defeated Oklahoma in overtime by one point, 43-42 using a trick play called the "Statue of Liberty". On the play, running back Ian Johnson completing a two point conversion to give Boise State the thrilling victory. At the end of the game, Ian proposed to his girlfriend, who was a cheerleader for Boise State. She accepted his proposal. I have witnessed many great bowl games, but this one was one of the best.

13) Coach Bobby Bowden—This Hall of Fame coach currently holds the second spot for the coach in Division I with the most wins—382 wins; one behind legendary coach Joe Paterno. Coach Bowden is a God-fearing man with great integrity and character. I have been a Bobby Bowden fan for nearly 15 years; thanks to my brother. He is the biggest Florida State fan. For the past ten years, he and his best friend Eric—who is a Miami Hurricanes fan—have gone at each other year after year because of this intense rivalry.

Given the history of "wide rights" and "wide lefts", predicting a winner for this match-up is not easy. Every year we watch the game at either my mom or my brother's house. One year, 2003 to be exact, I broke the tradition and watched it over a friend's house. Big mistake! He wanted "to talk" instead of watching the game. He actually turned the television off during the first half to get my attention. I could not believe it! Needless to say, I left his place at half-time to enjoy the second half at home with my brother and all of his friends. And guess what, I have not returned to his house since that day.

14) Tiger Woods—I said it before and I'll say it again, I am not a big golf fan. But my father is. And yes, Tiger Woods is his favorite golfer. I have watched a few rounds of Tiger Woods golf with him and he explained *everything* to me because I was totally confused. The 2006 PGA Championship was one for the record books. With this win, Tiger became the first person to win the PGA championship twice at the same venue. This win also moved Tiger into second place as golf's greatest champion with twelve major wins in ten years.

"They don't understand Tiger", my father said with a big grin on his face. "They just can't figure him out!"

I guess my dad was right because the player who came in second express those same sentiments at an interview after the tournament.

"What makes Tiger a great player?" They asked Shawn Micheel, the second place winner.

"I wish I knew what it was {is}. He does so many things so well" he answered.

So my dad was right—no one can figure out Tiger Woods.

15) Coach Bobby Knight—Okay, where do I begin with Coach Knight? Three adjectives come to mind when I think of Bobby Knight—passionate, sarcastic, and unrelenting. This explains his nickname, "The General". He spent most of his coaching career as the head basketball coach of the University of Indiana where he coached great players such as Hall of Famer Isaiah Thomas and Duke's head coach Mike Krzyzewski.

Just as other great coaches, Bobby Knight prepares his players for life after basketball. Although some of his motivational techniques are questionable, he makes certain his players understand they are students first and athletes second. Case in point: two weeks before the 2006 season began; Coach Knight suspended his star player, Texas Tech's Jay Jackson—for academic reasons. Jay was reinstated after his grades improved and was dubbed by Coach Knight as his "star student".

Coach Knight has celebrated many great accomplishments throughout his career at Indiana. Toward the end of his coaching career with Texas Tech University, he made basketball history. In January 2007, he surpassed North Carolina's Dean Smith with 879 wins—the most in Men's Division I college basketball. In typical Knight fashion, he down played the importance of the record by saying, "I'm glad this is over with". Of course, he recognized the importance of this historic endeavor; but he gave the credit to his players.

His critics do not fully understand his complex personality. But I do. You see, Coach Knight is a Scorpio, just as I am. Scorpios are very complex creatures. Some people may even say that we are crazy. And you know what, sometimes we are. But there is a method to our madness. Whether to raise awareness for a passionate subject or to simply get our message across, Scorpios will accomplish their mission—one way or the other.

To give more insight to Coach Knight, here is a small excerpt defining Scorpios: "unrelenting, strange and full of contrast, not flexible, not always liked but often admired". All of these adjectives explain Coach Knight. I love Bobby Knight! I love his passion for the game of basketball and life. I even like his sarcastic attitude; which may sound sort of twisted. But I do. I do not make many guarantees, but I am willing to make this one—once you've crossed Coach Knight, or any other Scorpio for that matter, you will never make the mistake again. Remember, Ron Artest, Tonya Harding, and the late Ike Turner are all Scorpios too.

16) Jim Brown—"The greatest running back in NFL history". That's what my father called Jim Brown. I was not privileged to witness him during his record setting years (1957-1967) as an NFL running back, so I questioned this statement. My father also said he was "better than Walter Payton, Barry Sanders, Emmitt Smith, or any other running back today". You know this was hard for me to believe. Better than Ladainian Tomlinson? But according to my dad, he was better than him. Jim Brown retired from the NFL in 1963 as the record holder in single season (1,863) and career rushing yards (12,312) and all time leader in rushing touchdowns (106), total touchdowns (126) and all purpose yards (15,549). He must have been the greatest running back to have set these records in just nine seasons.

17) Coach Pat Summit—She is one of the most respected coaches in college basketball—men or women. She coached great players such as Chamique Holdsclaw, Tamika Catchings, and Candace Parker. Over her thirty-four year career with the University of Tennessee, Coach Summit has defeated powerhouses Connecticut, Louisiana Tech, Duke, LSU, North Carolina and Stanford. She won her first national title in 1987; beating the Lady Techsters 67-44. Since 1987, she has won seven additional titles with the latest in 2007.

Coach Summit holds the record for the most wins in Division I—men and women. I was honored to witness a few of Coach Summit's match-up with the Lady Techsters in Ruston, LA and of course I rooted against her . . . sorry Coach.

18) Muhammad Ali—He said it himself, "I am the greatest!" And the greatest he is. This three time world heavyweight champion was named the "Sportsman of the Century" by *Sports Illustrated* in 2005. He was also given The Presidential Medal of Honor which is the highest civilian award in the country. He was born Cassius Marcellus Clay; but later changed his name due to his Muslim faith. He fought many unforgettable fights—"The Fight of the Century" against Joe Frazier, "The Rumble in the Jungle" against George Forman and the rematch between Joe Frazier "The Thriller in Manila". Ali retired from boxing in 1981 with a career record of 56 wins—which 37 were KO—and 5 losses. In 1983, he was diagnosed with Parkinson's syndrome. He is still one of the most recognizable sports figures today.

19) The Olympic Games—A sports fan paradise! Every sport that you could imagine are played during the Olympics. My most memorable Olympic teams are: the 1992 Original Dream Team, the 1996 U.S. Women Gymnastics team featuring Dominique Dawes and Kerri Strug, the 1996 Women's Basketball team and the 2004 and 2008 men's swim teams featuring the greatest Olympian of all time Michael Phelps who holds the record for the most gold medals at a single Olympics (2008). He also holds seven more world records in swimming.

The Olympics are held every four years in various cities around the world and they get more and more exciting! I look forward to the summer games every four years.

20) Bill Russell—Born in my hometown (Monroe, LA), Bill Russell developed into one of the greatest centers in NBA history. His shot blocking ability, rebounding and man-to man defense were key factors in the Boston Celtics' eleven championship titles during his 13 year career (1956-1969). Just as Jim Brown, my father praises Bill Russell as "the best player in NBA history". Well, that's my father's opinion and you know what they say—"Father knows best".

21) High school football in Northeast Louisiana—Ahh, high school football. Especially in Louisiana. You see, we love high school football. On Friday nights, high school stadiums are packed with screaming fans who may have left work early just to get the perfect seat for the Bastrop vs. Neville High game or the "Baby Bayou Classic"—Wossman vs. Carroll High.

I am a proud graduate of Wossman High School and I am not ashamed to admit that I attended *every football game* when I was a student from 1987-1991. I mean every game—home and away. Ask my mom, she'll tell you. She paid for the tickets each Friday and "the $30 Isotoner gloves that were lost on road trips". Call me crazy, but I was there rain, sleet, or shine.

I know there are high school football fanatics across the country. And for those who are not, you don't know what you're missing!

Okay, now, are you convinced that I am the Diva of Sports? A true sports fan? Many of the women I spoke with could not understand why sports is such a big deal for me. Yeah, many of them liked sports. They watched it from time to time. They were more interested in the athletes themselves, not the actual games, statistics, and rules. It was the athletes that really held their attention.

They didn't *live* for sports, like me. And I did not ask to be a sports fanatic. I said earlier, it is in my blood. I have always been exposed to sports. I played football in the street with my brother and his friends.

I followed my brother and his friends to the neighborhood recreation centers and cheered along the sidelines. I was also side-line cheerleader for my childhood friends, Sandra, LaTiesha, and Samantha, as they played basketball in jr. high school. In high school, I watched my cousin—Coach Z—yell plays from the bench . . . occasionally cursing. Okay, he cursed a lot. But that's besides the point.

I also watched my son participate in football, baseball, basketball, track and field, karate, and every other sport that he could think to play. I have seen a lot of sports history made. And from the looks of things, I'll be watching, yelling, and cheering for years to come. But you will *never* hear me complain about it.

CHAPTER 21

Will Smith, Blair Underwood, and Boris Kodjoe are Already Taken

"Help me somebody!"
Malvin S. Smith

We have arrived at the final chapter. And I know I have millions of witnesses who agreed with this subject. Come on now, Will, Blair, and Boris? I chatted with women, mostly sisters, around the world who all agreed—these three brothers are great catches indeed. But they are already taken. And how did this tragedy occur? Yes, it's a tragedy. A catastrophe! How did we, single sisters worldwide, allow all three to go down the aisle as single men and stroll back up the aisle as married men? Somebody, anybody, should have intervened at one of the wedding ceremonies. All three are taken and unavailable for single and frustrated sisters, including me, who cannot find a decent man to save our lives.

Well, they are not only married, they are happily married. So we, as respectable women, have no other choice but accept and embrace this fact. But their marital status cannot stop us from gazing upon them and admiring and appreciating their, Ahhh, talent?

Jada Pinkett-Smith has to be the luckiest woman in the world. Look at the man she managed to snatch—great father, entertainer, and role model. Yes, Will Smith! He began his career as a cool hip-hop artist from Philly; rapping about the *Summertime* and *Parents Just Don't Understand.* He later ventured into the acting world with his hit television series *The Fresh Prince of Bel-Air.*

He moved onto the big screen and acted in many great movies such as *Bad Boys, Independence Day, Men in Black,* and my favorite, *The Pursuit of Happyness.* He was nominated for an Academy Award for his work in *Ali* and *The Pursuit of Happyness* which he portrayed the life of Chris Gardner, a once homeless father turned millionaire.

Will Smith shattered the lives of single sisters who shared hopes and dreams of becoming "Mrs. Smith" when he married the beautiful Jada Pinkett in 1997. They have been blessed with three adorable kids (including one from a previous marriage) and are Hollywood's golden couple. (Sighing . . .)

Blair Underwood is another brother who broke the hearts of single sisters when he took "the stroll" down the isle. He married the lovely Desiree DeCosta in September 1994. From this union, three children were born.

He began his acting career in 1985 as Russell Walker in the movie *Krush Groove.* He also acted in many other films including *Set it Off, Rules of Engagement* and his latest role as Curtis in *Madea's Family Reunion* where he portrayed a ruthless businessman who physically abused his fiancée'.

Last, but certainly not least, Boris Kodjoe. Ahhh Boris! What a wonderful sight to gaze upon. His eyes, lips, muscular broad shoulders, his pearly white teeth, his everything! Simply put, this brother is fine. In 2002, *People Magazine* named him one of the Most Beautiful People in World. Women from all walks of life agreed, he is certainly a great catch.

During a late night, well, more like an early morning conversation, with my best friends, Boris Kodjoe's name emerged.

We were discussing an episode of his hit series *Soul Food* and she mentioned, "Every female in the universe wants Boris."

I added, "Yeah, I bet there are naked Neputinians and Plutonians drooling over him at this very moment." We burst into laughter deliriously for several minutes.

Boris Kodjoe branched into the entertainment industry as a model which soon led to an acting career. *Love and Basketball* was his first featured film; but he is best known for his role as the sexy delivery man—Damon Carter—in Showtime's hit series *Soul Food* which aired from 2000 to 2004. He also played the role of Frankie the bus driver in his most recent film *Madea's Family Reunion* in 2005.

Boris broke the hearts of women throughout the universe, female Plutonians and Neptunians included, when he married his sexy *Soul Food* co-star Nicole Ari Parker in May 2005. They have two beautiful children, Sophie and Nicolas Kodjoe who graced the cover of *Ebony* magazine in June 2007.

Yes, it is a crying shame that these three brothers are taken. They were taken by good women; but yet and still, they are taken. Too bad we were not able to clone a few more of each before they tied the knot. On second thought, it may not be too late. I feel another "Ah ha moment" emerging. Remember the episode of *The Flintstones* when aliens kidnapped Fred, loaded him into a huge space ship, and cloned about ten of him? You see where I am going with this? Maybe, just maybe, we could summon Fred's little green friend, The Great Gazoo, to help alleviate this frustration. If I could get a few sisters to help locate that same space ship, maybe, just maybe, we can clone about 10,000 of each one of these brothers. Just think; this would reduce the number of frustrated black women in the world by 30,000! Well, not exactly 30,000; my best friend and I have already claimed a Boris clone and my sister—a Blair.

AFTERWORD

"I got to be out my mind to think I need someone to carry me.
I've done enough crying!"
Mary J. Blige

Well, there you have it—21 of the most widely discussed frustrations among black women worldwide. Believe me, there were more. Many more. But these were mentioned more than others. And a few of them I kind of threw in myself; like sports for instance. Of course, sisters talked about sports, but they were more interested in the *athletes* than the actual statistics, facts, rules and procedures, and specific games. They left that part of the discussion to me—the self proclaimed "Diva of Sports".

For the most part, we vented about finances, unsatisfying jobs, school, single motherhood, and men. Lord, how many times did I mention men? Too many. And the guys I spoke with during research understood our frustrations too; well some of them understood.

I recall a very interesting conversation with two men—my son's barber and his client—in November 2006.

"What's your book about?" one of them asked.

I answered, "Frustrations of black women". To avoid being sliced with the recently sharpened clippers, he did not respond. He slightly nodded his head in approval.

"How did you come up with that idea?" was his next question.

I went through the entire process . . . "dinner with my sister, online research", etc., etc. He had plenty of questions for me, but I was not bothered. Actually, I had the attention of everyone in the shop. The back and forth conversation was very interesting. I felt like one of Elizabeth Hasselbeck's co host of *The View*. Out of all of the questions he asked, the most interesting, I thought, was

---

195

this—"Do you really feel like black women are more frustrated than any other race of women?"

"Yes indeed!" I quickly replied.

He thought, "Maybe the smile that non-black women portray is just a façade". If the smiles on their faces are fake, then he raised a very good point explaining the difference between black women and other races. Black women are real. Most of the time, what you see is exactly what you get. If we are angry, it shows. If we are hurting, it shows. Maybe if we were great at pretending or exemplifying "quiet frustration", as my best friend calls it, the world would not view us as angry black women.

Furthermore, the next time any of you witness a frustrated black woman, anywhere in the world, do not frown and say "Oh, she's just *another* angry black woman". No, she is not. Realize that she is frustrated, and rightfully so. And if you read this book in its entirety, you understand why. Hey, don't shoot the messenger, just listen, soak it all in, and take heed to the message. And fellas, do not fret. You will get your chance to vent as well. But Ladies first, right?

11 More Frustrating Things!

1) On again, off again relationships
2) Black on black crime
3) Hypocrites
4) Too tight underwear
5) Health problems
6) Rising gas prices
7) Buying the wrong shade of lipstick/gloss (for Rhonda)
8) Not having enough hours in the day
9) Helping kids with homework (for Flee and Sarah)
10) Long commutes to/from work
11) Dirty politics

MIKKI'S FAVORITE QUOTES

"The future belongs to those who believe in the beauty of their dreams."
Eleanor Roosevelt

"I believe that you are here to become more of yourself and live your best life."
Oprah Winfrey

*"Some say the blacker the berry, the sweeter the juice.
I say the darker the flesh then the deeper the roots."*
Tupac

*"Some people want it to happen, some wish it would happen,
others make it happen."*
Michael Jordan

"Fame is the worst drug known to man."
Jay-Z

*"Greatness isn't one big thing.
Greatness is a lot of small things done well."*
Ray Lewis

"How does it feel to be me?"
Eddie Cane

"Having money is not everything; not having it is."
Kanye West

"Mediocrity always attacks excellence."
Dr. Michael Beckwith

"Man gives the award. God gives the reward."
Denzel Washington

"Unless you've walked in the shoes of the oppressed,
you cannot understand how it feels."
Johnny Cochran

"I don't get motivated about making money.
I get motivated about making Black history."
Sean "P. Diddy" Combs

"Hell baby, tell them something about Grambling!"
Coach Eddie G. Robinson

"Success is not measured by the things you acquire
but by the number of obstacles you overcome."
Larry Flynn

"You can't handle the truth!"
Col. Nathan Jessep

"I'm cute! I'm cute! She said I'm cute!"
Rudolph the Red-Nosed Reindeer

"Seldom do I pause to answer criticism of my work and ideas."
Dr. Martin Luther King

"It is easier to build strong children than to repair broken men."
Frederick Douglas

"Excellence is to do a common thing in an uncommon way."
Booker T. Washington

"Talent is God given. Be humble. Fame is man-given.
Be grateful. Conceit is self-given. Be careful."
Coach John Wooden

"Everything in my world makes perfect sense!"
Mikki C. Zimmerman

11 BOOK CLUB DISCUSSION QUESTIONS

1) What inspired Mikki to write *"Can I Get a Witness?"*
2) How were the 21 frustrations listed in the book discovered?
3) According to Mikki's research, what seems to be the biggest frustration for black women?
4) What NFL star is referenced in the "Absent Fathers" chapter?
5) List 3 tips offered in "Meeting too Many Mr. Wrongs". Discuss each.
6) In the chapter "Constant Rise in Newly Diagnosed HIV Cases in Black women", what age group is at risk of contracting the deadly disease?
7) According to Chapter 8 (Down Low Brothers), what is the biggest problem with the Down Low phenomenon?
8) In the Stupid Lyrics chapter, do you feel that Mikki is biased toward the hip-hop genre of music? Explain your opinion.
9) Of the 21 stereotypes from Chapter 19, how many have you been exposed to?
10) Name three of your own frustrations that were or were not discussed in the book.
11) Was the advice and solutions given in the book helpful? Explain.

LaVergne, TN USA
10 November 2009

163646LV00004B/7/P